AFRICAN LACE-BARK IN THE CARIBBEAN

No other fabric invented by man's ingenuity has been accorded so much admiration as lace. The desire to possess it is found in all classes. As a handicraft it is one of the most fascinating; it requires no expensive apparatus . . . makes no untidy litter, and is equally suited to the lady in her castle; the cottager to relieve the invalid's tedious hours, and for training of youthful hand and eye in schools.

ELEANOR PAGE, *LACE MAKING*

The relationship historically between needlework and women has been far more complex than previously assumed and than commonly held views certainly grant. For women of all stations in life and in all socioeconomic classes, needlework has been both a domestic and domesticating labor, both a tool of oppression and an instrument of liberation. . . . Reviled and celebrated, it has nevertheless been a significant cultural practice of meaning-making.

MAUREEN DALY GOGGIN, "AN ESSAMPLAIRE ESSAI ON THE RHETORICITY OF NEEDLEWORK SAMPLER-MAKING . . ."

AFRICAN LACE-BARK IN THE CARIBBEAN

The construction of race, class, and gender

Steeve O. Buckridge

Bloomsbury Academic
An imprint of Bloomsbury Publishing Plc

B L O O M S B U R Y
LONDON • OXFORD • NEW YORK • NEW DELHI • SYDNEY

Bloomsbury Academic
An imprint of Bloomsbury Publishing Plc

50 Bedford Square	1385 Broadway
London	New York
WC1B 3DP	NY 10018
UK	USA

www.bloomsbury.com

BLOOMSBURY and the Diana logo are trademarks of Bloomsbury Publishing Plc

First published 2016
Paperback edition first published 2018

© Steeve O. Buckridge, 2016

Steeve O. Buckridge has asserted his right under the Copyright, Designs and Patents Act, 1988, to be identified as Author of this work.

British Library Cataloguing-in-Publication Data

A catalogue record for this book is available from the British Library.

ISBN:	HB:	978-1-4725-6930-1
	PB:	978-1-3500-5850-7
	ePDF:	978-1-4725-6932-5
	ePub:	978-1-4725-6931-8

Library of Congress Cataloging-in-Publication Data
A catalog record for this book is available from the Library of Congress.

Cover design: Louise Dugdale
Cover image courtesy of the Institute of Jamaica

Typeset by RefineCatch Limited, Bungay, Suffolk

For Gang-Gong, who was strong, black, and beautiful

CONTENTS

ILLUSTRATIONS

PREFACE

This study was conceived while working on the book, *The Language of Dress*; however, my interest in clothing and plants goes further back. As a child growing up in Jamaica, I was fascinated by the extraordinary skills of the needleworkers and seamstresses in my family. I enjoyed watching my mother pedaling away on her Singer sewing machine as she gently manipulated fabrics and guipure lace to create fashionable wedding gowns that delighted her customers. I often marveled at the breadth of knowledge required to be a good seamstress and needleworker. As visual rhetorician and material culture scholar, Maureen Goggin rightly implies, needleworkers need to understand the choice of threads, texture of fabrics, the appropriate colors, right stitches, and the ability to read her customer's mind and body. I would also add that they need to know how to harness their creative energy to make not merely garments, but works of art!

In decades gone by, home sewing, as well as other forms of needlework, such as embroidery, patch work, quilting, knitting and crocheting, were popular activities among women across many areas of Jamaican society. Needlework skills were often passed down from mother to daughter, and generations of women spent much of their lives sewing, knitting, and mending, styling and making lace. Among some Jamaicans, such as Rastafarians, knitting and crocheting colorful belts, caps, tams, and scarves have remained popular activities within their communities. Seamstresses, or dressmakers as they were more commonly called, took great pride in their ability to design and cut patterns and to create beautiful and sophisticated custom apparel for their female clients. Many dressmakers, like my mother, were able to earn an income, be financially independent, and simultaneously clothe their family. For many of these women, their sewing and needlework skills were an important "lifeline."

My mother and other dressmakers from the community organized sewing circles and gathered regularly in each other's homes to share sewing tips amongst themselves, exchange patterns and new styles, trade fabrics, and update each other on the latest neighborhood news. These communal work sessions were punctuated with bursts of laughter as the women engaged in gossip and bear tales or as we say in Jamaica "nuf labrish." Simply, this was the domain of women where stories were told and young women were counseled by the matriarchs of the community. Men were barred from these sessions. It was a space where female friendships were renewed, skills perfected, and bonds of solidarity were strengthened.

Although my mother's world of sewing and needlework was a source of inspiration for this study, it was to my grandmother, Gang-Gong, a committed feminist and loyal Garveyite, that I owe my love of plants and interest in natural history. Gang-Gong was an entrepreneur and business woman who raised cattle and traded goods. She also owned a large garden filled with beautiful flowering plants and numerous fruit trees. As a hobby, she loved to climb tall trees, a habit she maintained until in her seventies. Interestingly, my grandmother was well-known for needlework skills. She knitted and crocheted caps, sweaters, and socks. She was also admired for her "Sunday best" outfits, especially her church hats. Gang-Gong possessed an in-depth knowledge of Jamaican trees and the use of local plants, shrubs, vines, and roots in Afro-Jamaican herbalism. Gang-Gong, like many black women of her generation, had acquired the knowledge of herbalism from her mother and grandmothers and used the knowledge to protect and heal the sick in their families. Some women, who practiced the craft of herbalism and procuring customary remedies, passed the information down to their descendants. It was from Gang-Gong, for instance, I learned that the tea of the soursop leaf [*Annona muricata*] strengthened the nervous system and lowered hypertension, and devil's horse whip [*Achyranthes aspera*] was good for stomach complaints, including dysentery, as well as colic and coughs. The leaves of the aralia shrub [*Aralia guilfoylei*] as well as the leaf of life [*Bryophyllum pinnatum*], when steeped or boiled in water (boiled is the preferred term used in Jamaican rather than brewed), resulted in a tea that cured cold symptoms and fever. Meanwhile, the tea of the bitter cerassee vine [*Momordica charantia*] was considered an ideal remedy for colds, "cleaning the blood," and even treating diabetes. A few other remedies included chaney root [*Similax balbisiana*] tonic for strength and rheumatism, and the fragrant smelling fever grass, also known as lemon grass [*Cymbopogon citralus*], was good for fevers and served as a common carminative inflatulent, while pepper mint [*Satureja viminea*] and ginger root [*Zebrina pendula*] teas relieved cramps, stomach ache, and calmed indigestion. These remedies were supported not by science, but by common knowledge.

Like many Jamaican children, I endured the "wash out" ritual, which usually took place at the end of every summer and just before the new school year began. Children who had spent their summer holiday indulging dietary cravings were often given a popular purgative produced from the senna tree [*Cassia senna*], as well as the sinkle bible, better known as the aloe vera [*Aloes vulgaris*] plant, to "wash out" and cleanse their bellies so they could be healthy and ready for the new school term. Numerous Jamaican children detested these purgatives due to the bitter taste and pungent odors; nonetheless, resistance to the "wash out" was futile. It was my grandmother who introduced me to the mysteries and folklore associated with some local plants and trees—most captivating were the stories of ghosts or *duppies*, as they are called in Jamaica, that dwelled under cottonwood trees and the unsolved mystery of the Physic Nut Tree [*Jatropha curas*], which has a viscid milky sap that turns red at Easter—believed to be symbolic of the blood of Jesus Christ.

The use of plants for medicinal purposes has been the foundation of medical treatments throughout much of human history. Jamaica is blessed with a wide variety of flowering plants known for their medicinal properties that were used by indigenous people and enslaved Africans. Many of these plants can be found across the island's tropical habitat from the arid areas of the South Coast to the mist forest of the Blue Mountains. Jamaicans have long appreciated the beauty of their country's flora and fauna, and greatly value the healing properties of the island's numerous plants. Therefore, it is not surprising that herbalism has remained deeply rooted in Jamaican culture whether as part of a healing ritual, as a beverage or "bush tea," or even as an aphrodisiac drink produced from the Irish moss seaweed [*Chondrus crispus*] or strongback root [*Cuphea parsonsia*], Jamaican's fascination with local plants and trees is part of a long history, a continuum that goes back to our African ancestors and the continent of Africa.[1] Perhaps Gang-Gong explained this fascination best. She once remarked, "We are a people of the forest; it is to the forest we seek plants that will heal us, protect us, clothe us, and give us life!" These words have remained with me to this day and helped in shaping my thinking and approach to this study.

For some Jamaicans, the lace-bark tree was the "tree of life" that provided essential products used to protect, clothe, and heal the tortured black body. The lace-bark tree was not part of my childhood experience and, sadly, most Jamaicans, except for a handful of specialists, have never heard of this natural wonder among Jamaica's rich and varied plant life that prevails. I first came across references to lace-bark while conducting research on slave dress at the National Library of Jamaica. I was both stunned and excited by this revelation and immediately wanted to know more. This study is the result of that fascinating investigative journey across three islands to shed light on a forgotten lace-bark industry once dominated by needleworkers and dressmakers who were highly skilled at their craft.

This book is not a botanical study of Caribbean and Jamaican flora. It is a heartfelt celebration and acknowledgment of black women's resourcefulness, ingenuity, and creativity that has sustained and maintained families and communities for centuries. It is out of admiration for needleworkers, like my mother and grandmother, along with my own interest in clothing and textiles, dress history, and Jamaican herbalism that has led me down this path. I gladly share this study with love and genuine gratitude to the women and their needles, who have been marginalized, silenced, forgotten, or absent from the history books, but have enriched our lives in meaningful ways with beautiful works of art.

---

[1] G.F. Asprey and Phyllis Thornton, *Medicinal Plants of Jamaica*, Part 1-4 (Kingston: University College of the West Indies, 1953); Ivelyin Harris, *Healing Herbs of Jamaica* (Royal Palm Beach: Ahtto Press Inc., 2010).

FOREWORD

My knowledge of Jamaica and the Caribbean has been slim, and Steeve Buckridge has turned this around for me. Not only is *African Lace-Bark in the Caribbean* eye opening, but so was *The Language of Dress: Resistance and Accommodation in Jamaica, 1760–1890,*[1] a volume I pleasantly discovered at a conference. I relished reading his version of the early history of Jamaica and Jamaican dress, hoping for another volume extending into the twenty and twenty-first centuries, expanding the tidbits in his conclusion. His exceptional descriptions and analysis of Jamaican dress featured how enslaved women used dress in response to the brutality of slavery. Instead of my wished-for second volume, however, Buckridge has produced an equally fascinating book about lace-bark clothing and accessories, elaborating on a specific example of dress in the lives of Jamaican women.

What pleases me about both books is how he proceeds in presenting his argument, working from a general setting to clearly laid-out details. In *The Language of Dress*, he analyzed the influence of African customs of dress on Jamaican women's daily lives, followed by examining their experiences in reacting against colonial domination, but also about choosing carefully to embrace selected European styles, but with their own twist. Similarly, in *African Lace-Bark*, he begins by reviewing the general category of bark-cloth (of which lace-bark is less-known) as a global phenomenon, produced and used in tropical countries across the world at various times. He moves on to focus on bark-cloth in Africa, its relationship to general patterns of dress, including various imported and indigenous textiles used every day and in rituals. He finishes by zeroing in on the Caribbean and Jamaica. His expertise as a cultural historian shines as he documents production and use of lace-bark by analyzing paintings, historical documents, visits to Kew Gardens, London, and conducting interviews. He connects the making and use of lace-bark to the history of lace, its prestigious place in fashion, and why lace-bark found a place in Jamaican lives. Finally he discusses lace-bark in Victorian Jamaica and its

---

[1] Steeve Buckridge, *The Language of Dress: Resistance and Accommodation in Jamaica, 1760–1890* (Kingston: The University of the West Indies, 2004).

slide into disappearance as its source (the Lagetta lagetto tree) became decimated and is now rare, almost extinct. Most importantly, his emphasis in both books is on the place of women in Jamaican life and what they have contributed to material culture and Jamaican cultural history.

I find Buckridge's writing style fluid, thus easy-to-read, and captivating. He drew me into following his path of discovery regarding the scholarly details related to making and wearing Jamaican lace-bark. Items included blouses, collars, caps, and trimmings, later tourist trinkets and souvenirs like doilies, fans, and lampshades. The value of Buckridge's work is that it not only adds to a trove of Jamaican cultural history, but also to making global dress history more complete, going beyond "Western" dress with details of more than what the elite of a society wears, but also in Jamaica, what the middle class and peasant class devised in presenting themselves. As I write this, a book is being completed on a global history of fashion by Linda Welters and Abby Lillethun[2] to supply readers an appreciation of styles of dress around the world, not just a focus on "Western" attire and accessories. Research like Buckridge's enhances our knowledge of the variety of resources used, the styles fashioned from them, and the meaning attached by people about what they wear and why. Dress as a material resource is a rich source for understanding human behavior. Steeve Buckridge delivers a fine contribution, and with this completed, I hope for a second volume on Jamaican dress picking up from 1890 into the twenty-first century or perhaps an overview book on dress in the Caribbean.

Joanne B. Eicher
Editor-in-Chief of the *Berg Encyclopedia of World Dress and Fashion*.
Regents Professor Emerita at the University of Minnesota, USA

---

[2] Linda Welters and Abby Lillethun, *Fashion History: A Global View* (Bloomsbury Academic, forthcoming).

ACKNOWLEDGMENTS

I am reminded of the famous Yoruba proverb, *Igi Kan Kì s'igbo*, which translates as "One tree cannot make a forest," meaning that an individual working with others can accomplish much. An acknowledgment is proof of this fact. I wish to thank Claire Robertson, Joanne Eicher, and Verene Shepherd for their guidance, mentoring, and encouragement over the years. I am indebted to the late Hon. Rex Nettleford, whose insight and knowledge continues to shape my professional journey. I am most grateful to the Center for Scholarly and Creative Excellence at Grand Valley State University for supporting my research activities. These grants permitted me to explore the topic on lace-bark in a way that would otherwise not have been possible.

My tenure as a visiting scholar and fellow in residence at the Yale Center for British Art (YCBA) provided the opportunity to conduct research at the Center and to access archival material across the Yale campus that was useful to this project. The fellowship facilitated the chance to engage scholars, archivists, and curators to share ideas and to learn from my peers. My appreciation goes to the graduate students in Art History at Yale and all those who gave feedback on my presentations. I wish to express my thanks to Elizabeth Fairman, Sir Peter Crane, Ashley Duval, Ruth Barnes, Gillian Forrester, Carla Heista, and Tim Barringer for their suggestions and support. I also thank Amy Meyers and her excellent staff at the YCBA for their generous support of my work on material culture and dress in Jamaica. The staff in the library and reading rooms at the YCBA were especially helpful in guiding me through unfamiliar territory.

My research on bark-cloth and lace-bark in Jamaica has benefited immensely from the invaluable expertise of staff, curators, archivists, botanists, and librarians at the following institutions, the University of the West Indies Library and West Indies Collection, the National Archives of Jamaica, the Institute of Jamaica's Natural History Division and Museum of History and Ethnography, and the National Library of Jamaica. Special mention must be made of librarians Francis Salmon, Genevieve Jones-Edman, and Yvonne Fraser-Clarke. I am particularly grateful to Tracy Commock and Keron Campbell of the National History Museum in Jamaica for their critical and supportive contributions to this endeavor over the years. My thanks to Shelly-Ann Morgan and Margaret Stanley of Edna Manley College of the Visual and Performing Arts for their support. My everlasting gratitude to the staff and faculty of the Institute for Gender and Development Studies at the University of the West Indies for hosting me and making me feel at home. I extend a warm thank you to Leonard Notice in Geography at UWI who was helpful with images, and to Derrick Lennon who was kind to share his knowledge of lace-bark with me. I owe a tremendous debt to the Accompong Town Maroons, who opened their hearts to me and welcomed me into their community during my field research. They have taught me so much about my culture, and I will always be thankful to them.

In Cuba, I wish to convey my gratitude to the staff of the Biblioteca Nacional de Cuba José Martí and the Instituto de Ecología y Sistemática. I am particularly grateful to Miguel Barnet, Natalia Bolivar, Alfredo Noa, Iralys Ventosa, Juan Carlos Fernãndez, Sergio Valdés Bernal, and Henrietta Pryce for their guidance during my research in Cuba. Likewise, in Haiti, I am indebted to the staff of the Bibliothèque Nationale d'Haiti and Bibliothèque Haitienne F.I.C. They were patient and often went the extra mile to accommodate me. My gratitude to Erol Josué and Louise Bijoux at the Ministère De La Culture, Viviane Hoogendoorn and her staff of the Allamanda, and Ostine Louverture from the Department of Forestry in Haiti. Bayyinah Bello offered advice on Haitian sources and my colleague, Dan Golembeski, shared his Haitian pictures with me—my thanks to them both. I am most grateful to Ati Max Beauvoir, Chef Supreme du Vodou Haitien, for the opportunity to meet with him and to learn about Haitian plants in ritual. I cannot forget the assistance that came from Lillian Chinowa at the National Art Gallery in Harare, Zimbabwe, Ramón Morales Valverde of Real Jardín Botánico de Madrid, and Brigido Peguero and his staff at the Jardín Botánico Nacional de Santo Domingo. My thanks to the curators and archivists at the museums and galleries in the UK, who unfailingly responded to my queries and requests for images and sources. These include Emma Butterfield of the National Portrait Gallery, Edwina Ehrman of the Victoria and Albert Museum, Carolyn Wingfield of the Saffron Walden Museum, and Julie Crocker of the Royal Archives at Windsor Castle.

I am grateful to Alex Forist of the Grand Rapids Public Museum for his help, Tim Chester for his insight on conservation efforts, and to Christine Niezgoda at the Field Museum in Chicago, who was helpful and kind to show me the museum's lace-bark collection. In addition, tremendous thanks to Mark Nesbitt at the Royal Botanic Gardens at Kew who permitted me to range widely amongst the lace-bark collection and provided a valuable exchange of insights over the years. Emily Brennan was most supportive and my thanks to her for sharing my interest in Jamaican lace-bark.

Aspects of this study have been presented at various public and academic gatherings, including the African Studies Association annual meeting, and I have benefited from the comments and suggestions offered me on these occasions. There are many others with whom I have shared conversations and correspondence and whose responses assisted me through the course of this project, and I thank them all.

I wish to thank my colleagues and the staff at Grand Valley State University in the Department of History, Area Studies, the Brooks College, and the College of Liberal Arts and Sciences for providing a stimulating and collegial environment that has enriched my understanding of history and interdisciplinary studies. I would also like to thank the librarians and staff of the GVSU libraries for their thoughtfulness and support. My sincere appreciation to Michelle Burke and Brett Huddleston for their reading and suggestions with the manuscript, and thanks also to Lauren McCutcheon, Vince St. Germain, and the staff of the Digital Studio for their work on images.

This project has been long in the making; hence I am deeply grateful to the publisher and especially my editor, Hannah Crump, for her thoughtfulness and faith in me. Finally, I would like to acknowledge my friends who helped to make this journey easier, my teachers who enlightened me and, above all, my family members who have sustained me with their unconditional love, particularly the women of my family who have enriched my life with meaningful things.

INTRODUCTION

The "natural" beauty of cloth and the "natural" beauty of bodies have been taught to the eye by art, and the same has been the case with natural beauty of clothes. The tight-laced waist, the priwigged head, and the neck collared in a millstone ruff . . . have all been comfortable, beautiful, and natural in their time, more by the alchemy of visual representation than by the force of social change.[1]

ANNE HOLLANDER

Dress, material culture, and Caribbean historiography

In 2007, *The New York Times* published "Admit It. You Love It. It Matters." The article was written by fashion and cultural critic, Guy Trebay, to celebrate the launch of Fashion Week in New York City.[2] The article resonated with me as it conveyed what scholars of fashion studies and the history of dress have been arguing for years—that dress matters and that fashion is not a mere trivial whim as some might think, but an important feature in our lives beyond keeping us warm and protecting us from the natural elements. In fact, dress conveys a message about the wearer to the observer and, furthermore, it reflects a person's social identity.[3] Dress may reveal, for instance, an individual's group affiliation, gender, age, occupation, and even state of being. Certain types of clothing are used as a form of social control and humiliation, like prison uniforms, while some styles of dress represent evocative subtexts that differentiate and separate us or identify those who do not belong. For many people, the act of "dressing up" can make us feel good, boost our confidence, and make us feel like we can go out and conquer the world. On the other hand, dressing the body can flatter, attract the opposite sex, and complement our figure, but it can also "show us up" and make us look unattractive. Clothing is a "civilizing mask" that enables us to express ourselves and make a personal statement.[4] However, dress is more than adornment, or a reflection of status and personal taste. Dress is connected to structure and agency in society, and in some cultures dress and cloth are important ritual objects that represent harmony between the living and the world of spirits. Moreover, dress is inextricably connected to the body; it shapes us and molds us. Perhaps Virginia Woolf said it best: "Vain trifles as they seem, clothes have, they say, more important offices . . . they mould our hearts, our brains, our tongues to their liking."[5]

Sadly, as historian Barbara Burman has rightly pointed out, "some historians have regarded clothing as peripheral to historical enquiry, as too ephemeral or too every day to warrant attention."[6] Consequently, the everyday domesticity of seamstresses and home dressmaking, knitting and lacemaking, has been overlooked. Although there have been some strides made in Caribbean history, more research is needed to develop some understanding of the innumerable women who have been sewing and have defied the colonial patriarchal norms and confines of slavery to create beautiful clothing for themselves and their family members. In general, this study emphasizes the significance of dress, particularly bark-cloth among enslaved and freed people, and shows that dress was not a mere whim; rather, dress was an important feature in slave society and beyond. Apart from protecting and adorning the body, dress was used by enslaved people to showcase their creative talents, symbolically resist oppression, be culturally expressive, and at the same time convey that they too could be as beautiful and refined as their European colonizers.

The focus of this study is on the African custom of lace-bark production and its consumption in the Caribbean. Lace-bark is a form of bark-cloth, obtained from the bark of the *lagetto tree*. The fibers of the *lagetto bark* were removed by hand and dried, and the end result resembled fine lace or linen that was used by enslaved and freed women to make clothing as well as a substitute for manufactured lace. Although lace-bark is derived from the bark of a tree, it is different from other forms of bark-cloth. For instance, unlike most bark-cloth such as tapa, the bark of the *lagetto tree* was not beaten into malleable cloth. The scientific name for the lace-bark tree is *Lagetta lagetto*; however, common names and spelling vary across regions—to be discussed in later chapters. Aside from this, enslaved and freed women in Jamaica were not unique in their use of bark-cloth. Several cultures around the world have made cloth from the bark of trees such as *tapa* produced from the paper mulberry tree in the Pacific. In the text, I analyze how the skill of producing lace-bark was nurtured and retained in the Caribbean by African enslaved and freed women. This is also a story about the lace-bark tree, once thought to be extinct, it is now threatened. This research illuminates the complexities of cultural retention and enhances our knowledge of an important aspect of the Black Atlantic, revealing how African women were conduits for cultural transmission.

Plantation history has traditionally disregarded economic participation by women and how their services played a crucial role in urban and rural life. This study sheds light on enslaved and freed women's creativity and economic activity as vibrant traders and producers of exquisite plant material for use in clothing manufacture for members of the enslaved population. Lace-bark was closely associated with African women in Jamaica, but it was also of interest to European adventurers, scientists, tourists, natural historians, industrialists, and colonial authorities. Many Europeans who arrived in the Caribbean were engaged in bio-prospecting expeditions in search of knowledge about useful foods, plants for natural dyes and medicine, and even materials for clothing. Naturalists involved in colonial botany sought plants with valuable properties with the potential of providing lasting profits.[7] Some prospectors gleaned information about Caribbean plants from indigenous and enslaved African women.

Here, I focus attention on women's engagement with lace-bark and how its subsequent use helped shape identities. This study adds to the ongoing debate about women's contribution to the plantation economy by engaging new methods of explorations and interpretations of women's lives, particularly their involvement in a cottage industry based on bark-cloth and lace-bark. I argue that a vibrant cottage industry based on African bark-cloth and lace-bark developed in response to economic conditions, cultural taste of refinement, and the insufficient and poor quality of clothing slaves received from their enslavers. African women controlled this industry, and it fostered a creative space that enabled them to be expressive in their dress and simultaneously to escape, at least temporarily, the harsh realities of plantation life. Women who participated in the industry were able to achieve some financial independence. The study will portray the dynamics of race, class, and gender in Caribbean society and contribute to the larger scholarship on the history of African women in the Diaspora.

Several fundamental questions central to this study enable us to develop some understanding of how bark-cloth and lace-bark fabrics were used in colonial Jamaica. For instance, how did a lace-bark industry develop and who started it? What were the contributions of indigenous people? Did African slaves learn about local plants from indigenous people? What role did African heritage play in the process of obtaining bark-cloth and lace-bark? Was it the same as in Africa? What types of clothes and styles were made from bark-cloth and lace-bark? This study explores slaves' harmonious relationship with their environment and the degree of sophistication and ingenuity used in obtaining lace-bark and suitable new materials for clothing.

Throughout much of Jamaica's history, dress has been a major feature of cultural expression. African customs or "Africanisms" in dress have been maintained, nurtured, and adapted in Jamaica as in other parts of the African Diaspora. Many Jamaicans, for instance, are well known for "dressing up" when the occasion requires it and even more telling when it does not. Black style has often focused attention on the body in that the marginalized black body becomes a performance space for enslaved and freed people to contest, conform, or resist in the racially segregated society.

Aspects of enslaved Africans' culture, such as music, religion, food, and art, have been celebrated and examined in numerous scholarships, which reminds us of the incredible talents, inventions, and creative achievements of enslaved people in spite of them living in a repressive and harsh society. An example of such achievements was reinforced in 2010 on a visit to Royal College of Physicians' 350th anniversary exhibition in London, commemorating the birth of Sir Hans Sloane and the founding of the Royal Society. Amongst the exquisite lace-bark objects on display (on loan from Kew Gardens) was a wooden lock from Jamaica. The caption read, "Made by the Negroes of Jamaica: wooden lock and key – c. 1860." The lock and key were made from several types of wood, including Olive, Spanish Elm, and Mahoe. Interestingly, the caption further described the lock as identical to the wooden locks of ancient Egypt. I marveled at the sophistication and complexity of the design, and how each piece of the wood was a testament to the brilliance of the object's inventors (Figure I.1).

FIGURE I.1 Jamaican nineteenth-century wooden lock. Photograph: © Trustees of the Royal Botanic Gardens, Kew (EBC 50885).

This research continues the theme of exploring beautiful and sophisticated objects created by colonized people in the Caribbean, but unfortunately for too long many scholars have focused their attention on objects made by men, while others have labeled objects created by women as merely art and crafts rather than as significant artifacts that can represent the domains of female power.[8] This study demonstrates the incredible importance of "female artifacts" such as lace-bark.

This study builds on the foundation of earlier scholarship on women and gender studies in the Caribbean including the works of Lucille Mathurin-Mair (1975), Hilary Beckles (1989, 1999), Barbara Bush (1990), and Verene Shepherd (1995; Shepherd and Richards, 2002). Meanwhile, the analysis of Jamaican lace-bark reflects a continued interest in the refined culture of slaves and their dress as part of material culture studies. The emphasis on material artifacts is important to understanding the people who owned the artifacts. Therefore, what some people might consider as mere objects that are part of the ordinariness of everyday life experiences are in fact formative and significant to learning about individuals and societies, especially those who left no written records. Material culturists, Steven Lubar and W. David Kingery, have argued that "Studying the artifacts allows one to understand meanings of texts and illuminates the social history embedded in them."[9]

Moreover, material artifacts, such as dress and textiles, "not only shape bodies and perceptions, but allow their possessors to establish their place in society."[10] Artifacts play a key role in providing both "a place" in society and a "voice" for those who used these objects. Through the process of analyzing these objects, we begin to learn about the people who used them. According to cultural anthropologist Anna-Karina Hermkens, objects can be regarded as "materialized practices of human behavior and interaction"[11]; therefore, the study of artifacts enables us to develop some understanding of social relationships. Hermkens and others suggest that by "following the thing," or the object, in this case the way lace-bark is made and used as dress, art, and commodity, we are also following the people making these objects. As a result, issues of gender and identity are revealed.[12] This is what I have tried to do here.

Dress and textile production has been an integral part of human existence since early history, and dressing the body is one of the most intimate acts that transforms us and connects us to the outer world. Consequently, needlework, dress, and textile production deserve more attention from scholars. A few pivotal works that look at the intersection of material culture, dress, and needlework among women include Barbara Burman (1999), Sarah A. Gordon (2004), Kathryn Church (2004, 2007), and Maureen Daly Goggin and Beth Fowkes Tobin (2009).[13] Despite significant strides made in Material Culture Studies, and Textiles and Fashion Studies, the analysis of clothing among enslaved Africans in the United States and the Caribbean lags behind.

Scholars like bell hooks (1992) and Carol Tulloch (1997, 2004) have enhanced our knowledge on diverse contemporary approaches to style in clothing, textiles, hair, and accessories of African descendants in the United States, Britain, and the Caribbean. Over the years, a handful of scholars began to investigate enslaved people's dress, hair styles, and headdress to develop some understanding of how enslaved Africans and their descendants used dress to construct identity and negotiated cultural space. Early analysis of slaves' and freed people's dress focused primarily on the United States Antebellum South and included works by Eugene Genovese (1976), Gerilyn Tandberg (1980), Sally Graham Durand (Tandberg and Durand, 1981), Helen Bradley Foster (1997), and, more recently, Monica Miller (2009), to name a few.

Although there is much interest in contemporary Caribbean dress and black style, such as Rastafarian, Street style, and Dance Hall within literary and visual cultural studies, the analysis of dress in Caribbean historiography has been scarce. Some important scholarship that makes reference to Jamaican slave dress includes Edward Kamau Brathwaite (1971, 1973), Barry Higman (1984), and Roderick McDonald (1993). In addition, Patrick Bryan (1991), Glory Robertson (1995), and Brian Moore and Michelle Johnson (2004) have included some analysis of post-emancipation dress, while Carol Tulloch (1997, 2004) and Carolyn Cooper (1995, 2004), among others, have enlightened us about contemporary notions of beauty and style in Jamaican popular culture. In 2004, the publication of Steeve Buckridge's study, *The Language of Dress: Resistance and Accommodation in Jamaica 1760–1890*, filled crucial gaps in our knowledge on slave dress and focused exclusively on the dress of colonized women both enslaved and freed.

That said, the analysis of slaves' use of plant material for clothing and the development of a cottage industry based on lace-bark is even more scarce within Caribbean historiography. The island of Jamaica was one of the earliest and best botanized areas of the Caribbean. Some of the first floristic studies of the island published included Sir Hans Sloane (1669, 1707, 1725), Patrick Browne (1756), Edward Long (1774), John Lunan (1814), and James Macfadyen (1837), while later works by George Proctor (1958) and Charles Dennis Adams (1972) made major contributions to the study of Jamaican plants. The works of Sir Hans Sloane, Patrick Browne, and Edward Long provide rich information on Jamaican lace-bark.

Economic botanists, such as Alfredo Noa (1992) and Victor Fuentes (1999), have produced detailed descriptions of various fibrous plants in Cuba and their use in making industrial ropes and some textiles. Similarly, Joel Timyan (1996) has crafted a descriptive study of Haitian plants, including some reference to fibrous trees used in clothing production and rituals. Most of these published scholarly works were done predominantly by agricultural scientists, ecologists, and botanists who in most cases sought to describe and catalogue the lace-bark tree as part of a larger effort to document the flora and fauna of the region. Steeve Buckridge's (2003, 2004) research on lace-bark examined the uses of fibrous plants in colonial

Jamaica and showed how flora and fauna were valuable commodities in enslaved people's lives. A few scholars, including Georgina Pearman and Hew D.V. Prendergast (2000) and, recently, Emily Brennan, Lori-Ann Harris, and Mark Nesbitt (2013), have published fascinating articles on Jamaican lace-bark from the perspective of economic botany. Despite this, more scholarship is needed on lace-bark and the material culture of Caribbean enslaved people. This text expands the scholarly focus on lace-bark to provide a microscopic view of women's role and provides an in-depth description of the lace-bark industry and its development over time. This is the first book-length study of its kind in Caribbean historiography that focuses exclusively on lace-bark production in Caribbean society.

By no means is this study exhaustive, nor is this a complete history of lace-bark. Rather, more research is needed on lace-bark in Cuba and Haiti, where the knowledge of this wonder plant, as in Jamaica, is lost and few people today are familiar with the tree. Several challenges developed while conducting this research. The botanical name for lace-bark, for example, is consistent throughout the scientific community, but not in the public domain. In those territories where the tree grows, there were many common names for lace-bark. Names varied from country to country according to linguistic differences, as well as within each territory and even across provinces, as in the case of Haiti. In some situations, common names for lace-bark were determined by secular and religious uses of the plant. Consequently data collection and locating surviving lace-bark trees in their natural habitat was daunting at times. Although several exquisite lace-bark artifacts and specimens from Jamaica have survived due to excellent conservation efforts, many of which are currently housed in several museum collections and herbariums around the world, to date no lace-bark artifacts on the same scale as those from Jamaica have been found for Cuba and Haiti. Understandably, most lace-bark clothing, like all plant materials, is difficult to preserve, and would not have survived the ravages of time without proper care and protection from the natural elements and wood-eating pests such as beetles and termites. Archeological evidence of lace-bark is also rare since buried cloth tends to decay quickly unless it survives under unique conditions. The analysis of artifacts, along with written descriptions from the period in question, provided the opportunity to piece together some semblance of how lace-bark was used and its contributions to the culture of refinement of enslaved Africans and their descendants.

Equally challenging was how to measure enslaved women's contribution to the local economy when in fact they worked in an informal and unregulated cottage industry that left no written or official records. The scarcity of evidence and the absence of slave testimonies required new methods of enquiry to uncover enslaved women's use of lace-bark. Incorporating an interdisciplinary approach with various methods and previously neglected sources proved useful in this regard, but at times I have had to generalize from specific examples due to the lapse of evidence and the absence of slave testimony. My approach to the analysis of lace-bark is informed by current trends in material culture studies. Although I examine lace-bark from an aesthetic perspective in which semiotics and structuralism are incorporated to explain the object, I have heeded to Alfred Gell's call for a new perspective to analyze the "the agency of things."[14] In so doing, I am able to explore the construction and ambivalence of the performance of race, class, and gender within the colonial society.

This study crosses several geographic and linguistic boundaries, while the inter-disciplinary nature of the study is heightened by the use of sources, deriving not only from material culture studies, Caribbean and African history, and women and gender studies, but also from art history, geography, anthropology, sociology, geology, ethnography, economic botany, historical linguistics, and textiles and clothing. Particular attention has been paid to the works by Sir Hans Sloane and eighteenth-century historians Edward Long and Patrick Browne to provide descriptive accounts of lace-bark production and the various uses of the lace-bark tree in Jamaican colonial society. The works of eighteenth- and nineteenth-century natural historians of Haiti, like Michel Etienne Descourtilz, and of Cuba, such as Alexander Humboldt, guided my approach to the study of early plant life in these territories. Investigative studies, including *Flowering Plants of Jamaica* by Charles Dennis Adams (1972), are used to shed light on the diversity and richness of Jamaican flora. Meanwhile, travel journals from the period of study, like those of Cynric Williams, are used to convey some ideas of how slaves and freed women used lace-bark in clothing manufacture. Numerous articles from the *Jamaica Gleaner* and the *Jamaica Gazette* help track the development of the lace-bark industry and its changes over time, while documents from the world exhibitions and fairs, along with women's self-help society records and government publications from the nineteenth century, reveal the height of lace-bark popularity and achievements in Victorian Jamaica.

Scientific studies and articles from botanical journals, dictionaries, and agricultural digests, like *Revista del Jordin Botanico Nacional* from Cuba, provide valuable information on the state of lace-bark trees, conservation efforts, and various fibrous plants in Cuba. Furthermore, correspondence from the field, along with conversations, interviews with scientists, conservationists, government officials, scholars, spiritual leaders, and Maroon descendants about bark-cloth and lace-bark, is woven throughout the text. This study relies on ethnographies to establish the African roots of lace-bark production in the Caribbean and an abundance of plantation records from Harmony Hall Estate, Worthy Park Plantation, and Radner Coffee Plantation to uncover the use of textiles among colonized people in Jamaica.

Sources related to material culture practices of Africa have been utilized to provide a framework for this study. The expertise of textile specialists has been enlisted to assist with the analysis and cultural significance of bark-cloth in Africa and the Caribbean. Several scholarly works, like *Cloth in West African History* by

Colleen Kriger (2006) and *African Textiles Today* by Chris Spring (2012), provide valuable information on textiles in Africa. Meanwhile, studies related to bark-cloth in the Pacific, such as the works of Anna-Karina Hermkens, Rod Edwins, and Robert Neich, are included for comparative analysis of production and to gauge how these textiles might have influenced Europeans' interest in bark-cloth.

In addition, lace-bark specimens and artifacts from the Natural History Museum of Jamaica, Field Museum of Natural History in Chicago, and Royal Botanic Gardens at Kew in London, which has the largest collection of lace-bark artifacts from Jamaica, are included throughout the study. Besides artifacts that provide tangible evidence of how lace-bark was used, the illustrations and paintings of colonized subjects by artists from the early period are incorporated. The images by Agostino Brunias and Isaac Mendes Belisario reveal dress styles and lace accessories among enslaved and freed people in the Caribbean. Likewise, the illustrations by Joseph Bartholomew Kidd provide glimpses into the Jamaican landscape with its spectacular beauty of the island's flora and fauna. Oral history obtained during field research in Jamaica, Cuba, Haiti, and the Dominican Republic is incorporated where possible. In Jamaica, these sources are the results of open-ended questionnaires conducted with Jamaican Maroon descendants and those who harvested lace-bark for a livelihood.

Terminology and organization

There is no such thing as an object out of context. There are objects in the right context, in which they beam meanings from others, or in the wrong context, in which their power to instruct is diminished through weak or improper association[15]
HENRY GLASSIE

Some discussion of terminology and the organization of this text is advisable.

Lace-bark is also a form of "natural lace" and should not be confused with other plants or trees with similar names, such as lace-bark pine [*Pinus bungeana*] or the Chinese Elm, also called lace-bark elm [*Ulmus parvifolia*], which is native to China, Korea, and Japan, but now is abundant in North Carolina and spreading to other parts of the Southern United States. These trees derive their names from the peeling or exfoliating of their outer bark, to reveal an interesting pattern that makes them popular as an ornamental.[16] Unlike these trees, the *lagetto* is unique due to its fibrous inner bark and is found only in Cuba, Jamaica, Haiti, and the Dominican Republic. I use the term "lace-bark" frequently throughout this study in reference to the cloth obtained from the tree, however, other common and regional names are incorporated when appropriate. I have also included the botanical or scientific names of most plants mentioned in the study, but at times I have chosen to avoid these names as a means of appealing to a wider audience and at the same time evoking a sense of everyday use among the subjects of this research. Nonetheless, I have added an Appendix with corresponding scientific names for some of the plants referred to in the text.

Comprehension of bark-cloth production requires some knowledge of tree anatomy and the topography of the environment or natural habitat of bark-cloth trees. Therefore, references will be made throughout the study to plant anatomy and environmental features. Topography or the surface characteristics of the earth, from the soil and landscape features to the climate and level of rainfall, are essential to the survival of trees, including those from which bark-cloth is obtained. Climate conditions play a key role in bark-cloth production and often determine the success of a bark harvest. In West Africa for instance, the rainy seasons provide high humidity and moisture, thus enabling easy removal of the bark from the trunk of trees for processing. In dry season the process is more difficult due to lack of sufficient moisture and sap in the bark.[17] For thousands of years, forest dwelling people around the world, including numerous cultures in West and Central Africa, have lived by gathering food and raw materials from the forest for their daily existence.

Consequently, knowledge of plants and animals, their uses for food, medicine, and clothing were transmitted orally from one generation to the other and passed down among descendants, including people of African descent in the Diaspora.[18] The impact of the natural world on the life of people is undeniable. Historian and ethnographer Jennifer Newell has rightly argued that "the natural environment is inextricably woven into the unfolding of human histories."[19] History and the natural world are very connected whether it is in Africa, Polynesia, or the Caribbean among people who sought "sustenance" such as food, clothing, and medicine from the rain forest; our lives are shaped by the natural environment. As Geoff Parks summed up nicely, "The ecology of a stretch of country and its history are far from unrelated. They work on one another . . . if you go in search of one; you are led to the other."[20]

The subjects of the study are slave and freed women who were African or of African ancestry living in Jamaica from the late seventeenth to early twentieth century. Although the subjects are primarily those living in Jamaica, there is some comparative analysis with the use of lace-bark in Cuba and Haiti among diverse groups of people in these regions. As I have argued in earlier studies, the focus on women rather than men or both is due to several reasons. Universally, women have not been responsible for the production of textiles; however, throughout much of human history and across many cultures, women have been the ones primarily in charge of the maintenance and care of clothing.[21] In colonial Jamaica, large numbers of enslaved and freed women took care of the clothing needs of their families and even their enslavers. Countless women, for instance, have been actively engaged in sewing, mending, knitting, and washing and ironing clothes, and numerous women continue these customs today. Many men, on the other hand, have been the recipient of clothes maintained in the home. Nevertheless, there is some discussion of men's activities to provide a sociocultural context to comprehend how women negotiated cultural space to be expressive and feminine, and how gender was socially constructed, understood, and lived within the patriarchal colonial society.

This study focuses on Jamaica because of the abundance and availability of sources on lace-bark and the substantial number of lace-bark artifacts from Jamaica that have survived. The period of study spans a broad time frame from the seventeenth century to the turn of the twentieth century, culminating with the collapse of the lace-bark industry. The time frame enables us to grasp some sense of how the industry developed and the transformation that occurred over time. Even though the religious significance of the lace-bark tree is briefly discussed, such a topic deserves more in-depth attention that is beyond the scope and focus of this study. Here, I am more concerned with the secular uses of lace-bark and the role women played in creating a cottage industry based on natural lace. The narrative style and organization of this book is intended to appeal to a wide audience beyond the scholarly and academic community. I have adapted the term "African lace-bark" to suggest that lace-bark production was primarily an African activity in Jamaica that subsequently gave rise to an informal industry based on natural lace. The success and popularity of lace-bark was due to the skills and expertise of African women and their descendants who controlled this industry. The tendency here then is to illuminate the "Africanness" of lace-bark production and the function of dress and textiles as a cultural link between the Caribbean and Africa.

Considering that this study is about lace-bark, some clarification of the term "lace" might be useful. The origin of lace is an ongoing debate among scholars, but a few scholars such as Emily Jackson and Ernesto Jesuram have suggested that lace has existed throughout much of human history.[22] Basically, as long as there has been some form of twisting fibers for netting, there was lace. Regardless, lace as we know it today is often a lightweight fabric patterned with open holes or spaces that can be hand or machine made. Lace comes in many varieties with different names in various cultures and is constructed in multiple ways. One way to construct the web-like pattern in the fabric is not by weaving, but by removing threads of previously woven cloth through a process where thread is looped, twisted, plaited, or braided to other thread independently of any backing fabric.[23] Other methods of making lace include knitting, crochet, tatting, bobbin lace, and machine-made Leavers lace. Even though open work fabric is traditionally classified as lace, there are other techniques that can be used to construct open work fabric similar to lace, but not usually classified as lace, including sprang and macramé. By contrast, linen is a lightweight but durable fabric made from the fibers of the stem of the flax plant.[24] Arguably, lace-bark is not "true" lace in the sense it was not handmade or machine made; nevertheless, the physical characteristics of lace-bark are surprisingly similar to manufactured lace and linen. Throughout this study, I use the term "cottage industry" to refer to the pre-industrial mode of production centered on the home. Cottage workers, mostly women, provided for themselves and family by producing bark-cloth every available minute. I also use the term "dress" as it is more inclusive. Dress includes not just garments and jewelry but also dyed skin, tattoos, or any sort of "assemblages of modification of the body and/or supplements to the body."[25]

I have taken an eclectic theoretical approach to the study of women and their production of lace-bark. I examine how enslaved and freed women who owned some capital operated as entrepreneurs, producing natural lace within the confines of the colonial society. In attempting to investigate the role of women in the lace-bark industry, I found the most useful theoretical framework to be symbolic interactionism, particularly in the area of visual art and the construction of identity. In other words, identities are conveyed by dress as it reveals the social position of the wearer to both wearer and observer within specific interaction situations.[26] Material artifacts and objects such as dress, bark-cloth, and lace-bark are considered semiotic because they convey meaning within social and cultural contexts. As Henry Glassie has pointed out, "all objects exist in context."[27] Furthermore, objects themselves function as signifiers in the production of meaning. Cultural theorist Stuart Hall states, "We give things meaning by how we use them or integrate them into our everyday practices. . . . In part, we give things meaning by how we represent them—the words we use about them, the stories we tell about them, the images of them we produce, the emotions we associate with them, the ways we classify and conceptualize them, the values we place on them."[28]

Hall's explanation of the meaning of things along with Glassie's articulation of contextual importance provides an important conceptual framework for this study and enables us to comprehend the "construction of meaning" and cultural significance of lace-bark in enslaved women's lives. By following Hall's approach, the term "culture" in this study has multiple meanings and suggests various concepts. I incorporate the anthropological perspective of exploring what is distinctive about the societies or people in question, and the more traditional concepts—what is thought to be best of the society along with shared values.[29] I also include critical race theory and post-colonial theory to critique the oppressive social structures of the Caribbean slave society, while black feminist theory provides the final anchor that grounds this study. Black feminist theory as a form of cultural criticism helps us probe the intersectionality of race, class, gender, and sexuality. Moreover, it challenges the invisibility of black women's lives and achievements, and simultaneously interrogates the culture of male dominance within the colonial plantocracy.[30]

This text is divided into several sections including this Introduction, three chapters, followed by a Conclusion, Appendix, and Glossary. The first chapter,

Pre-History to Early Slave Trade: "People of the Forest," looks at Africa as source and origin of a rich bark-cloth tradition brought to the Caribbean by African slaves. The chapter includes a brief discussion of bark-cloth production in the Pacific for comparative analysis and highlights bark-cloth production in West Africa during the pre-colonial period and beyond. I analyze whether or not the indigenous people knew about lace-bark and other fibrous plants and if they shared this knowledge of local plants with enslaved Africans. The chapter highlights the structure of Jamaican slave society and the policies that regulated the slave clothing and dress customs of enslaved Africans.

Chapter 2, Plantation Jamaica: "Controlling the Silver," focuses on Plantation life in Jamaica and addresses the social, economic, and cultural factors that led to the creation of a lace-bark industry in Jamaica. The chapter reveals why women dominated the lace-bark industry, how it was produced, and the role of the Maroons and free blacks in lace-bark production. The chapter examines the role of seamstresses, and how the lace-bark industry created some financial independence for enslaved and freed women. Sections of this chapter are devoted to lace-bark in Cuba and Haiti and how lace-bark was used in these territories. I investigate why lace-bark production had a greater presence in Jamaica and how the industry changed over time.

Chapter 3, Victorian Jamaica: "Fancy Fans and Doilies," begins with the shift from an economic to a "civilizing" mission during the post-Emancipation era, and the renewed interest in lace-bark for different reasons. In this section, I analyze lace-bark clothing, and explore how the commercialization of lace-bark production impacted women's lives. I also examine the popularity of natural lace on the world stage, and the role of Women's Self Help societies in promoting lace-bark crafts and needlework for the emerging tourist market. In addition, the chapter discusses how lace-bark clothing reflected the material environment of Victorian Jamaica and the colonial government's attempts at marketing lace-bark, and their failure at industrializing the lace-bark industry.

The text concludes with a summary of the findings and emphasizes the contributions of enslaved women and their descendants to the colonial economy as active participants in the lace-bark cottage industry. The Conclusion reiterates the significance of women's collective strength and the fundamental importance of women's role and labor in creating a new beginning in spite of an oppressive environment. Most importantly, it reinforces women's role as the conduits for the transmission of African cultural characteristics. The Conclusion closes with some assessment of conservation efforts to protect the remaining lace-bark trees and whether a lace-bark industry can be revived and whether it is sustainable.

Throughout the study, I use the terms "Caribbean" and "West Indies" interchangeably to mean the same region. Several of the early sources on lace-bark use the term "West Indies" simply because the term "Caribbean" became popular much later. The Caribbean is geographically diverse and is located in the tropical zone consisting of a chain of islands, stretching in an arc from Florida to Venezuela. The islands are nestled between the North and South American continents, and they enclose the Caribbean Sea as well as specific continental countries whose borders meet the Caribbean Sea (Figure I.2).

These nations have a closely related history and follow a similar pattern of development. The region encompasses hundreds of islands with twenty-eight major territories, ranging from sovereign states and overseas departments to dependencies. The island nations are divided into several geographical groups, including the Greater Antilles, consisting of Cuba, Hispaniola (Haiti and the Dominican Republic), Jamaica, and Puerto Rico. Cuba is the largest island nation in both size and population; however, Jamaica is the largest of the British West Indian islands. The Caribbean and its sea are named after the indigenous people of the Lesser Antilles in the region, called the Kalinagos, but formerly known as the "Caribs." The term "West Indies" was first used by early Spanish explorers and adventurers to differentiate the "Indian looking" indigenous people of the region from those in India or the East Indies. Today, while much of the region self identifies as the "Caribbean," the term "West Indies" remains popular in some areas of the English-speaking Caribbean.[31]

Beyond the shared history and similar patterns of development among regional nations, the Caribbean is profoundly one of the most complex and culturally diverse areas on the globe. This phenomenon is a result of vast numbers of different people who arrived in the region over the centuries from other parts of the world,

FIGURE I.2 Map of the Caribbean. Courtesy of Leonard Notice at the University of the West Indies.

bringing with them aspects of their culture. The diversity and vibrancy of Caribbean cultures is reflected in the dress of the people. Lace-bark was an important feature in the history of Caribbean dress, and it represented a rich African legacy that dared to survive against the backdrop of an oppressive, white-dominated society. The overall goal, then, of this study is to acknowledge the creativity of enslaved African women and their descendants, and reveal the beauty and refinement of a remarkable form of visual art that until now has been obscure to all except a few specialists.

1 PRE-HISTORY TO EARLY SLAVE TRADE: "PEOPLE OF THE FOREST"

We are a people of the forest . . . It is to the forest we seek life!

GANG-GONG[1]

Bark-cloth, a global phenomenon

Bark-cloth has a long and varied history, dating back to the pre-historic period and, even though we do not know exactly when or where bark-cloth was first produced, archeological evidence in the form of stone and wooden bark-cloth beaters suggests that bark-cloth had a wide distribution around the globe.[2] In tropical areas where suitable trees existed for the purposes of making cloth to cover and protect the human body, bark-cloth was a popular item of consumption among many people. As human beings industrialized, and with readily accessible machine-made textiles, bark-cloth production gradually declined and eventually disappeared from many regions. Bark-cloth was made in Asia, including in the Philippines, Indonesia, and the Malay Peninsula. It was made in many areas of Oceana, Africa, North, South and Central America, including the Caribbean. Across many of these regions, except for lace-bark in the Caribbean, the production of bark-cloth often consisted of stripping the tree bark from the parent tree, then soaking and scraping the bark, followed by a process of "thinning" and softening by pounding the moistened inner bark with a beater or mallet to transform it into malleable, smooth cloth.[3]

The cloth obtained from vegetable or plant materials is divided into three broad categories: bark-cloth, a non-woven cloth made by macerating the inner bark of certain plants and shrubs; non-spun fibers, which can be woven; and the third, spun fibers such as cotton.[4] Woven cloth made from the bark fiber thread is called bast fiber cloth. In principle, cloth is made of fiber; however, not all fibers are spun into thread, and not all threads are woven into textiles.[5] Among the Kuba of the Congo, leaf fibers from the young leaves of the raphia palm [*Raphia vinifera*] were used and processed but not spun. Raphia leaf fibers were woven into textiles that served many functions in the society. In some cultures, fibers were spun and then twisted into heavier threads or cordage that would then be plaited or twisted by hand to make clothing, blankets, and mats. The thread, fibers, and tools used in the process of making cloth and other articles for consumption are important material artifacts as they convey the level of expertise and sometimes the identity of the cloth's producers.[6] Furthermore, bark-cloth and its uses varied from one culture to the next. Bark-cloth designs could be as simple as the undecorated bark breeches among some of the forest cultures of Central Africa to the colorful bark-cloths of Polynesia and Melanesia that were beautifully decorated with geometric patterns and culturally defined motifs rich in symbolism.[7]

Bark-cloth also differed in texture. The cloth could be as "thick as a wool blanket or as thin as a silk scarf, as stiff as parchment or as soft as chamois leather."[8] Even though yards of flowing bark-cloth were draped and sometimes wrapped around the human body, it was also fashioned into exquisite forms of dress, while in some communities, the cloth was fringed, embroidered, layered, and feathered to create fine mats, cloaks, bedding, and blankets, often richly decorated according to cultural standards of taste and individual creativity. Scholars of bark-cloth have argued that some of the most refined bark-cloth traditions are found in Southeast Asia and the Pacific.[9] Yet, despite the beauty of this unique art form, bark-cloth and its symbolic interplay with the body surface, especially in ritual was often misunderstood. Consequently, the clothing practices of the "other" were prescribed contrasting images and meanings.

There is much evidence of cultural misinterpretation associated with cloth and clothing during early cross-cultural encounters between indigenous producers and consumers of bark-cloth and Europeans. Perhaps it seems strange to think of cloth as the root of erroneous interpretation, but considering Europeans' Judeo-Christian and Western perspectives on dressing and undressing the body as opposed to the very public display of "nakedness," undoubtedly, misconceptions were inevitable.[10] Cross-cultural encounters gave rise to distorted images associated with the "natives'" naked black bodies that were stereotypical and racist. On one hand, there was the African as naked savage, uncivilized and decked out in tree bark and loin cloth; on the other, the exoticized naked Polynesian in grass skirt and a perpetual state in anticipation of sex. The corporeal price for the indigenous was catastrophic as the native body became an object for Europeans' viewing pleasure that fostered a sense of Imperialist sex paradise. The racial stereotypes, or what Stuart Hall called "racialized regime of representation," helped shape the relations between Europeans and the colonized and fostered Europeans' sense of entitlement. These racialized images persisted beyond the colonial era into the contemporary period.[11]

The projections of these images through the white gaze emboldened the indigenous body as it engaged these images and meaning. Ultimately, the body became a site of contestation, a battlefield that is fought over continuously across a spectrum of historical moments. As philosopher George Yancy has argued, this does not mean the body has no material force of its own, but how we "interpret that force is through historical discourse even as that discourse may falter."[12] The European colonial world was obsessed with the Black body. It was an object of fascination and abhorrence, and Europeans sought to control it.[13] In the process, some Europeans either dismissed or failed to recognize the cultural significance of cloth, particularly the role of bark-cloth, whether as sacred cloth or as a medium between the spirit world and the living.[14] As we will see in this study, bark-cloth was more than cloth and design. It was an impressive work of art that revealed social class and gender, state of being, religious affiliation, as well as ethnicity and regional origin. In fact, bark-cloth was a vocabulary that was deeply connected to the body and intertwined with daily life of the community, a powerful material object that exercised a form of cultural agency.[15] In other words, bark-cloth influenced social behavior and attitudes.

One of the most well-known forms of bark-cloth is *tapa* from the Pacific region. The word "tapa" has become synonymous with all forms of bark-cloth around the world.[16] The word was popularized in the nineteenth century during the period of increased European contact and is derived from two sources—the Samoan word "tapa" for the uncolored edges of the bark-cloth and the Hawaiian word "kapa" (pronounced *tapa*), which means beaten or the beaten thing.[17] In tropical areas around the world, the fibers for bark-cloth were derived from the inner bark of the tree's anatomy, the secondary *phloem*, located just beneath the outer bark in a variety of tree species. The main plant sources of bark-cloth were the *Ficus* and *Artocarpus; Broussonetia papyrifera*, and *Hibiscus tilliaceus*.[18] Even though bark-cloth around the world was made from various fibrous plants and shrubs, in the Pacific Islands the main source of tapa was the inner bark of the domesticated, non-indigenous, paper mulberry tree [*Broussonetia papyrifera*]. The paper mulberry belongs to the Moraceae, or the mulberry family, one of the largest groups of tree and shrub species with an inner bark suitable for making cloth and paper.[19]

The paper mulberry originated in Southern China and Southeastern Asia more than 5,000 years ago and was first used for paper manufacture in China around 100 AD. It was introduced into Oceana by early Southeastern migrants 3,000 years ago, traveling down through the islands of Melanesia and out into the Pacific region. The mulberry tree was one of the earliest plants cultivated in Southeast Asia.[20] Women and men carried their knowledge and skills of making bark-cloth with them, thus spreading and refining the technique of cloth production in the area. Tapa was an important feature of Oceana culture and was produced in certain areas of Melanesia, from New Guinea to Vanuatu, Fiji and most of the highlands of Polynesia, from Hawaii to Tahiti, the Marquesas, Tonga, Samoa, as well as New Zealand.[21]

It is worthwhile noting that bark-cloth production was a gendered activity in some cultures. In Polynesia, Captain James Cook remarked in 1769 that "the making of cloth is wholly the work of women in which all ranks are employed."[22] Observing the women making bark-cloth, the botanist Joseph Banks revealed that the stalks of the paper mulberry were slit up longitudinally and drawn off the stick. The bark was then soaked in water for several days, after which the material was scraped until all the outer green was rubbed and washed away—nothing remained but the very fine fibers of the inner bark.[23] Next, the bark material was laid in overlapping sections over a wooden anvil or log with a hard surface, and beaten with carved wooden hand beaters called *i'e* in Samoan. Beating the bark expanded the fibers, creating cloth and ultimately sheets, measuring four and more yards wide and dozens of yards long. The bark-cloth was then stretched out on the ground and dried, before it was ready for use.[24] Some tapa was so refined it may have been mistaken for woven cloth (Figure 1.1).[25]

FIGURE 1.1 Tapa cloth scattering forms like oak leaves. Samoan Islands (51 in. x 48 in.). Siapo Mamanu. © The Grand Rapids Public Museum.

Beyond the beauty of tapa, there were production challenges associated with this type of bark-cloth. After five to six days of beating inner bark fibers into sheets, and then bleaching the materials, the cloth could be torn and soiled quite easily. Tapa artists had to be highly skilled and careful in how they handled the material. Moreover, insects such as termites liked to eat it, and it gets worn out rather quickly. Tapa disintegrates if it gets wet, which explains why many Polynesians found European fabrics, namely white linen which looked like unpainted tapa, very appealing, giving rise to a demand for European fabrics.[26] Unlike tapa, lace-bark did not present the same challenges.

African bark-cloth: a rich heritage

"Aboa bi bɛka wo a na ɔfiri wo ntoma mu"—An insect that bites you will surely be hiding inside your cloth.[27]

GHANAIAN PROVERB

While Polynesia has been the focal point for beautiful tapa productions, for centuries West and Central Africa has been amongst the world's great producers of textiles. Whether as a valued trade commodity for local and foreign consumption or as a form of currency, adornment, ritual object and signifier of status and identity, African cloth has been widely celebrated. Dating back to the Greek and Roman presence in North Africa, Europeans have long admired African textiles and, as early as the fifteenth century, Portuguese travelers to the region brought home exquisite textiles from Africa to decorate their homes and to present as gifts.[28] The textile industry during the pre-colonial era in West and West Central Africa was extensive with professional weavers, spinners, and dyers among the important craftspeople. In the mid-nineteenth century, the missionary Rev. R.H. Stone surveyed the Yoruba city of Abeokuta from the top of a granite boulder and reaffirmed this notion. He wrote, "They [Africans] were dressed and were industrious ... [providing] everything that their physical comfort required. The men are builders, blacksmiths ... weavers, basket-makers, hat-makers, mat-makers ... women ... most diligently ... spin, weave, trade, cook, and dye cotton fabrics. They also make soap, dyes, palm oil, nut-oil, all the native earthenware, and many other things used in the country."[29]

Cloth manufacturing was an integral part of the domestic economy, but in some regions of West Africa manufacturing had commercial significance, as with the Ashanti (Asante), Yoruba, and Nupe, who produced beautiful cloth for market distribution.[30] In the kingdom of Luango, the textile industry manufactured large quantities of cloth for regional markets as opposed to production for only household consumption. Textile manufacturing was one of the most important industries on the Slave Coast.[31] Cotton cultivation and indigo production were auxiliary industries to textile manufacturing: as early as the 1790s, the European explorer Mungo Park noticed the making of bark-cloth in the Gambia. Raffia cloth was made from palm bark by softening a long strip of bark in water, then beating the softened bark with a mallet until it flattened out as a single, supple piece of cloth several times larger and wider than the original piece of bark.[32]

In contemporary society, cotton and woven textiles are easily available due to machine mass production the world over. However, in pre-colonial West Africa, cotton was not as plentiful as one might think and cloth was not always readily available to the majority of people.[33] Although cotton has been cultivated across the Sahel and savanna regions of Africa for more than a thousand years, cloth was considered highly valuable and thus the monopoly of the ruler. Many West African monarchs distributed cloth as gifts to worthy and deserving subjects. In the West African Kingdom of Dahomey, the visitor R. Norris recorded in 1772 that the King's annual custom included "presents of Indian damask, or some other handsome silks"[34] and those who "acquit themselves to his satisfaction receive large cotton cloth."[35] Henceforth, countless commoners who did not have access to manufactured cloth utilized bark-cloth.

African communities manufactured complex woven textiles with vibrant colors and rhythmic patterns that reflected high levels of refinement and achievements, from *Kente* and *Adinkra* cloths of the Ashanti, and the mud-dyed *Bogolanfini* of the Bamana people of Mali to the *Aso oke* of the Yoruba and the brightly embroidered cottons of the Cameroon. Nor can we forget the luminous metal thread embroidered velvets of the Amhara, the prestigious *Kasai* velvets, also called *Raphia cutpile* and the *raphia applique* of the Kuba confederacy, or the silks of the Malagasy.[36] The array of beautiful and intricate textiles in Africa is astounding and dispels the racist imagery of the naked "savage." Yet, despite this, scholarship on bark-cloth in Africa is limited and most people are unfamiliar with this type of African cloth with a few exceptions. The dynamic textile industry in Africa, along with widespread imported fabrics over time, has overshadowed and, in many cases, displaced the bark-cloth industry. The resulting situation is that African bark-cloth is often considered a sign of "backwardness" and a poorer version of cloth as compared with woven cloth, and is viewed as not significant, today being worn only by the poor.[37]

Interestingly, bark-cloth was one of the earliest cloths made throughout sub-Saharan Africa and is considered the oldest branch of the cloth industry on the African continent, followed by textile weaving, which developed later on. Besides bark-cloth, animal skin and leather was in widespread use in Africa long before extensive use of imported cloth from Europe, India, and the United States. Furthermore, weaving was known to many Africans before trade with India and Europe.[38] However, the origins of African bark-cloth is an ongoing debate among scholars and Africans; regardless, beaten bark-cloth was reported in West Africa as early as the middle of the sixteenth century in countries such as Liberia, and bark-cloth production continues today on a small scale in Ghana, and Nigeria.[39] Bark-cloth was cut and sewn as patch work; it was also embroidered and painted with natural dye pigments. Like Polynesian tapa, it was very fragile, particularly if wet and readily replaced when new durable textiles became available.[40] The best known areas for bark-cloth production in Africa were the Congo, Rwanda, Uganda, Malawi, and Zambia. Bark-cloth was also made among the Ashanti of Ghana and in Madagascar.[41] Of this list, only Ghana and the Congo supplied slaves to Jamaica.

There were some parallels between bark-cloth production in Polynesia and the African context, but there were also major differences. The most common source for bark-cloth in many areas of Africa was the tropical fig or *Ficus* tree. The *Ficus* was the genus of 800 species of woody fibrous trees in the Moraceae family of plants. While most of the tapa produced in Polynesia was obtained from the paper mulberry, much of the bark-cloth beyond the Pacific was produced from species of wild or cultivated fig. Several of these *Ficus* or fig species were scattered across the continent of Africa and thrived extremely well in the forest zones. For forest dwellers, the tropical fig tree was easily accessible, abundant, and a valuable commodity for its cloth and medicinal properties. As a flowering plant, it was most important to the forest ecosystem as its fruits were a major source for frugivores, especially birds.[42]

Although the bark of the breadfruit and the paper mulberry was used in Polynesia to make cloth, in Africa these plants did not become major sources for bark-cloth. The paper mulberry was introduced to Ghana, Tanzania, Zimbabwe, and Uganda to produce fibers for the production of paper. This did not materialize, as the paper mulberry in sub-Saharan Africa, unlike the Pacific, was used primarily for firewood, and in Ghana paper mulberry wood was used to make crates, picture frames, and plywood.[43] While the breadfruit did not become a major food source in Africa, it became a major staple in Jamaica. Introduced into Jamaica by Captain William Bligh in 1793, breadfruit saplings were distributed across the island, not as a potential clothing option for enslaved Africans, but to fulfill the demands of the planter class who sought affordable nourishing food for their slaves.[44] Still, the breadfruit did not become right away the successful economy food enslavers and plantation owners in Jamaica had hoped for. Enslaved Jamaicans did not like it and preferred to produce their own food in their small plots of land. It was not until after emancipation in 1838 that the breadfruit became part of the local Jamaican diet.[45]

Within many African economies, including the textile industry, labor was often divided according to gender. In several regions of West Africa, women did the spinning and men did the weaving. There were specific looms for men and women. Where the narrow strip loom was found, it was often used by men, while the vertical loom was used solely by women. In other parts of Africa, particularly in the Congo River basin, where the strip loom was absent, the men used the vertical loom to produce raffia cloth.[46] Gender division of labor applied to some bark-cloth producing cultures where men did the pounding of the bark while women did the design. Among the Imbuti people of the Epulu and Ituri forests of Central Africa, bark was historically obtained from the topical fig trees that they found in the forests and beaten, however, Imbuti women designed bark-cloth with complex, asymmetrical symbols that continue to be a source of debate among art historians. Designs on the cloth varied and sometimes depicted flora and fauna, and cosmological concerns.[47]

Critical to our understanding of lace-bark is the cultural significance of West Africa as source and origin of Jamaican bark-cloth. In Ghana, formerly the Gold Coast, bark-cloth was manufactured and many towns and villages in pre-colonial Ghana had art and craft industries that utilized the skills of both male and female slaves.[48] Knowledge of the bark-cloth industry of this region during the early centuries is scarce. Nor do we know the exact date when bark-cloth technology emerged in Ghana. Due to the lack of sufficient evidence, we are left to hypothesize about the early bark-cloth industry. Nevertheless, bark-cloth is known to have been made and used throughout the region long before the introduction of weaving. The famous woven cloth in Ghana called *Kente*, developed in the seventeenth century by the Ashanti people, the dominant ethnic group among the Akan people, was produced in various designs, most of which had cultural or historical significance. *Kente* was originally made from unraveled imported silk fabrics, which were then locally woven into narrow strips and sewed together. In 1841, the visitor John Beecham remarked that the Ashanti "purchased the richest silks in order to unravel and interweave them with their own thread; and their best clothes are extolled for their fineness, variety, brilliance and size."[49] Customarily, *Kente* was the cloth of Kings and all new designs of the cloth came under the control of the Asantehene (King), who would either reserve them for himself or allocate them to important men and women in the kingdom as symbols of their status. Woven cloths by the Akan people in Ghana were expensive due to the slow and laborious process involved in their production. Only the wealthy and officials could afford them, while the common people wore cheaper imported cottons or bark-cloth.[50]

In Ghana and other areas of West Africa, the *Antiaris* genus of the Moraceae family was used for bark-cloth production while in East Africa, among the people of Buganda, the species of tree used was of fig, *Ficus natalensis*.[51] Among the Ashanti people of Ghana, cloth was made from the "bark-cloth" tree [*Antiaris africana*] called the *kyenkyen* tree in the *Twi* language of the Ashanti. The tree was also known as *tsobo* by the Dangme people of Ghana and *ofu* in *Guang*, the language spoken by the Boso people, but more widely known as the "bark-cloth" tree due to the strong white cloth made from the bark. The West African *Antiaris* seemed less toxic than its Asiatic counterpart [*A. toxicaria*] and therefore posed no harm during the cloth production process.[52]

The *kyenkyen* tree grew mainly in the forest zones of West Africa; hence, the bark-cloth industry was found in the forest areas. Northern Ghana was covered with wooded savannah; therefore, it has never been known to produce bark-cloth.[53] The large *kyenkyen* tree grew to 100 feet or more in height with a diameter of 3 feet or more and emanates from the West coast of Africa. In Nigeria, the tree was sometimes called *false iroko*. The wood is soft, and the tree is easily distinguishable since its smooth bark is at times pale or off-white in color with many wart-like growths. The tree required extreme care after the cut otherwise bacterial infection could develop and ultimately kill the tree. In West Africa the wood was used in manufacture of canoes, but some logs were exported for the manufacture of veneers.[54]

African bark-cloth production was also strenuous and time-consuming. In West Africa, men searched the forest until a suitable *Antiaris* was found. The tree was cut down, and the trunk sectioned into logs of suitable length. In some cases, the tree was not cut down, but large branches were cut off instead. The bark was cut vertically along the length of the log then across at the top and bottom, thus creating a cylindrical-shaped piece of bark that was easy to peel away from the harvested log. The inner bark was separated then placed horizontally on a wooden beam, hoisted on two Y-shaped posts at each end for support and beaten with wooden mallets called *abore ayifore* in *Guang* and *ayitin* in *Twi*.[55] The corrugated wooden mallet was used diagonally so that the fibers of the bark were spread out. The result was a soft piece of cloth much wider than the original cut from the bark. The cloth was then rolled up and washed thoroughly. Afterwards, the cloth was positioned between two pieces of sticks securely bound with a vine and rotated to squeeze out the water, then dried in the sun for three hours after which it was ready for use. Bark-cloth in Guang was called *ofuta*, and among the Ashanti it was called *kyenkyen* cloth.[56] This type of cloth production was an essential part of the rainforest economy in West Africa. For example, Ashanti bark-cloth was traded amongst the forest people of the Ivory Coast.[57] The primary difference between West and East African bark-cloth was the color. In West Africa the cloth was off-white to gray, while in Uganda and Tanzania it was brown or a deep terra cotta red.[58] Furthermore, not all bark-cloth making was restricted to the forest zones. The *baobab* tree [*Adansonia digitata*] did well in drier places, and its bark was utilized for several purposes including cloth making. The smooth gray bark of the *baobab* was softened and pounded, until it was transformed into pliable cloth for household use.[59]

Bark-cloth: ceremonial and secular purposes

Throughout history, bark-cloth served many functions in diverse societies. The semiology of bark-cloth was embodied in its role and use in the community, not only as clothing and signifier of status and identity but also as an important iconography representing the sacred and secular interwoven in an integrated fashion. In Ghana, for example, the *kyenkyen* cloth was ideal for sleeping mats for bedding as the cloth was impermeable to ticks and bed bugs.[60] Bark-cloth adorned and delineated sacred spaces and was hung from the ceiling in the Ashanti King's residence.[61] Likewise, in numerous African communities bark-cloth was used as a ritual object and medium that connected humans with the divine, as well as with each other. Bark-cloth was used in ceremonies associated with birth, naming a child, marriage, illness, and succession rites.[62] Meanwhile, some cultures utilized bark-cloth as powerful medicine. In the seventeenth century, the Portuguese priest Father Merolla reported that, among the Songo of Angola, "When women are with child they clothe themselves ... with a sort or rind taken off a tree ... receiving them at the hands of wizards who tell them they [the cloth] ease their burden of great belly and cause them to be easily delivered."[63] In Ghana, the Asantehene donned bark-cloth during the *Odwira* ceremony, an annual festival of renewal and ritual cleansing of shrines and the nation; and in Nigeria, the Igala people used bark-cloth in some of their costumes for masquerades.[64]

In several regions where bark-cloth was used, the source trees, such as fig species and *baobab*, were revered and valued for their medicinal properties. The *kyenkyen* bark was used in the Ivory Coast as a purgative and in the treatment of leprosy,[65] and the sap of the paper mulberry [*Broussonetia papyrifera*] was used as a laxative, while the ash of burned tapa was used to treat thrush.[66] Some trees were closely associated with religion and the spirit world. The Igbo of Eastern Nigeria believed the *iroko* tree [*Chlorophora excelsa*] was sacred, as it furnished the souls for newborns and pieces of its bark were used as a popular ingredient in customary medicine.[67]

Besides the many uses of bark-cloth and source trees, gender identities were constructed through the production and use of bark-cloth. The gendered division of labor in many communities established cultural ideas that defined men's and women's roles within the confines of society. Women in Polynesia, for example, were expected to make tapa; otherwise, their customary roles in society as wives, mothers, and women were "questioned." Such notions were a reflection of the patriarchal norms that envisioned what women ought to be and do in society. Women's lives in Polynesia were so intertwined with the making of bark-cloth that the ideas of "woman" and "making tapa" were inseparable.[68] Unlike in Polynesia, bark-cloth production in the Ashanti society was dominated by men.

As discussed earlier, in several African cultures there were certain obligations and prescribed activities deemed appropriate for men and women. In some cultures this concept included plant rights based on gender. In other words, just as there were gendered spaces, there were also gendered species or "women's crops" and "men's crops."[69] Throughout several areas of Africa, trees were usually associated with male privilege; as a consequence, men dominated tree planting and bark-cloth production was considered a typical male responsibility.[70] Engendering bark-cloth in Ashanti as exclusively male was not only a major source of income for men but it also shaped their identity as men. Moreover, within cultures where bark-cloth was gendered male, like the Ashanti, men were the transmitters of bark-cloth knowledge from one generation to the next.[71] The role of men as artists who produced bark-cloth was important to the local economy and essential to the daily functioning of society that relied on bark-cloth for trade revenue, ritual, and clothing. As woven cloth was introduced to bark-cloth regions, the trade textiles became more fashionable and bark-cloth lost its appeal. In some areas, bark-cloth was relegated to work attire or completely abandoned. On the Gold Coast of West Africa, bark-cloth was replaced by *Kente* cloth and European textiles. Today, mostly hunters and the very poor in the Brong-Ahafo region of Ghana still wear clothes made from *kyenkyen* cloth.[72]

Of particular importance was the role women played as traders of cloth. In West Africa, for instance, where trading was a significant part of the socio-economic culture of African women, many traded in local markets as wholesalers and retailers, and in some cases women held a monopoly over trade in several coastal ports. Ga women, like women of other West African ethnic groups, were actively engaged in trade as early as the sixteenth century, and visitors to the Gold Coast observed the pervasiveness of women who traded a wide variety of goods produced by men, such as cloth.[73] Women exercised dominance over several trade goods, such as fish, meat, prepared food, and a wide selection of cloth. Henceforth, women's activities as traders were essential to the local economies of the region and most likely to the very survival of the bark-cloth industry. Bark-cloth not only privileged men and women differently, it reinforced gender and social differences.

By following the process and the artists who transformed bark into meaningful things that influenced and shaped people's lives and society, we learn how identities were constructed and material objects such as lace-bark became meaningful things. Stuart Hall reminds us that objects by themselves rarely ever have one single or fixed, unchanging meaning; instead, the objects acquire meaning by how they were used and integrated into everyday practices.[74] Certainly, bark-cloth acquired different meanings within societies based on how it was used and represented. Bark-cloth was a functional object, a sacred cloth, valued trade commodity, and a decorative art within specific cultural contexts. It is in the representation of bark-cloth that we see important connections and intersections across various social groups and between generations over time.

Threads of our ancestors

Believe me, Sire, these countries far surpass all the rest of the world in beauty.[75]
COLUMBUS TO KING FERDINAND, FROM CUBA, 1492

Among the early inhabitants of the Caribbean were the indigenous Taínos, whose culture developed around 1200 A.D. Taíno society was part of a continuum of successive cultural developments that characterized Caribbean history for thousands of years.[76] The Taínos, the word meaning "good people" or "good men and not cannibals," were considered the most culturally developed people of the Caribbean, living in the islands of Cuba, Hispaniola, Jamaica, and Puerto Rico at the time of the Spanish conquest in 1492.[77] The Taínos of the Greater Antilles were the first Americans to come into contact with Europeans and explorers led by Christopher Columbus and the first to endure the effects of Spanish conquest.[78] Much of our knowledge of the Taínos is based on archeological evidence and the relatively few written records of Europeans from the fifteenth and sixteenth centuries during the period of conquest.[79] Despite the gaps in our knowledge, what little has survived in terms of material objects portrays a culture with a rich heritage of artistic expression.[80]

Early European accounts of Taíno dress customs seemed more focused on their "nakedness" than on their weaving techniques and rituals associated with cloth.[81] Columbus, for instance, was preoccupied with their nakedness and was reported to have used the adjective *desnudos* (nude) some fourteen times in his journal from his first Atlantic voyage.[82] In his letter to King Ferdinand and Queen Isabella, Columbus wrote, "The people of the island ... all go naked, men and women, as their mothers bore them, although some women cover a single place with the leaf of a plant, or with a net of cotton which they make for the purpose."[83]

In this case of cross-cultural contact, cloth (or in this instance, the absence of it) is a source of misinterpretation. Columbus and his contemporaries failed to recognize that perhaps, for some Taínos, semi and full nudity was appropriate within their cultural context due to the tropical heat. By contrast, the Spanish colonizers wore heavy woolen coats as they would in Europe, which was most inappropriate and perhaps unhealthy in the warm climate. It was claimed that Europeans often failed to apprehend the Taínos because the Indians could easily detect them by their smell[84]—most likely from their damp woolen coats soaked with perspiration from the heat. Europeans had long equated European-style dress as a visual representation of civility and the clothed body as a reflection of moral aptitude. Columbus's emphasis on the "nakedness" of the Taínos suggests concern and cultural bias on his part. Furthermore, Columbus's cultural assumptions and biases dismissed the excellent weaving skills of the Taínos and singularly exposed them, even though some Taínos did wear clothing. Several chiefs or leaders wore clothes studded with gold nuggets.[85]

The Taínos consisted of diverse groups of people scattered throughout the Caribbean with a long history dating back thousands of years prior to the arrival of the Europeans in 1492. The ancestry of the Taínos can be traced to the Arawakan-speaking Ronquinian Saladoid people living along the Orinoco River in South America, whose culture was closely related to the Cedrosan Saladoid culture of Northern South American coast.[86] These people migrated from the rivers and coasts of present day Venezuela and the Guianas into the Lesser Antilles, and then moved northward, settling on the Virgin

Islands, Puerto Rico, Hispaniola, and the rest of the Greater Antilles.[87] They mingled with the local inhabitants, referred to in archaeological studies as "Archaic," thus giving rise to a new culture over time called Ostionoid.[88] This culture developed a distinctive artistic expression in pottery, bone, shell, and stone. By the time of cross-cultural contact with Europeans, the Taínos had begun the final phase of Ostionoid cultural development.[89] Recent archeological studies have divided the Greater Antilles Taíno population into two distinct groups: Western Taínos, composed of those cultures in Jamaica, Central Cuba, and the Bahamas; and the Classic Taínos of Hispaniola and Puerto Rico, whose cultures were more developed.[90] Despite the variations in cultural development and diverse groups of Taínos, they all had the same culture and shared a common language.[91]

One important feature of Taíno society was the cultural significance of cloth and its gendered association with Taíno women. Taíno society had a matrilineal descent system; hence, inheritance ran through the female line with women inheriting positions of power such as chieftainship.[92] While kinship was passed from father to son in Europe, among the Taínos the chief or *cacique*'s predecessor would be his mother's brother and his successor would be his sister's son.[93] Through the matrilineal system, women achieved empowerment, such as inheritance rights, and became the recipients of sacred objects called *zemis*, which represented the lineage's ancestors. Women, therefore, were reported to have been both the producers and distributors of certain high status commodities, including wooden stools, household objects, and a "thousand things of cotton."[94] For Taíno women, cloth and cotton were important forms of material wealth.

As producers and distributors of cotton, women were centered as key players in the daily political, social, and economic functioning of Taíno society. Even though women had access to political power as chiefs, it is not clear how the resources were regulated or managed by means of matrilineal inheritance. This raises the provocative question: did women control these resources including cloth, or was it a matter in which inheritance was passed through her, but not to her? Further, did Taíno women serve as a type of repository for their male relations? We really do not know. The few European sources that exist on the Taínos do not address this issue.[95]

Cloth and cotton were highly valued and were produced from wild and domesticated cotton shrubs [*Gossypium* spp.] across the region. Early accounts from Hispaniola reveal there were vast cotton fields, but little is known about these cotton productions or if the fields were irrigated. Comparable to cultures we examined earlier, labor among the Taínos was divided by gender; however, women seemed to do most of the daily work activities. Columbus wrote, "It appears to me that the women work more than the men"[96] and, according to the nobleman Michele de Cuneo, who accompanied Columbus on his second voyage, "the women do all the work. Men concern themselves only with fishing and eating."[97] Hence, we can infer that if the men concerned themselves only with fishing and eating, women most likely were the ones predominantly engaged in cotton production.

Gender division of labor often prescribed how women and men should behave in social contexts. In Taíno culture, women, and not men, were the ones who made cloth. Early European accounts refer to women spinning and weaving for the purpose of making fish nets and hammocks. Spanish observers noted, "It is well . . . told what kind of beds the Indians had on the island . . . called a hammock, and it is or follows, a blanket woven in part or parts open, crossed with a checker-board pattern like a net. . . . And it's of cotton spun by hand by Indian women."[98] Amongst the Taínos, cloth served complex functions that were both practical and highly symbolic. Articles of dress woven from local cotton and other fibers provided some protection against the natural elements and simultaneously communicated visually information about individuals and the community at large.

Although some Taínos wore a limited amount of clothing, cloth was produced and used for several reasons. Cotton was used to make belts that signaled an individual's marital status. Cotton belts were worn by men and women who were virgins, and married women wore small skirts called *naguas*, which were woven from cotton and resembled a short apron; however, the length determined the rank of the woman. Elite Taíno women wore longer *naguas* to reflect their status in the community. A fine example of a *naguas* can be seen in the painting of a Carib family by the eighteenth-century artist and visitor to the Caribbean, Agostino Brunias (Figure 1.2).

Although Caribs were a distinct ethnic group from the Taínos, there were some cultural similarities in dress customs. The Caribs who had settled in the Leeward Islands were the enemies of the Taínos and were known for their warlike lifestyle. The painting beguiles any notion of aggressiveness and evokes a sense of tranquility while alluding to the importance of family. Brunias pays close attention to dress while portraying several aspects of indigenous family life; a hammock, for instance, can be seen in the background. The women are both depicted wearing *naguas* while the man is wearing a breech cloth, perhaps of cotton, bark-cloth, or vegetable fibers.

The painting is important because it provides visual evidence of pre-colonial dress customs in the region and suggests the importance of cloth and its use as a form of adornment among indigenous people in the Caribbean. More subtly, Brunias' painting is riddled with complex meanings. At the same time as Captain Cook's artists were drawing images of Polynesians on the other side of the globe, Brunias' ethnographic art identified his subjects as Caribs and distinguished them from others in Caribbean society. Arguably, the painting depicts taxonomic images of specimens rather than "individuals."[99] Similar to illustrations of plants and animals in natural history, Brunias' Caribs are "exoticized" with an air of authenticity. At any rate, Brunias' depiction of the Caribs' dress is matched by the narratives of European visitors and plantocrats.[100] The indigenous term *naguas* was eventually adopted by the Spanish colonists, and the word later became *enaguas* for petticoats.[101]

FIGURE 1.2 *A Leeward Islands Carib family outside a Hut.* Oil on canvas. Agostino Brunias (1728–1796). Yale Center for British Art, Paul Mellon Collection.

As with earlier cultures we examined, cloth was profoundly embedded in customary Taíno practices. Cloth was fashioned into exquisite forms of dress that reflected identity, status, and gender. On special occasions, such as festivals, *caciques* and priests wore cotton mantles and vestments decorated with tropical bird feathers in a variety of colors, perhaps a sign of their Arawakan South American roots.[102] Such outfits, as compared with those of commoners, signaled the chief's status as "leader" and distinguished *caciques* from others in the community. Cultural historians Mary Ellen Roach-Higgins and Joanne Eicher have argued that dress in any culture bestows identities on individuals as it communicates positions within social structure.[103]

Taínos transformed their bodies into works of art. They used cloth and natural pigments from local plants and colored clay to decorate their bodies for rituals, war and to protect their skin from the sun.[104] Cosmetic decorations of the body were based on individual and communal standards in aesthetic taste. Even though Taíno women spun cotton to make household items, such as mats and nets for fishing,[105] most significantly, cloth was made to wrap their most sacred icon, *zemis*. Therefore, women as producers of cloth were linked to the sacred.[106] Women had contact with spiritually powerful objects through the medium of cloth and may have experienced considerable access to the sacred through their association and production of cloth. For Taíno women, cloth produced for the purpose of wrapping their scared objects suggests a symbolic commitment of the living to the ancestors and the continuous link between the living and the spirits across time and space. Indigenous women in many areas of the Americas have long been connected to the spirit world through the medium of cloth. Among the Yucatec Maya, for example, women were chief custodians of the domestic shrines housing the gods of the lineage, and their weaving skills were "essential to the sustaining of ceremonial displays."[107]

In Taíno society, cloth was so valuable it was presented as gifts and tributes. Columbus received gifts from the *cacique Guacanagari*, consisting of "numerous objects of gold, woodcarvings and items of woven cotton and feathers."[108] Besides the generosity of the *cacique*, the gifts reflected a level of superb craftsmanship attained by the Taínos and some semblance of a trade system. Anthropologist Irving Rouse argued that trade was widespread throughout the region and involved parties or individuals who undertook long sea voyages for that purpose. Some Taínos, like those on the island of la Gonâve, off the western coast of Haiti, were well known for their wooden bowls and traded their distinctive products.[109] Cotton and woven cloth, as highly valued items, were part of this trade network throughout the Caribbean and perhaps women, as "producers" and "distributors" of high end goods, were involved as befitting their status and role within the matrilineal society.

The ancestors of the Taínos emigrated from South America where several forest cultures were familiar with bark-cloth. Fragments of bark-cloth, dating from 2000 BC, have been found in archeological digs in Peru, while geographical distribution of stone and wooden beaters found suggests that at one time bark-cloth production was carried out over a broad area of the northwest regions of South America.[110] Forest cultures that relied on plants for medicine, food, and even poison for arrowheads in hunting and warfare would have encountered numerous fibrous plants in the rainforests. Several species of the *Daphneopsis* genus, a member of the same plant family as the lace-bark tree, existed throughout the northwest regions of the Amazon and were easily identifiable due to the unique arrangement of the fibers commonly occurring in the phloem. The tree branches tend to be flexible, and once broken the fibers often conspicuously stick out.[111] Some forest cultures of the Amazon were very creative at using bark-cloth in elaborate forms of dress. The Cubeo and related Tucanoan people of the northwest Amazon fashioned bark-cloth into elaborate masks, while the Tikuna of Brazil made a wide range of masked costumes even more elaborate and fanciful than those of the Cubeo and Tukano. Bark-cloth was also worn by the Jivaro people of Peru and Ecuador, though wearing bark-cloth today is considered a sign of poverty. In addition, bark-cloth was produced and used throughout Central America from the Aztecs to the Mayans.[112]

Trade and migratory patterns among the Taínos and their ancestors facilitated the spread of bark-cloth knowledge and technology throughout the region. Archeologist Irving Rouse pointed out that the resident Taínos of Eastern Hispaniola and Western Puerto Rico were said to exchange daily visits across the Mona Passage; therefore, transmission of knowledge and skill was possible due to a common language.[113] Jamaican Taínos were well known to be active traders and provided cotton cloth and hammocks to the islands of Cuba and Hispaniola, and even made sails for some Spanish ships.[114] Most likely, knowledge of bark-cloth was passed along these trade routes and transmitted from one generation to the next, particularly on the islands of Jamaica, Cuba, and Hispaniola, where the lace-bark tree grew abundantly.

Taíno woodworkers, who cut timber to build their houses, carved wooden stools, dug out canoes for sailing, and made bowls and sacred objects from wood, most likely encountered fibrous trees suitable for making cloth. Wooden objects that survived convey some sense of Taínos' in-depth knowledge of trees and various types of wood used for making household items and ceremonial sculptures. Taíno wooden sculptures were exquisite works of art that garnered the attention and admiration of Europeans.[115] Columbus was among the first to acknowledge and compliment the Taínos on their wooden sculptures. After landing on the northeast coast of Cuba on Monday, October 29 in 1492, Columbus recorded in his diary, "They found many statues of female figures and many head-shaped masks, very well carved. I do not know if they keep these for their beauty or if they worship them."[116]

The Taínos used specific woods for the construction of religious furniture and household items. In Jamaica, the lignum vitae [*Guaiacum officinale*] was used to create *zemis*. Other woods used to carve religious figures included West Indian cedar [*Cedrela odorata*], Santa Maria [*Calophyllum calaba*], and the blue mahoe [*Hibiscus elatus*].[117] In addition to stone, shells, bones, coral, and ceramic artifacts found over the years, wooden stools called *duhos* used in rituals, as well as *zemis* carved from solid wood and representing Taíno deities, have been found in

Jamaica, Puerto Rico, and the Dominican Republic.[118] The Taínos hid their ceremonial objects from the Spanish in caves that were used for rituals and burials. The beauty and diversity of these objects reflect the complexity of their iconography and provide some insights into Taíno development over time.[119]

Agricultural practices applied in Jamaica and the Greater Antilles by the Taínos were influenced by methods used in the Amazon region.[120] To clear farm land, an agricultural system based on deforestation (forest burning and ash-bedded sowing), commonly called *slash and burn* cultivation, was introduced in the Caribbean as early as 400 BC. Flora introduced to the region were generally domesticated plants that originated in the Amazon basin.[121] Some of the plants brought to Jamaica and other islands were essential to maintaining Taínos' lifestyles and included the cassava or manioc [*Manihot esculenta*], amaranth [*Amaranthus* spp.], peanuts [*Arachis hypogaea*], as well as cotton [*Gossypium* spp.], maize [*Zea mays*], and pineapple [*Ananas comosus*], to name a few.[122] The Taínos developed their agricultural skills over time and expanded their knowledge of local trees and plants, eventually creating an extensive pharmacopoeia of curative plants and a vast vocabulary of trees and shrubs suitable for dyeing and making cloth. The Taínos also cultivated gardens with their prized foods, and medicinal plants. Such expansive knowledge of plants, dye pigments, food, and medicine was of great interest to colonial prospectors who sought to profit off the treasure trove of Amerindians' local knowledge. Colonial authorities, for example, sought medicine to cure tropical maladies thus keeping their troops and plantation owners alive in the colonies. Some European physicians established close ties with Taíno healers to learn about indigenous pharmacopeia. In Hispaniola, Antonio de Villasante, for example, learned the significance and properties of local plants from his Christianized wife, Catalina de Ayahibx, a Taíno chief (or Cacica).[123]

The Taínos obtained natural dyes from tree bark, berries and seeds, to color cotton cloths. Indigenous plants used for dyes included the annatto [*Bixa orellana*], called *bija* by the Taínos, which provided a reddish-orange dye. Dyes were obtained from the brazilwood or brasiletto wood [*Caesalpinia brasiliensis*] and the red mangrove [*Rhizophora mangle*], as well as guava [*Psidium guajava*], which was used to produce black pigment.[124] Even though the Taínos made cloth and used leaf fibers, archeological evidence of bark-cloth production in the form of mallets is scarce. Perhaps they deteriorated, or stones with smooth surfaces were used to beat bark. Another likely solution is that lace-bark was so unique it did not require tools such as mallets for beating as is typical in bark-cloth production. Many of the artifacts unearthed that were associated with plants, like woodcarvings and grinding stones for grain, suggest the importance of plants and how they were used in indigenous societies.[125] Amongst the Taínos bast fibers were obtained from "tough feather grass [*espata*] or hemp, which they cord, tan and spin . . . it is a strong pretty thread."[126] Anthropologist Sven Lovén revealed that hemp grew in many areas of Hispaniola, particularly near cotton areas. Leaf fibers were obtained from the henequen [*Agave fourcroydes*], and the Taínos in Haiti obtained leaf fibers from the American agave [*Agave americana*]. Lovén argued that those early Indian methods of harvesting leaf fibers from culture plants, such as agave, were passed on to Africans in some cases by Europeans who acquired the knowledge from the Taínos.[127]

The Taínos were among the earliest people of the Caribbean to use bark-cloth and lace-bark in their daily activities. The seventeenth-century natural historian and physician Sir Hans Sloane reported while in Jamaica that the Indians "peel the cassava with shells and [were] putting it into bags made from tree bark, pressing it and putting it over fire."[128] The bags, which were used as sieves in preparing meals, were more than likely made from lace-bark—a custom to be adopted later by enslaved Africans in Jamaica. The use of lace-bark in food preparation reveals how functional and important this form of bark-cloth was in women's lives. Lace-bark was undeniably essential to women's work in preparing meals for themselves and their family. Likewise, the eighteenth-century local historian Edward Long revealed that "the Indians employ it [lace-bark] in a variety of different fabrics."[129] Long does not elaborate on how lace-bark was "incorporated" into other fabrics, nor does he explain what styles were fashioned out of these "varieties of fabrics," but the evidence confirms that some indigenous people were well aware of the lace-bark tree and used its fibers to their benefit.

One of the most interesting examples of the Taínos' use of lace-bark comes from the island of Hispaniola. In the nineteenth century, a few Europeans ventured into the interiors of Hispaniola to visit one of the few remaining Taíno villages not destroyed or displaced by colonial settlers. The Taíno retreat was hidden deep in the rainforests of the interior. During their visit and a walkabout with the *cacique*, the visitors noticed a flutter of butterflies and enquired of the *cacique* if they could catch some. After searching through the woods for a few minutes, the *cacique*'s "quick and trained eye soon detected a young *Lagetta* tree, the bark of which he cut then by a longitudinal slit and with the help of his knife-point, he took off the cylinder of bark."[130] The *cacique* "readily separated a thin stratum which when pulled open, presented a loose fibrous texture, hardly to be distinguishable from manufactured lace."[131] He then took a bamboo shoot, which he stripped and shaped into a circle, and attached the lace with string-like fibers from a palm leaf, hence creating as good a "butterfly net as could be desired ... and soon half-a-dozen of the splendid butterflies were seen and admired at leisure."[132] The visitors were not only amazed and delighted, but it was obvious that the *cacique* had done this before, especially since the entire process took about a quarter of an hour.[133]

The scene from Hispaniola is both pleasant and informative. On one level, the tranquil scene of catching butterflies in the woods alludes to the harmonious relationship and connectedness between the indigenous people and nature. Meanwhile, the Europeans were able to connect with "otherness" in a picturesque scene with exotic trees. Although we do not know the identity of the European travelers, the experience to an unknown place was an adventure that introduced them to new plants and the beauty of the forests. However, the scene serves as a troubling reminder and a stark contrast to a colonial landscape later polluted by commercial enterprises and an indigenous population decimated by the brutal policies of colonial rule.

In Taíno society, cloth was symbolic of social relations, and the way people adorned themselves provided some clues as to their identity in terms of gender, ethnicity, and class. Within the Taíno cultural context, cloth was gendered in that Taíno women were the ones engaged in spinning and weaving cotton into cloth. Taíno women as producers and distributors of cloth bore the responsibility of producing cloth for trade and gifts, and especially for ritual. Of particular significance, they wove cloth to bedeck and clothe their most sacred objects, the *zemis*, thus creating a spiritual link for women through the medium of cloth to the world of the ancestors and divinities. Taíno society was dependent on women's role as producers and distributors of valuable commodities for its social and economic survival. Accordingly, cloth was an important source of material wealth for women and the basis of women's power, strategies, and agency. This would come to an end in the sixteenth century. Cross-cultural contact between Spanish explorers and the indigenous people of the Caribbean ushered in an era of European colonization that destroyed populations and transformed gender roles in Taíno society. Women's empowerment (and their role as producers and distributors of valuable commodities) was displaced by Spanish hegemonic masculinity embodied in patriarchal institutions and capitalist commercial enterprises seeking wealth and profit.[134] Despite the genocide unleashed on the Taínos by their Spanish conquerors, some aspects of Taíno culture survived and knowledge of local plants such as lace-bark was transmitted to enslaved Africans who mingled with the declining Taíno population to create a plural culture consisting of Spanish, Taíno, and African influences.[135]

The new arrivants and social setting

The Caribbean is the story of arrivants from across the Atlantic and beyond, each group bringing a cultural equipage.[136]
REX NETTLEFORD, *CARIBBEAN CULTURAL IDENTITY*

The early Spanish colonists in the Caribbean used a few African slaves to replace the declining Taíno population. It was not until the eighteenth century that the transportation of enslaved people from Africa by means of the Trans-Atlantic Slave Trade had steadily increased and continued to grow until the abolition of the trade in 1807. Enslaved Africans in the Caribbean came from different regions of West and Central Africa, spanning a coastal distance of over 5,000 miles, including the Senegambia, Sierra Leone, Windward Coast, Gold Coast, Bight of Benin, Bight of Biafra, and West Central Africa. In Jamaica's case, the majority of enslaved Africans came from the Gold Coast (part of present day Ghana) and the Bight of the Biafra in present day Nigeria.[137] Many Africans were forcibly extracted from their homelands, including areas historically well-known for bark-cloth production, and compelled to march to the coast where they were hoarded into slave pens and fortresses to await their fate.[138]

Further disoriented, African men and women were stripped of their humanity by their enslavers, thus exposing their naked bodies as a means of subduing and humiliating the captives.[139] The enslaved Africans were "thrust into the hold of the vessel in a state of nudity, the males being crammed on one side, and the females on the other."[140] For Africans, whose clothes represented their ethnicity and identity, stripping them was symbolic of the painful severance of cultural, social, and kinship ties.[141] Despite this, enslaved people could not be stripped of their body modifications and knowledge of dress customs and practices. In the bowels of the slave ships, "the naked human beings, their bruised and festering flesh, the foetid air, the prevailing dysentery, the accumulation of filth, turned these holds into a hell."[142] Africans who survived the horrific violence of the transatlantic crossing called the Middle Passage and arrived in Jamaica and other plantation economies of the Caribbean were branded like cattle, auctioned, and distributed among buyers and plantation owners.

As chattel slaves, Africans were denied their status as human beings; instead, they were reduced to the level of property and commodity to be traded, sold, and purchased at their enslavers' will. Enslaved Africans were not passive; they resisted the institution of slavery from the moment of capture and continued to reject their status as slaves and subordinates throughout slavery and beyond.[143] In many areas of the colonial world, enslaved Africans engaged in numerous resistance activities from feigning illness to sabotage and rebellion. Maroonage was a key feature of slavery and occurred in several areas of the African Diaspora. Numerous slaves chose to escape from the oppressive routine of plantation life by running away and establishing sovereign communities in the mountains. These freedom fighters became known as Maroons who kept much of the African customs alive.[144]

Jamaican society was divided into the three broad social categories: whites, free nonwhites, and enslaved persons. Slave society in Jamaica, however, was not homogenous, but rather complex and diverse.[145] Historian Elsa Goveia argues that the slave society "consisted of ordering of separate groups all held together within a social structure."[146] For example, slaves were divided according to class, ethnicity, and occupation, as well as urban and rural slaves or those who worked on plantations and estates. These differentiations were often reflected in the dress of both male and female slaves.[147] Colored slaves consisted of all persons of African and another ancestry. Miscegenation in Jamaica gave rise to gradations of coloreds based on lightness of complexion. The more common term for this group was *mulatto*. Some coloreds had special privileges granted by private acts, and they considered themselves to be a distinct group of higher social standing and separate from enslaved Africans. Consequently, they distanced themselves from African slaves. Meanwhile, Creole slaves or those locally born also viewed themselves as separate from the "unseasoned" or newly arrived slaves from Africa. The largest group was enslaved Africans and their descendants. Europeans used two kinds of generalization to refer to this group, *Negro* and *slave*; the terms were synonymous until abolition.[148]

Jamaican slave society included different ethnic groups. Some of the groups included the Yoruba, Igbo, Congo, Coromantee, and Mandingos.[149] Enslaved people on estates or plantations were further grouped according to their skill, age, and occupation. Some slaves were classified as domestic or house slaves separate from field slaves. Overall, the social consequences of the sugar revolution and demographic changes were very significant as they gave rise to a complex society. Apart from the servile population, there was a small white minority in almost all the Caribbean islands. In Jamaica the term *whites* referred to colonists of unmixed European descent, mainly English, Scottish, and Irish. Some Europeans were well known for their skills in knitting and weaving and passed some of these skills such as knitting to their African slaves. Knitting continues to be a popular needle work activity in Jamaica; however, textile weaving and spinning cotton as in other parts of the Americas was not prevalent in Jamaica.[150] Amongst this group of Europeans, there were poor and elite whites, including those who were born locally. Although the white community was socially and economically diverse, as a group, they saw themselves as the superordinate race that wielded authority over a subjugated population.[151]

Enslaved Africans and their descendants in Jamaica labored in various economic activities. Many worked on sugar plantations, which was the dominant economic institution. Others labored on ginger, coffee, and pimento estates or in pens that produced livestock. Enslaved Africans also labored in urban areas as domestic servants, sailors, longshoremen, canters, builders, and even delivery aids and hospital attendants.[152] On plantations and estates, enslaved African women worked side by side with male slaves toiling in the fields, yet their contribution to the plantation economy was often overlooked. While male slaves were valued for their contribution to the plantation economy, slave women were expected to perform both sexual and economic duties.[153] Slave women were restricted, exploited, and confined to an economic space constructed by white masculine power that sought to deny them their identity and rights as persons. The Euro-ethnocentric biases of the period perpetuated stereotypes that characterized enslaved women as "Jezebel" and "Quashiba" on one hand or as submissive and promiscuous on the other. Enslaved women resisted these stereotypes and were not afraid to confront their oppressors.[154]

Jamaican Sunday markets and plantation dress

Enslaved Africans brought their knowledge and expertise in weaving, bark-cloth production, beading, dyeing, and tailoring with them to the Caribbean and other parts of the African Diaspora. Some slaves brought their talents and skills in trading cloth and clothing. Slave women who could sew became seamstresses and played important roles both in the informal slave economy by sewing for their family, friends, and members of the enslaved community. Some seamstresses were able to hire out their services when permitted while some labored as house slaves sewing for their enslaver. Seamstresses used their skills to make clothing from lace-bark and available fabrics, thus giving rise to a cottage industry based on sewing and lace-bark production. Archeological digs over the years at slave villages on plantations such as Drax Hall and Seville in Jamaica have unearthed numerous sewing artifacts from successive periods over time, including thread spools, buttons, and brass thimbles, suggesting the development of a cottage industry based on sewing among the enslaved population.[155] Bark-cloth, lace-bark, and woven textiles would have been major commodities of this cottage industry.

There is much evidence of West African dress, cloth, and weaving techniques transplanted to the Americas. A West African narrow loom for weaving strips of textiles was found in a black Maroon village in French Guiana in 1748, where they would "weave cotton cloth which serves to make skirts for the women and loincloths for the men."[156] Ritual cloths, similar to those in West Africa, meant for Condomblé ceremonies in Bahia, Brazil, were woven locally and included colors symbolic of Yoruba-Dahomean meanings. West African narrow looms have also been found in the Brazilian city of Salvador, and cloth made by slaves in the same region reflected strong Mende influence in design.[157] Enslaved Africans were creative in their dress, and women's attire often reflected a preponderance of African characteristics. In Jamaica during holidays women were "decked out with a profusion of beads, coral and gold ornaments of all description,"[158] and they "proudly displayed their tribal marks . . . as testimonies of distinction [from] Africa."[159] Headdress in some places included plaiting and twisting hair into cornrows as in Africa. Many women donned the headwrap, the most visible symbol that represented the continuity of African heritage in dress.[160] These cultural characteristics reflected an African aesthetic that visually enriched the slave community and signaled enslaved people's tenacity to survive in an alien environment.

On many estates, enslaved individuals received small plots of land to cultivate their food in their spare time. The Jamaican Slave Law of 1816 required estate owners to provide rations where no suitable land was available for slaves to cultivate or where drought had caused crop failure. Regardless, plantation owners provided their slaves, in many cases, with salt and pickled fish. Slaves were granted Saturday afternoons and Sundays to "feed themselves" from the ground or plots of land given to them by their enslavers.[161] Crops cultivated in these provision grounds and slave gardens included cassava, yams, corn, and plantains, which enabled enslaved people to feed themselves and sell surplus food. Originally slave gardens were meant to be cost savings for enslavers and to bind slaves to the plantation; instead, some slaves earned money to buy their freedom while others transformed their gardens into a base from which to dominate local markets.[162] For many enslaved Africans, survival depended on their ability to work in their gardens after an exhausting and grueling hot day in the fields. Successful producers of excess food in rural areas played an intrinsic role in the development of an internal market giving rise to a slave economy that involved independent economic activity.[163] In addition to selling produce and vegetables, enslaved Africans raised livestock, produced and traded lace-bark, and crafted brooms, furniture, and ceramics for Sunday markets.[164] Since slave owners' involvement in these markets was limited beyond the usual inspection required by slave regulation, markets became centers for enslaved persons to "transgress the social and geographic boundaries imposed by the plantation."[165]

Sunday markets bustled with trading between urban and rural slaves, and free coloreds, who ventured into the towns to sell their wares. As in many West African markets, the majority of traders were women.[166] This was not unique to Jamaica. In the city of Charleston, South Carolina, the majority of slaves who traded were market women.[167] Likewise, in the French Caribbean, women sold agricultural products as they had done in Africa, and free Creoles, along with slave women, dominated markets as it was difficult for male slaves to get passes to leave estates.[168] In markets, slaves flirted with freedom and created a space from which to resist, organize, and verbalize their resentment at slavery.[169] Evidence of linen or cloth markets in Jamaica is scarce; perhaps they went unnoticed by Europeans who distanced themselves from mingling with their slaves in "Negro" spaces. In the Eastern Caribbean, linen markets were common and dominated by women traders (Figure 1.3).

Typical of Jamaican markets, cloth traders and their wares were disbursed throughout the market space. The seventeenth-century historian Bryan Edwards revealed that over 10,000 people gathered every Sunday morning in the market of Kingston, where they bartered for "salted beef and pork, fine linen and ornaments for their wives and children."[170] The visitor John Stewart, in describing the transactions in Kingston's markets in 1808, noted that "the town where the markets are held is a scene of the utmost bustle, thousands of negroes being assembled to dispose of their merchandise, and various descriptions of buyers necessarily augmenting the crowd."[171] Linen [cloth] was an important trade item, and enslaved Africans could sell unwanted fabrics and clothes they received from their enslavers.

Slave owners in Jamaica were legally required to provide their slaves with adequate clothing, and those who refused to furnish clothing for their slaves could be fined. Over time, the slave codes gradually changed from requiring ready-made

FIGURE 1.3 *Linen Market, Dominica*. Oil on canvas. Yale Center for British Art, Paul Mellon Collection.

garments to sufficient dress and textiles be distributed to slaves.[172] The growth in the slave population due to natural increase and the continuous importation of enslaved Africans was too costly and impractical for slave owners to distribute ready-made garments to the large slave population.[173] By the latter half of the eighteenth century, many slave owners resorted to the importation of inexpensive, coarse European textiles and Indian cottons for slave clothing. The eighteenth-century planter, historian, and politician Edward Long recorded that slaves received "a large abundance of checqued linen, striped hollands, sustain blanketing, long ells, and baize, Kendal cottons, Oznaburg [sic], canvas, coarse hats, woolen caps, cotton and silk handkerchiefs, knives, scissors, razors, buckles, buttons … thread, needles and pins"[174] to sew their own clothes.

Osnaburg was the most common fabric distributed to members of the enslaved population in Jamaica, especially on plantations because it was the cheapest and most durable cotton fabric, ideal for rigorous field work. On some estates, large quantities of osnaburg were imported for distribution to slaves. On the Windsor Lodge and Paisley estates in Jamaica, between 1833 and 1837, approximately 2,676 yards of flax osnaburg were purchased for slaves.[175] Slave owners did not distribute European lace to their slaves, and very few enslaved individuals had access to manufactured lace. Historically, lace was a mark of status and wealth, a luxury item, and highly specialized art associated with the elite. Considering this, lace was too expensive for slave owners to provide. Neither could some local whites afford lace. Members of the planter class did not desire their slaves to "out dress" them or dress beyond their slave status by wearing luxurious fabrics such as European lace. In some areas of the Caribbean, like the Danish West Indies, slaves were forbidden by law to wear lace;[176] those who wore it could be arrested. Magistrates refused to believe that slaves could afford such items and slaves risked being accused of theft.[177] The Atlantic trade in textiles between Britain and the colonies focused on mass quantities of European fabrics and Indian cottons to clothe the large slave population, and did not include lace. Enslaved people in Jamaica who desired European lace had to find alternative methods of obtaining lace or look for suitable materials that were affordable, accessible, and could function as a substitute for lace. After Emancipation, lace was more accessible due to the development of retail stores and the mass production of affordable European machine Leavers lace.[178]

Slave laws regarding dress were enforced and administered by parish vestries.[179] Jamaica had no sumptuary laws, like the Danish West Indies, regulating private expenditure and dictating exactly what enslaved Africans could and could not wear.[180] Consequently, enslaved people in Jamaica exerted considerable control over their dress and could wear lace of their own choosing if available. Slaves were able to be culturally expressive in their dress as some enslaved people were "expert at their needles,"[181] while female house slaves were generally "good seamstresses."[182]

Across Jamaica, enslaved people's dress reflected a multitude of styles. Urban slaves occasionally received cast-off clothing from their enslavers; thus, they tended to be better dressed than field or rural slaves, and their clothing reflected their occupation and elite status within the servile community.[183] Urban slave women preferred long, brightly colored skirts made from refined cloth, such as muslin or cotton, instead of osnaburg, with beads and gold jewelry.[184] Among rural and field slaves, the standard slave dress for men included an osnaburg or checked frock or smock, a pair of osnaburg or sheeting trousers, and a coarse hat; and for women, an osnaburg or coarse linen shift, a petticoat, and, based on their taste and circumstances, a handkerchief to be used as a headwrap. Shoes were not common and were usually reserved for special occasions, such as dances and carnival.[185] Enslaved women in the rural areas wore their skirts pulled over a cord tied around their hips, thus exposing their legs as high as the knees. This "pull-skirt" enabled women to move easily while carrying out their tasks, and to keep their skirts dry when crossing rivers and streams. The dress was complemented with a headwrap and occasionally a broad-brimmed straw hat, placed over the headwrap to protect their faces from the hot sun while toiling in the fields.[186]

Many enslaved women's adherence to an African aesthetic in dress was reinforced by the continuous arrival of African slaves until the end of the slave trade in 1807, and by African indentured laborers who arrived in Jamaica between 1841 and 1867.[187] Enslavers were not concerned when their slaves retained elements of African dress, since they differentiated and set Africans apart from Europeans, nor did they want to provide additional and more expensive clothing and cloth for their slaves.[188] The role women played in African societies as agricultural workers, mothers, teachers, and healers provided them with the opportunity, knowledge, and expertise to be agents of transformation and the transmitters of African knowledge.[189] Enslaved women in Jamaica who desired to elevate themselves within the community sought to transform their appearance from a slave aesthetic to a more pleasing mode of dress. To achieve this goal and resist the stereotypical images associated with enslavement, many looked for opportunities to adorn themselves and show that they too could be as beautiful and refined as their European colonizers. One fabric that embodied this notion of refinement was lace. Since machine and handmade lace were out of reach for most slaves, many resorted to natural lace.

The origin of Jamaican lace-bark

Bwa kwochi pa janm dwat'—A crooked tree is never straight.[190]
HAITIAN CREOLE PROVERB

As mentioned earlier, lace-bark was unique in that it was both a natural lace and a form of bark-cloth. It was also the most popular form of bark-cloth produced in Jamaica. Natural lace was obtained from the lace-bark tree called *Lagetta lagetto*. The *lagetto* was one of the three species of the genus *Lagetta* which belongs to the Thymelaeaceae plant family known for its fibrous plants.[191] Of all the lace-like fibrous plants known to have been used in dress and clothing accessories, like the lace-bark tree of New Zealand [*Plagianthus betulinus*], none is as unique as the *lagetto* in terms of quality, versatility, refinement, and resemblance of the fibers to manufactured lace. Successive research and new data on the Jamaican lace-bark tree has led to several botanical reclassifications of the tree by scientists. The plant was once identified as *Daphne lagetto* in 1788, then became known as *Lagetta lintearia* in 1792, and was finally renamed in 1908 as *Lagetta lagetto*.[192] Since then, the name *Lagetta lagetto* has been widely accepted by scientists as the current official name of the tree. Despite this, there were numerous common names for the tree based on region, language, and even ritual context. The lace-bark tree was widely known in Cuba and the Dominican Republic as *daguilla*.[193] Other terms in Cuba included *dahile* or *dahlia*, and "lace-stick" or *palo de encaje*.[194] In Haiti, the lace-bark tree was called "lace-wood" or *bois dentelle* in French, or *bwa dantèl* in Haitian Creole. Additional names in Creole included *dagwi* and *laget* or *malaget*. In Jamaica, the tree was simply known as lace-bark tree or "gauze tree," and in a few areas of

Jamaica, the plant was referred to as "sweet scented spurge," "white bark," "Indian lace," "linen lacebark," and "alligator bark."[195]

Interestingly, the word "Lagetto" (changed by the botanist Jissieu to *Lagetta* to form a genus-name) was once believed to be an Indian term derived from the Arawak language spoken by the Taínos. Arguably, the word is a corruption of the Spanish word *latigo* by enslaved Africans (by metathesis of the letters "t" and "g"), meaning "horse-whip."[196] Meanwhile, in Cuba, the origin of the word *daguilla* remains a source of debate. Cuban linguist Sergio Valdes Bernal argued that the word was either of Arawak origin or a derivation of the Spanish word *daga*, "dagger," due to the form or shape of the *lagetto* leaves.[197] The *Lagetta lagetto* was native to Jamaica, Cuba and Hispaniola. Of the three species of the genus, the *Lagetta lagetto* was the most widespread in the three islands, but evidence of its distribution in Cuba and Hispaniola has not been well documented locally as in Jamaica. Furthermore, extensive documentation of the uses of the tree in Jamaica suggests that the tree was more prevalent in Jamaica and utilized more widely for its properties than in other islands.[198] The lace-bark tree had laurel-like leaves of ovate to elliptical, short acuminate shape and rounded at the base, hence it was commonly referred to as *arbor lauri-folia* by Sir Hans Sloane in the seventeenth century.[199] The tree ranged in height from two to ten meters (thirty feet high), and the trunk could be as wide as two feet. It took twenty to twenty-five years for the tree to reach full maturity. The flowering tree blossomed in April and May, and the flowers were white and produced in terminal racemes (Figures 1.4, 1.5).[200]

According to Edward Long, the Jamaican non-domesticated lace-bark tree was "common in the woods of Vere, Clarendon, and St. Elizabeth."[201] However, the tree had a much wider distribution as it thrived in wet limestone forests far from the coast at an altitude of 1,500–2,600 feet, where the annual rainfall was over 75 inches (and may range up to 150 inches per year). Within the wet limestone forests, the lace-bark tree grew on the hillsides where the soil graded to bare rock on slopes and formed part of the sub-canopy of the wet limestone forests (Figure 1.6).

Undergrowth was often sparse due to either the rocky substratum or the dense shade.[202] Unlike many other Caribbean islands, some two-thirds of Jamaica is limestone plateau, and this is composed of hard limestone rock and derived soils that are about equal in area. Wet limestone forests in Jamaica are found primarily in three regions of the island: the Cockpit Country, located in the western to central part of the island nation, the Bull Head Mountain range, stretching across the central axis of the island, and along the John Crow Mountains in the eastern part of Jamaica.[203] The Cockpit Country has the largest wet limestone forest on the island, and the region is a fine example of karst topography (egg-box shaped hills and valleys with many caves formed as limestone was dissolved by acid rain and ground water). It has a mixture of wet evergreen forest and seasonally dry deciduous forest, high in endemic species of plants (more than one hundred) and animals. The region has many caves and rivers that disappear into the ground and reappear further downstream.[204]

FIGURE 1.4 *Lagetta lintearia* from *Curtis's Botanical Magazine* vol. 76, p. 4502 (1850).
Biodiversity Heritage Library.

The topography of this region is important for several reasons. The soil in the wet limestone forest along the central axis of Jamaica helps explain why the tree is found mainly in these parts of Jamaica (Figure 1.7) and a few isolated areas of Cuba and Hispaniola.

Even though the wet limestone forest is considered rocky hills, there are depressions in the rock and sinkholes in which soil consisting of residual bauxite has accumulated at varying depths over the parent limestone. These circular depressions are filled with humus from the surrounding rim of the limestone rock. The lace-bark tree grew in these crevices or honey combs where the tree roots became entangled with the porous limestone.[205] In 1844, local botanists, hoping to collect plant saplings with roots, complained of difficulties as they had to use "a hammer or large stone . . . to break away the porous limestone."[206] Approximately 1,300 square kilometers of the Cockpit Country was designated territory of the Leeward Maroons, the descendants of early African run-away slaves who established settlements in this region. From their main settlement at Accompong Town, founded by the Ashanti warrior Accompong from West Africa, and brother

FIGURE 1.5 Lace-bark tree in Haiti. Photograph: Dan Golembeski, Associate Professor at Grand Valley State University.

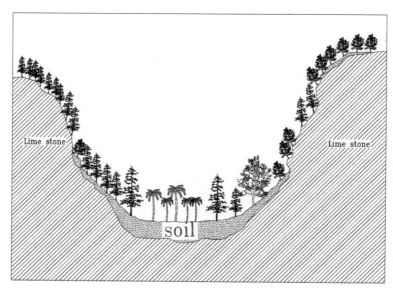

FIGURE 1.6 Diagrammatic profile of Wet Limestone Forest. Courtesy of Leonard Notice at the University of the West Indies Library, Mona.

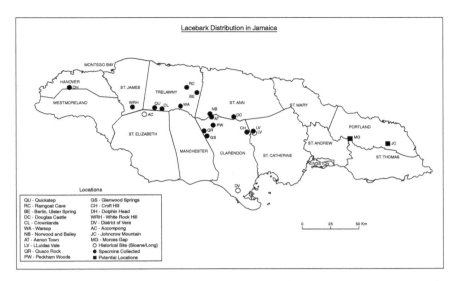

FIGURE 1.7 Map showing lace-bark distribution in Jamaica and specimen sites. By Leonard Notice in collaboration with the Institute of Jamaica. Data Courtesy of the Institute of Jamaica.

of Maroon leader, Cudjoe, they carried out a sustained campaign of armed resistance in the eighteenth century against the British, who sought to suppress them. The Maroons successfully secured their freedom and established an autonomous community from the rest of Jamaican society.[207]

The Accompong Town Maroons had access to lace-bark as the trees grew in Maroon territory in the western part of the island, and the region was inaccessible to outsiders. Obviously, it makes sense that the Maroons would become core participants in the lace-bark industry.[208] Unlike the Accompong Town Maroons, the Windward Maroons on the eastern part of Jamaica did not have easy access to lace-bark as the tree did not grow in those areas, nor did the tree grow on the metamorphic rocks of the Blue Mountains where they settled. Although wet limestone forests exist in eastern Jamaica along the John Crow Mountains, this region does not fit the profile suitable for lace-bark trees to grow, due to the heavy rainfall of some 300 inches per year and the region's height of almost 6,000 feet, hence no tree specimens have been found in this region. Even so, it is possible that some lace-bark trees could thrive at lower altitudes, but this requires further investigation. In contrast to bark-cloth trees such as paper mulberry in Polynesia and *Ficus* in Africa, the lace-bark tree required such a unique environment and soil type to grow it was difficult to propagate.[209]

The origin of the lace-bark tree is a matter of ongoing debate. Botanists in Cuba explained that Cuba has the most fibrous plants of all the Caribbean islands and therefore the *Lagetta lagetto* most likely came from there and spread to other parts of the Caribbean.[210] Wind-borne seeds from the flowering lace-bark tree might have migrated to Jamaica by means of strong winds that blow down from Cuba to Jamaica in the months of November and December. Furthermore, sea and wind currents, often with hurricane force, may have contributed to the spread of seeds. In addition, birds and bats played a key role as migratory agents, transplanting lace-bark seeds. Nor can the human factor be ignored. Early inhabitants of the region, such as the Taínos, could have introduced the tree to the other islands of the Greater Antilles.[211]

Irrespective of how lace-bark trees spread throughout the region, within Taíno culture, cloth and lace-bark were intertwined with Taíno women's daily lives in both a functional and spiritual manner. Just as cloth was significant in the lives of Taíno women, so too will lace-bark become an important vehicle for personal and social transformation in the lives of enslaved African women. Nor will it take long for lace-bark to capture the attention of British Imperialists and awaken the economic interest of the colonial authorities engaged in bio-prospecting.

2 PLANTATION JAMAICA: "CONTROLLING THE SILVER"

Having had from my youth a strong inclination to the study of plants and all other productions of nature; and having through the course of many years with great labour gathered whatever could be procured . . . being fully convinced that nothing tends more to raise our ideas of the power, wisdom, goodness, providence, and other perfections of the Deity.[1]

—SIR HANS SLOANE, 1749

Natural history and Jamaican lace-bark

In 1687, the European physician Hans Sloane arrived in Jamaica as the personal physician to the new governor of Jamaica, the Second Duke of Albemarle. During his fifteen months of residence on the island, Sloane studied his new surroundings and soon developed an obsession for collecting natural and artificial objects, which dominated the remainder of his life. Sloane was one of the first European scientists to travel to Jamaica, and the Caribbean plant and animal specimens he collected were described in careful detail and lavishly illustrated in his two-volume magnum opus, *Voyage to the Islands Madero, Barbados, Nieves, S. Christophers, and Jamaica, with the Natural History of the Herbs and Trees, Four-footed Beasts, Fishes, Birds, Insects, Reptiles, etc. of the last of those Islands* (1707–1725).[2] Sloane's natural history of the Caribbean captivated the British public and established him as a literary genius of his day.[3] Hans Sloane's visit to Jamaica coincided with the onset of the Sugar Revolution, when the local plantocracy had rushed to transform the economy and labor organizations into massive agro-industrial operations for overseas markets. It was also a time when economic-botany was taking shape, and several European bio-prospectors scoured the Caribbean region in search of food, medicine, dyes, raw materials, and luxury goods. Transatlantic explorations were primarily European male enterprises, and among those who came were men of science, including naturalists, physicians, and botanists. Artists and collectors of curiosities also traveled to the region. The published works of Sloane and other natural historians of the period circulated widely in Europe among scientists,[4] and by the eighteenth century, interest in the natural history of the Caribbean had become so popular among the upper classes in Britain that the Caribbean became an important zone of nature enquiry and colonial bio-prospecting.[5]

During the early period of cross-cultural contact between Europeans and Amerindians, the conquistadors sought wealth in the form of gold and silver but, by the eighteenth century, bio-prospectors who arrived were seeking bio-resources or "green gold" that would yield vast fortunes. Some bio-prospectors sought to make Europe pharmaceutically efficient and at the same time assist the colonial power in controlling the colonies by learning how to combat tropical disease.[6] Ironically, European bio-prospectors turned to the Amerindians whom they once considered as "savages" for useful medicines. This is no different from today where pharmaceutical and drug companies are engaged in genetic and medical research amongst indigenous people that lead to new drugs. In the eighteenth century, as the Amerindian population declined, the medicine of African slaves in the West Indies became very important to bio-prospectors. Countless Africans were new to the island as they arrived as slaves, but they were familiar with tropical diseases and knew how to cure them. Still, many enslaved Africans were not always willing to share their medicinal secrets with European physicians.[7]

The rise of bio-prospecting within the region was an important phenomenon that greatly impacted the metropolitan's view of the colonial world and its inhabitants. Sloane, like many of his contemporaries, was interested in bio-resources and prepared for his bio-prospecting expedition to the Caribbean. Before leaving for Jamaica, he collected all the data available in Europe on tropical plants so that he could recognize them. Upon arriving in Jamaica, he turned to local residents for information about the natural products of the island, which he later recorded and published.[8] Sloane's natural history books included colorful works of art and detailed narratives of the flora and fauna of the colonies; these depictions captivated the imagination of the readers back in Europe. Natural history publications served several important functions. On one level, they enhanced Europeans' knowledge of the Caribbean; they also illuminated the hidden treasures, wonders, and fascinating objects of the Caribbean's natural world and fostered an awareness of commercial enterprises one could pursue for profit, such as lace-bark.

Samples of specimens and knowledge of how indigenous people and Africans used local plants in Caribbean medicine were introduced in Europe to help save

European lives and provide better healthcare for British Imperialists who sought to control these valuable plants and the medicines derived from them.[9] Even so, natural history publications were important in documenting the flora and fauna of the Caribbean, while collected specimens, seeds, and saplings provided an opportunity to help conserve these plants that were threatened by ecological challenges of the period. Historian David Watts has asserted that the rise of a sugar industry in the Caribbean changed the physical landscape and nature of the environment, which led to deforestation, soil erosion, run off from sugar mills, and the invasion of pests that resulted in the extinction of some species. These changes in the environment were directly related to the social and economic transformations brought by colonial tropical plantations.[10]

Obviously, not everyone celebrated the works of the natural historians and bio-prospectors (or bio-piracy). The debate has divided scholars in the field. Michel Foucault believed that natural history in the eighteenth century represented "the eradication of history, fable, hearsay, anatomy, smell, and touch from a field of knowledge restricted to surface visibility, and a language shorn of memory."[11] Basically, it was a time of "pure tabulation of things," while feminist historian of science Carolyn Merchant has argued that this was the period of the "Death of Nature" when nature was detached and distanced from God, who authorized the human exploitation of the environment.[12] Merchant and others felt that the collectors of curiosities seemed more interested in the process of "thingification,"[13] in general, harvesting natural resources and imposing European names, claiming land, and displacing and enslaving indigenous people.[14] What Europeans considered as improvement to the colonial environment was blatant appropriation and exploitation of subjugated people. Underlying these differences, natural history participated in the production of meaning and, therefore, is undeniably crucial to our understanding of the colonial environment.

Natural historians, artists, and collectors of curiosities who sought to study Caribbean plants and animals in their natural environment included observation and scientific research as methods of analysis. Published information about local flora and fauna became historical representations that shaped the colonizers' view of their colonial possessions and simultaneously provided the British public with a window into the natural world of distant colonies and their subjects. Artists throughout the period and beyond also played a significant role in providing a window into the life and natural environment of colonized people and their domains. A fine example is the sketches and paintings by Scottish academician Joseph Bartholomew Kidd (1808–1889).[15] Kidd's painting, *The Date Tree* (see Figure 2.1), beautifully illustrates some sense of the diverse flora of the island of Jamaica, yet there is no semblance or point of reference in the work to the harsh environment created by British merchants and plantocrats who sought to expropriate and enslave Africans for the sole purpose of generating profits based on sugar.

FIGURE 2.1 "Plate 6. The Date Tree/Sugar Works in the Distance" from *Illustrations of Jamaica in a Series of Views Comprising the Principal Towns' Harbours and Scenery*, London & Kingston, 1840, hand-colored lithograph. Joseph Bartholomew Kidd (1808–1889). Yale Center for British Art, Paul Mellon Collection.

Paintings from artists like Kidd are invaluable to understanding the past as well as the tensions and contradictions of "colonialist doctrines and practices ... more or less successfully, on an aesthetic level."[16] Kidd's botanical illustration is an extension of Linnaean botany, part of scientific imperialism that sought to exert some control over the earth's natural resources. Yet, perhaps most perplexing is an attempt on the artists' part to present British imperial landscapes of the island colonies as aesthetically pleasing and morally satisfying.[17] Caribbean landscape scenes like those of Kidd played essential roles in helping us to understand the impact of colonialism on native people and the colonial spaces beyond the metropoles in Europe. Art historian Christopher Iannini argues that natural historians of the Caribbean in this period "developed a rich repertoire of linguistic and pictorial techniques for cultivating a vivid understanding of the region."[18] Preeminent among them were Sir Hans Sloane (1660–1753) and Mark Catesby (1683–1749).

Sloane became one of the most influential cultural and scientific figures of the period, and the items he brought back from his voyage to Jamaica formed the basis of a vast collection, which, after his death in 1753, became the foundation of the British Museum, and later the British Library and the Natural History Museum in London.[19] Commenting on his activities in Jamaica and how he was able to amass a large collection, Sloane wrote in 1707, "I took what pains I could at leisure-hours from the business of my profession, to search the several places I could think afforded natural production and immediately described them in a journal.... When I return'd into England, I brought with me about 800 plants.... And shew'd them very freely to all lovers of such curiosities."[20] Among Sloane's prized collection of Jamaican objects he took with him back to England and "shew'd them very freely" were specimens and illustrations of Jamaican lace-bark.

Lace-bark was known to inhabitants across Jamaica and a few Caribbean territories, but relatively unknown in Britain. Sloane's European audiences were mesmerized by the beauty, uniqueness, and refinement of lace-bark, and soon the plant became known in Britain as the "wonder tree of Jamaica."[21] While Sloane's achievements have been widely celebrated within the medical and scientific communities, it is imperative not to forget the contributions of the indigenous people, and enslaved Africans whose knowledge of herbalism, food, and medicine enriched Sloane's repertoire and pharmacopeia of Jamaican plants and curiosities. The collectibles, plant specimens, and medicinal herbs acquired in Jamaica secured Sloane's fame in the halls of British science and endeared him to the British public at large.

Sloane did not "discover" lace-bark, but received a specimen of the plant from European resident Mr. Leming, who sent it to him "from Luidas [Lluidas Vale], an inland, mountainous plantation, where the tree grew in great plenty."[22] In the seventeenth and eighteenth centuries, the lace-bark tree prospered and was abundant in Jamaica. In 1774 Edward Long affirmed that the tree was "common in the woods" of Jamaica.[23] However, Sloane was credited as the person who introduced lace-bark to "civilized Europe."[24] Sloane did not see the tree in its environment, nor did he see the flowers or the seeds. Perhaps time constraints prevented him from venturing into the tree's habitat since he was in Jamaica for a short period. It was not until 1777 that botanists became aware of the tree when European physician, William Wright, brought a complete specimen of the plant from Jamaica and settled on it as a plant species of *Daphne*.[25]

The fact that most Europeans had never heard of lace-bark during this early period is not surprising. Only a few Europeans resided in Jamaica year round as many plantation owners were absentee landlords who lived in Europe off the profits of their estates. The few who remained in Jamaica distanced themselves socially from slaves to maintain their status. Europeans were more concerned with exploiting their slaves for maximum profit rather than paying close attention to what their slaves wore. Others may have confused lace-bark with handmade lace or gauze and would not have been aware unless they were curious to enquire. Lace-bark was difficult to distinguish from handmade lace. Sloane explained, "Unless one knows them [lace-bark] well and look attentively he will not perceive the difference."[26] Sloane was entranced by Jamaican lace-bark to the point where he sought to promote knowledge of the tree not only in print, and lectures, but also in art.

The famous portrait of Sir Hans Sloane painted in 1736 by the artist Steven Slaughter (1697–1765) (Figure 2.2) depicts the naturalist seated upright and dressed in fashionable attire of the period. He is wearing a velvet coat and lace cravat, which at first thought might be lace-bark but, on closer examination, is not. Sloane strikes a regal pose befitting his rank and influence in London society. In the painting, the image is framed by the festooned cloth hanging behind the subject, thus creating a gratuitous, decorative drapery, yet evoking a sense of royalty. The drapery alludes to the "Cloth of Honor" that was popular in portraits of influential people from the fifteenth to the nineteenth century.[27] Sloane's elaborate wig with curls is nicely coiffed and draped over his shoulders, and his family crest looms in the background. Of particular significance, Sloane is depicted unrolling a scroll to reveal an instructive sketch of Jamaican lace-bark. The prominence of the sketch in the artwork not only speaks volumes but piques the viewer's curiosity and captivates the observer.

Of the 800 plant specimens Sloane took with him to England from Jamaica, he chose Jamaican lace-bark to be part of his official portrait. Sloane does not explain why, but we can assume that he greatly admired this Jamaican tree and chose to singularize and elevate it above all the other plant specimens in his collection. Indeed, Sloane's collection of plants like the Jamaican lace-bark cannot be viewed entirely as a leisurely activity in the curious. Plants in Jamaica were not mere items for curiosity or collection, but essential commodities in people's lives, both as items of utility and resources of profit.[28] Sloane does not discuss enslaved women's association with lace-bark in his treaties, even though women have been engaged with lace-bark for decades prior to Sloane's arrival in Jamaica. Perhaps this lapse on Sloane's part was a reflection of the colonialist mentality. Albert Memmi argues that this is one of the great travesties of colonialism, "the most serious blow suffered by the colonized is being removed from history and the community."[29] From this perspective, the most dehumanizing aspect of colonialism is not being recognized. The subjugated became merely objects of history and not active participants. Then

FIGURE 2.2 *Sir Hans Sloane*. Steven Slaughter (1697–1765). © National Portrait Gallery, London.

again, maybe one should not be too harsh on Sloane; after all, it can be argued he was a product of his time and his collection of curiosities was a response to a higher call, a divine one, and therefore such details might not have been viewed as significant. Historian James Robertson has pointed out that Sloane's presence in Jamaica was too short, a mere fifteen months, hence gaps in his knowledge may have been created.[30] Beyond this, Sloane was clearly fascinated with Jamaican lace-bark. In 1725, he explained why:

What is most strange ... is that the inward bark is made up of about twelve coats, layers, or tunicles, appearing white and solid, which if cut off for some length, clear'd of its outward cuticula, or bark, and extended by the fingers, the filaments or threads thereof leaving some rhomboidal interstices, greater or smaller according to the dimensions you extend it to, form a web not unlike gause, lace, or thin muslin.[31]

Up to that point in time, no one could imagine anything such as "natural lace." Botanists were both puzzled by its beauty and texture, while natural historians of the period, such as Patrick Browne, were "equally at a loss with respect to it."[32] (Figures 2.3, 2.4) Like Sloane, one cannot help but admire the delicacy and intricate network of the lace-bark fibers, yet one is left in awe of nature's uncanny ability to seemingly imitate art.

It is easy to see why Sloane was intrigued, but one does wonder if there may have been commercial interest on his part. Sloane took many Jamaican plant specimens with him back to England and spent six years observing, describing, and comparing his Jamaican samples with existing literature before publishing *Catalogue Plantarum* in 1696.[33] Sloane published recipes for ointments and ingredients for treating eyes, among other ailments.[34] However, Sloane does not say whether he saw lace-bark as a potential business opportunity; we can only surmise, considering that during the period some natural historians and collectors of curiosities were bio-prospecting for commodities and lucrative business ventures. In the eighteenth century, several Europeans saw lace-bark as possible

FIGURE 2.3 *Lagetta lagetto*. Field Museum of Natural History © Field Museum.

FIGURE 2.4 *Lagetta lagetto*. Field Museum of Natural History © Field Museum.

raw material for exploitation. Edward Long suggested, "It may, perhaps, be of service to Great Britain as a manufacturing nation."[35] Colonial commercial interests during this early period may have been deterred due to the tree's inaccessibility and the challenges in propagating the plant on a large scale. At any rate, the idea of a natural substitution for handmade lace would have caught the attention of entrepreneurs who sought to capitalize on lace-bark. One can only imagine lace makers across Europe in a state of fright at the thought of losing their jobs, or their services becoming obsolete, due to lace "growing" on trees! Regardless, since most enslaved Africans and colonized people did not have access to European lace, the opportunity to own a piece of natural lace was most appealing.

The history of handmade lace

It is the one costly wear which never vulgarises . . . lace in its comparatively quiet richness never obtrudes itself and is recognized in its true worth and beauty only by those whose superior taste has trained them to see its value.[36]

F. NEVILL JACKSON

Throughout much of its history, lacemaking was considered a high artistic skill that has charmed men and women for centuries with its beauty and intricate designs. Handmade lace, with its exquisite ornamental openwork spaces of thread, has served many purposes, including as decorative art, a source of wealth, trade commodity, covering for sacred spaces and objects, and adorning and accessorizing the body and dress. Perhaps no other fabric is as transformative of the human body as lace. For instance, lace can both feminize and embolden the body; while for others it is the epitome of gracefulness, gentility, and refinement.[37] As clothing, it has served as a signifier of luxury, extravagance, and elitism.

It is not clear where or when the first handmade lace developed. Cut linen, also a form of early lace, has been unearthed at ancient funerary sites in Egypt and elaborate netting of gold and cotton has been found in mummy wrappings, dating back ten centuries before the Christian era. The knotting of gold, silver, and colored threads and fibers for beauty, even in the most primitive form, were the first attempts at lacemaking.[38] The next step in the evolution of lace included the drawing of threads, followed by "cutwork" involving removing portions or small sections of material and filling the open spaces with stitchery.[39] As discussed earlier, such threads were looped, plaited, or twisted together in one of several ways: with a needle, known as needlepoint lace; with a bobbin, hence bobbin lace, sometimes inaccurately called pillow lace; or by machinery, producing imitations of both needlepoint lace and bobbin lace.[40] An exquisite artifact of bobbin lace can be seen in the handkerchief from the Convent of Notre Dame de Visitation (Figure 2.5).

The Greeks, as far as we know, are believed to have produced the earliest needle-made lace, called reticella, which was entirely geometrical in design with an open-work ground or an open bit of lace that was used to fill in between other usually denser patterns or designs. These simple grounds were called "nets" while bobbin grounds became known as réseau (French for "network").[41] Handmade lace, as we know it today, originated in Italy in the fifteenth century, and the cities of Venice, Milan, and Genoa all gave their names to unique and distinctive creations of lace. The Venetians became world-renowned for one of the most beautiful laces, called Venetian Point or Point de Venise.[42] The art spread from Italy to Spain, and Barcelona became the chief Spanish lace center. Although Spain produced beautiful works of lace, such as the Mantilla of Point d' Espagne, which was introduced into the Spanish Americas and Caribbean, Venice remained the center of fashion for royal courts and the elite in the Middle Ages.[43]

Lace became a symbol of wealth henceforth, "the early simplicity of dress had given way to extravagance and luxury, and many rich people impoverished themselves by purchasing scarves, sashes . . . cushions of gold brocade embroidered with pearls . . . and trimmings of lace made with spun gold."[44] Extravagance led to sumptuary laws that sought to control the expenditures of the elite, but the laws had an adverse effect on the lacemaking trade and industries. Moreover, lace became, for centuries, the monopoly of rulers and the aristocracy. As early as 1299,

FIGURE 2.5 *Handkerchief;* Convent of Notre Dame de Visitation, Belgium, Ghent; cotton bobbin lace, circa 1865. Metropolitan Museum of Art. www.metmuseum.org

the Great Council of Venice forbade any trimmings which cost "more than five lire an ell."[45] In France, during the reign of King Louis XIV, "the lace wearing period," there were numerous ordinances against lace, and in seventeenth-century England, handmade lace was frequently used to decorate garments and would be one of the most costly elements of an outfit. Queen Elizabeth I is said to have left 3,000 dresses behind upon her death and nearly all of them ornamented with lace in a lavish manner.[46] The Renaissance period, which is often described as the "beginning of fashion," saw an increased interest in lace as well as greater ability for more people to afford lace.[47] However, by the eighteenth century, stringent laws were imposed across Europoe for the protection of home-based lace industries. To the annoyance of officials, a risky trade of lace smuggling developed across borders and many people lost their lives participating in the illicit trade. Some citizens were very creative in trying to evade the laws. In 1764, several women were arrested in England for transporting baked pies containing valuable foreign laces, and in 1731, the sum of £6,000 worth of French lace was smuggled into England in the coffin of Bishop Atterbury, who had died in Paris that year.[48]

The French Revolution of 1789 led to more simple and less extravagant forms of dress and eventually a decline in the demand for handmade lace. Nevertheless, lacemaking skills continued to spread throughout Europe and beyond. As people migrated they carried lacemaking skills with them. Such was the case in 1568 when religious persecution drove many Flemings to England, and groups of lace makers settled down in London.[49] Over time, countries extended the skill to their colonies. Equally important was the role and popularity of French fashion dolls and puppets, which reached their peak of fame in the eighteenth century. These dolls were not toys, but rather models used for the displays of fashionable laces from France and Italy. The dolls were circulated throughout Europe's capitals and continued into the nineteenth century as a popular form of advertisement for ladies' dresses.[50]

The art of handmade lace developed rapidly and the skills circulated widely. Experts of lacemaking argue that the seventeenth century produced the finest lace. During the Renaissance period in Europe, the splendid skill, delicacy of the artistry, and design elevated lace-making to lofty heights as the embodiment of beauty, yet at the very climax of its perfection, it began to decline.[51] A stunning example of exquisite seventeenth century lace can be seen in Figure 2.6.

The painting depicts the Duchess of Chandos in 1579 and portrays her in her glorious finery of lace. The Duchess dons a dress with sleeves heavily laced and her standing band (flared collar) is made of reticella lace with punto in aria lace attached to reveal a delicate work of artistry.[52] Such bands were popular among the elite throughout the period. The Duchess's attire reflects high maintenance and English opulence. Her impractical clothing conveys a clear message to the viewer that the subject of the portrait was of high standing, enjoyed a privileged lifestyle, and had plenty of spare time to indulge in the pursuits of fashion and the lengthy process of dressing. The Duchess's elaborate band of copious folds of lavish lace required the assistance of servants to set the band's layers and pleats with hot pokers and heavy starch once per week. The band most likely required daily pinning to keep it in place.[53]

By the nineteenth century, most handmade lace remained very expensive and beyond the reach of all but the wealthy. During the early period of Queen Victoria's reign, patterned machine-made lace emerged on local markets, offering lace at more affordable prices for the less affluent. The public wedding of Queen Victoria in 1840 rejuvenated the lace trade and awoke interest in the art when she wore a veil of honiton lace. By the ending of the 1860s, lace was popular again and lace making, along with embroidery, crochet, and tatting, became ideal fancy work as pastime activities for English ladies.[54]

In earlier centuries, both men and women wore garments accessorized with lace, but as men's fashion changed and became more practical and adaptable to most work environments, women's dress became more complex and ornamental with draped fabrics and heavy skirting in need of trimmings such as lace. Gradually, lace became

FIGURE 2.6 *The Duchess of Chandos; Frances, Lady Brydges* (ca. 1553–1623), 1579, unknown artist sixteenth century. Oil on panel. Yale Center for British Art, Paul Mellon Collection.

more associated with women's fashion. This did not preclude lace as part of religious garb worn by clergy. Lace continued to charm both men and women, and perhaps its charm lies in the ability of the lace maker to imitate nature with patterns from the simplest to the most sophisticated flower of nature. Such designs exemplified the gentle touch, steady hands, much patience, excellent vision, and countless hours of labor to bring beautiful designs to fruition that can last for many years.[55]

Lacemaking was predominantly women's work during the pre-industrial era. While some women, such as nuns in convents, worked on making lace covers for altars, vestments, and the occasional social elite who had commissioned a piece of lace art, most women in the secular world of lacemaking were linked to a household industry or family economy, which functioned as a unit. As a result, many women became responsible for producing goods and reproducing future workers. Nor did women's involvement in manufacturing in the home liberate them from their customary domestic duties, even though women's relatively poor wages served to confirm unequal gender roles.[56] The advent of machine-made or more specifically warp knitted lace democratized the once elite accessory and at the same time transformed both the body and our perception of lace. Historically, lace was used to adorn the body and accessorize, but gradually lace acquired new images, including a symbol of sexual enticement. Warp knitted lace came within easy reach of many for use as underwear, whereas for hundreds of years intricate handmade lace had been an outer adornment that appeared in formal portraits of the elite such as Duchesses (as seen earlier). Anne Hollander charges that as lace became more accessible the feminine became more disheveled, and pornographic works of art then came to depict female nudity emerging from lacy garments.[57]

European women who arrived in the Caribbean and the Americas brought with them needlework and lacemaking skills and transmitted these skills to local women. In many cases enslaved women learned by watching, studying, and copying the lace making techniques of their enslavers. Lacemaking was not prevalent in Jamaica during slavery, but in other areas of the Caribbean and Latin America the art was widely practiced. For example, the curriculum for eighteenth-century elite school girls in colonial Latin America consisted of sewing, lace-making, and spinning,[58] and today some convents have maintained this tradition. The Franciscan Missionary Sisters in Jamaica for example continue to teach young women needlework skills.[59] Furthermore, lacemaking was viewed as regular work for nuns in convents across many areas of Latin America.[60]

Other types of needlework from the colonial era can be seen in Brazil, where bobbin lace (*venda di bilros* in Portuguese) was brought to the Brazilian coastline by Portuguese colonists in the nineteenth century. Portugal had a rich tradition of lacemaking, and colonists continued to practice in the Americas. In Brazil, lacemaking was mostly the province of women; the art form was passed down from mothers to daughters who learned by watching and repeating their motions.[61] Enslaved African women of Bahia appropriated the lace fashions of their plantation mistresses to create ornate lace outfits for priestesses in the Afro-Brazilian religion of Candomblé. The priestesses wore elaborate eyelet lace dresses with stiff underskirts. The popularity of lace dress in rituals reflected a large home industry of embroidery and lacemaking that developed in Brazil and is still evident today.[62]

In Mexico City, many Mexican women, like their counterparts in Spain, continued the tradition of wearing black lace mantillas,[63] and in Puerto Rico, the bobbin lace called *mundillo* was widely admired for its beauty.[64]

Some enslaved Africans were already familiar with European lace and dress. On the West African coast, Africans were influenced by European customs in dress, which led to a synthesis of various dress customs in several African Kingdoms. Many African rulers and dignitaries received cloth and clothing from European visitors and traders throughout the centuries of trade. In 1701, for example, Dutch officials on Gold Coast brought to the Asantehene at Kumasi a "red velvet cloth bordered with gold lace,"[65] and in Southern Africa, the Dutch colonists who had settled the Cape region in the seventeenth century introduced both European customs in dress and lace-making skills to indigenous people. Eventually, lace-making became a "white art" among some African women, and in more recent history, it was introduced as a major craft activity for black women in South African prisons.[66]

From early in Jamaica's colonial history, lace was associated with affluence and conspicuous consumption. Commenting in 1687 on the economic success of the Port Royal merchants, Reverend Francis Crow suggested it was befitting "for a cooper's wife ... [to] go forth in the best flowered silk and richest silver and gold lace that England can afford with a couple of Negroes at her tail."[67] Such lavish spending on lace was not unique to Jamaica. In 1732, Justin Girod de Chantrans wrote in his journal of his voyage to Saint Domingue (Haiti) that he was concerned about the "attachment of white men to free négresses and mulattas, the devotion to pleasure, [and] the money spent on linen, lace and jewels."[68] In this regard, lace represented a lifestyle and signaled one's ability to consume. Europeans of financial means in the Caribbean could order lace directly from Europe for personal adornment and display to reflect their wealth and social standing. Lady Nugent, wife of the Governor of Jamaica from 1801–1805, received numerous cargos of dress from London so she could entertain in clothing appropriate to her social role and status in the colony.[69]

A few enslaved Africans in Jamaica did obtain European clothing trimmed with lace. Occasionally, African slaves received castoff or hand-me-down clothing as gifts from their white enslavers. Some clothing gifts most likely included garments trimmed with lace as enslavers ensured their house slaves were decently dressed as a reflection of their owner's wealth. Lady Nugent, on one occasion, "distributed to the women gowns, petticoats and various presents"[70] so they could attend her wedding celebration. Other enslaved individuals purchased cloth with money they saved up from selling their produce in the local markets. The visitor Cynric Williams, in 1823, observed slaves purchasing "finery" (cloth) and, "[They were] laying down pieces of money that I had never thought to see in the hands of slaves."[71] Some slaves may have had the opportunity to purchase European handmade lace, but this was rare as refined fabrics available for retail purchase locally were limited and usually prohibitively expensive. The majority of enslaved Africans in Jamaica did not have access to European lace. This will change after Emancipation in 1838. Enslaved women who were literate followed the London fashions and observed images published in local papers like the *Falmouth Post* and the *Royal Gazette*.[72] These papers were full of advertisements with detailed descriptions of appropriate dress materials suitable for specific occasions. Seamstresses and washer women who worked in the plantation Great House had access to their owners' garments and could study them, and become familiar with lace.[73]

Several intriguing images from the Caribbean portray colonial subjects' familiarity with European lace and its use as a status symbol. In Agostino Brunias' paintings from the Eastern Caribbean, much attention is paid to dress, therefore emphasizing the importance of cloth and dress in the colonial society. Since cloth was imported, it was highly valued, both as a commodity as well as a medium of exchange. Cloth and dress were also signifiers that expressed social meanings in addition to their functional roles. In this instance, his painting is colorful, and the art work depicts interesting subjects, but what is most relevant is the use of lace in the subjects' clothes. In the painting *A West Indian Flower Girl* (Figure 2.7), the mulatto women can be seen wearing the most ornate headdresses imaginable. The dress and elaborate headwraps of the mulattos set them apart from the rest of the society and signals their elite standing. For enslaved women, especially mulatto women, acquiring the most expensive and extravagant dress was one way of achieving differentiation and social mobility. The rarity and uniqueness of the outfit usually commanded social admiration within the community.[74]

The women in the painting are dressed in brightly colored long skirts and shawls called fichus as typical of European women's fashion at the time. The two subjects facing the viewer are wearing blouses with lace sleeves that was fashionable among the elite of the period, and symbolic of gentility and refinement,[75] meanwhile the central figure accessorized her outfit with a high cap, ornamented with black and white lace. The headgear and dress is reminiscent of the lace caps and lace fichus of the Normandy peasant women in France who prided themselves on the fineness of their lappets (decorative folds attached to heardress), and elaborate lace caps, and lace-trimmed halo headgear; these exquisite headdresses in France identified the peasants' village.[76] The headdress of the other women in the painting are reminiscent of the African woman's headwrap and their dress reflect a Creole aesthetic. The Creole dress was subversive by nature and fundamentally radical because it defied easy categorization due to its blending of African and European styles in dress. In essence, it visually and symbolically challenged the colonial regimes' apparent deep-seated desire to divide the colonial world into clear-cut opposites of black and white, African and European.[77]

The most prominent feature of dress depicted in the painting is the headwraps although one subject imitates the European high style of some years before, wearing a straw hat on top of a headwrap. The women's headdress captivates the viewer due

FIGURE 2.7 *A West Indian Flower Girl and Two other Free Women of Color.* Agostino Brunias (1728–1796). Oil on canvas, Yale Center for British Art, Paul Mellon Collection.

to the height, vibrant colors, and texture of the wraps. An interesting synthesis in dress customs, such a headdress could have been a popular trend or a fashion statement among some enslaved women, perhaps a symbol of the wearer's wealth, status, and prestige.[78] Agostino Brunias' subjects are portrayed as "exotic others" with an air of elegance, beauty, and sophistication. Perhaps he has exaggerated or embellished his subjects' dress; this we will never know.[79] Nonetheless, his subjects are positioned in a space that could be identical to any urban center in Europe of the time. The reality of a harsh environment based on plantation slavery and brutal punishments is absent, and instead the viewer is deceived by the world of bright colors and the beauty of "exoticized" mulatto women in high fashion, idly indulging in a tranquil moment of buying tropical flowers.[80]

Similarly, *Sketches in Character*, by the Jewish Jamaican artist, Isaac Mendes Belisario (1795–1849), provides visual evidence of Jamaican slaves dressed in magnificent carnival costumes, ornamented with lace and bedecked in sumptuous finery[81] (Figures 2.8 and 2.9). Colonial authorities allowed enslaved Africans and their descendants in Jamaica to hold carnivals and Crop-Over celebrations on Christmas holidays. Slave carnivals contained subtexts of subtle resistance not obvious to whites, which enabled slaves to make merry and simultaneously poke fun at the institution that denied them their rights as human beings.[82] Such revelry reflected a blending of African and European masquerade combined with mimicry, British mumming plays, and Shakespearean monologues. Carnival was also a performative space, in which slaves appropriated the symbols of their enslavers and experienced some fleeting or temporary power. Carnival was the

FIGURE 2.8 Queen or Maam of the set girls. *Sketches of Character: in illustration of the habits, occupation, and costume of the Negro population, in the island of Jamaica*; Isaac Mendes Belisario (1795–1849). Yale Center for British Art, Paul Mellon Collection.

FIGURE 2.9 Koo, Koo, or Actor-Boy. *Sketches of Character: in illustration of the habits, occupation, and costume of the Negro population, in the island of Jamaica*; Isaac Mendes Belisario (1795–1849). Yale Center for British Art, Paul Mellon Collection.

embodiment of creolization and cultural adaptation in action.[83] Often, the celebration included masquerades called Jonkonnu, consisting of masked troupes, dancers, and a procession of women called Set Girls led by a queen or Maam for the occasion.[84]

In the procession, the queen or Maam was more elaborately dressed to reflect her status in the parade as compared with other women in the procession. In Figure 2.8, the queen or the Maam is dressed in a spectacular costume, decorated with rosebuds and designed with puffed sleeves and a low neckline. Her outfit is accessorized with a broad brim hat and large plumage, and she carries a decorated whip. One of the most striking features of her dress is the falling band of lace frills accentuating the queen's low-cut neckline.

Equally intriguing, the image of Koo, Koo, or Actor Boy (Figure 2.9) provides visual confirmation of slaves' use of lace. The masked participant is dressed in a magnificent costume with heavy plumage above a well-coiffed wig. He wears a skirt with flounces extending all around to create several layers with edgings of lace. These elaborate costumes were funded by white sponsors and enslavers who enabled their slaves to go all out with their fancy outfits, consequently heightening the rivalry in dress among enslaved individuals. Some sponsors sought to outdo each other. Nonetheless, lace remained a popular accessory in carnival costumes during slavery and into the present.[85]

The Jamaican bark-cloth industry

"When chubble tek yu, pikney shut fit yu"—When you find yourself in trouble, a child's shirt fits you.[86]

JAMAICAN PROVERB

There were several factors that led to the development of a bark-cloth industry in Jamaica. Many enslaved Africans received insufficient clothing from their enslavers and were expected to supplement their yearly rations. Most slaves received "as much Oznaburgh as will make two frocks, and as much woolen stuff as will make a great coat."[87] Clearly, this was not enough for most slaves since the intense labor in the fields, along with the weathering of garments, often rotted the meager clothing rations slaves received.[88] Meanwhile, "[h]ead negroes [usually men] on estates generally received some present in the way of clothing upon the conclusion of crop."[89] Of critical note, slave laws regarding dress did not require equal distribution of clothing between enslaved men and women. In 1793 on the Worthy Park Estate, skilled male slaves received ten yards of osnaburg and three yards of Baize. A few skilled enslaved women received the same amount of osnaburg, but no Baize. On Harmony Hall Estate, a similar pattern of distribution existed. Slave men received more clothing than slave women, regardless of the fact that women's clothing of the period required more cloth for skirting. Likewise, in 1811, male head slaves received twelve yards of osnaburg and six yards of blue Baize each, while each regular male slave received eight yards of osnaburg. Female slaves, on the other hand, received seven yards each, and children five yards.[90] Generally, enslaved women received smaller clothing rations, and therefore had a greater need than slave men for sufficient dress. The custom of rewarding male slaves for their skills with more clothing, even though enslaved women worked side by side with enslaved men in the fields, reflected the colonial misogynistic perspective that women's contribution to the colonial economy was not valued as much as that of men. Deprived of validation, the dismissal of women's labor reaffirmed the patriarchal norms of colonial society and at the same time reinforced African women's subordination to African men.

Enslaved Africans had to find alternative means of supplementing their clothing rations. A few women stole clothes from their enslavers. White mistresses complained regularly that their washerwomen had a tendency to "lose" clothing;[91] others received additional dress in exchange for sexual favors. The slave mistress Phibbah received gifts of clothing from her enslaver, Thistlewood, including "six pairs of shoes and much cloth for herself."[92] Several slaves purchased extra garments and cloth with money saved up from selling their produce. In 1833, "[a] slave in the parish of Clarendon admitted that he made by this means, forty pounds annually."[93] Seamstresses were also able to earn money by offering their services to prospective customers. In 1786, Phibbah gave Thistlewood a present in silver, money she had earned by "sewing, baking cassava, selling musk melons and watermelons out of her ground."[94] In some instances, women received clothing on special occasions and as a reward for bearing children.[95] The planter Matthew Gregory Lewis gave "each [slave] mother a present of a scarlet girdle with a silver medal in the centre ... [which] entitled her to marks of peculiar respect ... and receiving a larger portion [of dress] than the rest."[96] During the commemoration of a new hospital on Lewis' estate, every woman received "a flaming red stuff petticoat."[97] Enslaved women who received extra clothes and European dress were socially elevated within the slave society but for planters like Lewis the slave woman's body was the focus of economic interest and sexual exploitation. Historian Hilary Beckles asserts that the enslaved woman's sexuality and maternity were no longer her own, but were placed on the market as capital assets to be manipulated for the benefit of plantocrats.[98]

Some slaves and freed people could not afford the cost of imported textiles and looked for a less costly and more viable means of obtaining dress. Enslaved Africans from bark-cloth and textile producing areas of Africa utilized the skills they acquired locally and in Africa to obtain suitable raw materials for dress from their environment. They acquired some knowledge of native plants from the Taínos, and built on this knowledge and developed it further.[99] They looked for plants in the Jamaican forests that could be used to make dyes to color the drab fabrics they received from their enslavers. Several dye pigments were used, such as indigo-berry (*Randia aculeate*), annotto or roucou tree (*Bixa orellana*), and vine sorrel (*Cissus trifoliate*).[100] The extensive list of dye sources (see Appendix) recorded by early natural historians and residents suggest the development of an auxiliary industry in dye production. As in West Africa, the Jamaican dye industry engaged in a vibrant and fluid relationship with lace-bark and bark-cloth producers, seamstresses, and cloth traders within the slave economy. Several smaller auxiliary cottage industries associated with plants developed, including soap, perfume, and tanning for leather. Enslavers did not provide the basic necessities for personal hygiene. These industries developed out of a need and a desire on the part of slaves to be healthy, to look good and feel good. Contrary to racist beliefs of the time, slaves were concerned about their appearance and personal hygiene in spite of living in a harsh environment. The bark-cloth industry thrived, as the amount of cotton grown in Jamaica during this period was not enough to have an impact on the local economy, and mass scale cotton production was not encouraged as some feared it would compete with Britain's textiles industry.[101] Bark-cloth seemed an ideal alternative.

The Jamaican bark industry was extensive and important to the livelihood of many slaves and freed people. The industry included the services of herbalists and healers, tree spotters, loggers, bark cutters, artisans, dyers, seamstresses, and tailors, to traders, tanners, and perfumers. Those involved received some financial rewards for their participation. The earliest historical evidence of bark-cloth in Jamaica dates to the seventeenth century when Charles II, king of England from 1660 to 1685, was presented with a lace-bark cravat by the Governor of Jamaica, Sir Thomas Lynch, who governed the island twice from 1671 to 1674 and again in 1682 to 1684.[102] Sloane mentioned this event and provided the earliest description of lace-bark in Jamaica. Undoubtedly, the governor's presentation brought Jamaica some prestige and awareness of Africans' creativity and superb craft skills.

As indicated, bark-cloth production existed earlier among the indigenous Taínos, while a few Spaniards who had settled the region prior to the British were already familiar with lace-bark and bark-cloth.[103] Within a few decades after the British arrived, the bark-cloth industry in Jamaica had developed to the level worthy of royal recognition. Chief among the participants in the bark-cloth industry were the Maroons, many of whom were of West African heritage, who had successfully escaped the plantations and secured their freedom in the mountains. They had greater flexibility and more time to engage in the cottage industry compared with many slaves who labored under harsh conditions for long hours in the fields. Furthermore, the Leeward Maroons controlled vast areas of the Cockpit Country with trees suitable for bark-cloth and lace-bark production.[104]

Several enslaved and freed Africans obtained bast fibers from plants for use in clothing manufacture, including mountain cabbage [*Euterpe oleracea*] and the down-tree-down [*Ochroma pyramidale*].[105] Reminiscent of raffia cloth production in Central Africa, these barks were stripped, beaten soft, and the fibers pulled out, separated, carded or combed to untangle, and dried. The dried fibers were then woven into textile, sewed or tied, and worn. Banana leaf fibers (abaca) obtained from the banana tree were treated in the same manner. The bark from other trees used to make clothing included the trumpet tree [*Cecropia peltata*]. In this case, the bark was cut away in narrow strips, peeled down to the inner thin layer. Similar to aspects of bark-cloth production in Polynesia and Africa, the thin strips were removed, beaten, dried, and then sewn together.[106]

Unlike the production process in Polynesia and Africa, there were no carved mallets for beating in the Jamaican context. We can only speculate that artisans improvised with heavy pieces of wood or suitable stones with smooth surfaces for beating the bark. The exact weaving technique is unclear since this is no longer done and the knowledge has been lost over the decades. Nor do we know if some weaving was done on specific looms. In the absence of archeological evidence of working looms in Jamaica, we can surmise it was done primarily by hand twisting and plaiting of fibers, perhaps similar to weaving baskets or fine mats, which is still done in rural Jamaica and particularly among the Maroons. Ingeniously, enslaved Africans learned to "make fashion" with what was available and accessible to them. The most popular form of bark-cloth was obtained from the Lagetta lagetto or lace-bark tree.[107]

Lace-bark: the tree of life

Let us praise now market women: higglers,
who maintain our solid, hidden economy
in soft money banks between full breasts.
Gold next; now these women control silver.[108]

LORNA GOODISON, JAMAICAN POET, "CONTROLLING THE SILVER"

Just as the paper mulberry, *Ficus*, and *kyenkyen* trees were valued for their properties, the lace-bark tree was valued in Jamaica, Cuba, and Haiti for the many properties derived from its bark for use in industry, agriculture, and the home. Lace-bark was used as functional decorative art, medicine, and clothing. Strips of fiber from the thick inner bark were twisted into ropes for industrial uses, making hammocks, and restraining farm animals. Thin pieces of inner woody bark were woven into "hampa" baskets for storage and to carry produce to market. The lace-bark tree provided wood for fencing, and small slender branches that were sturdy and ideal as support sticks for yam vines in slaves' produce gardens and on large farms. Additionally, in Cuba, Jamaica, and Haiti, the bark of the lace-bark tree was sought after by both colonialists and slaves for its medicinal properties. It was used to cure "chronic rheumatism and pain in the bones from lues or the yaws."[109] Field slaves used the macerated bark with water to heal skin eruptions, rashes, and other skin problems, as well as sun stroke from laboring long hours in the hot climate.[110] Some enslaved women used the green bark (from young plants) as an abortifacient.[111] There is much evidence of indigenous people using plants to commit infanticide to resist slavery and colonial oppression. There is no evidence to suggest that African women learned about lace-bark for this purpose from the Taínos. Regardless, some enslaved women engaged in "gynecological resistance" to express their anger at slavery and their refusal to allow their unborn children to endure such oppression.[112]

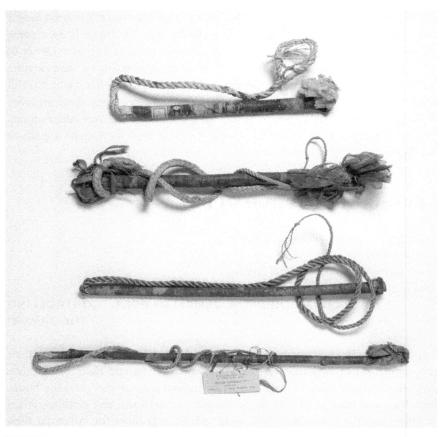

FIGURE 2.10 Lace-bark whips made from branches of the lace-bark tree. The inner woody portion and outer bark have been partially removed and the remaining inner bark twisted into the whip tails.

Lace-bark was fashioned into instruments of brutalization. As depicted in countless narratives and seen in numerous films, perhaps, no other emblem was as ubiquitous and emotionally charged as the planter's whip. Enslavers utilized the bark to make whips to flog their slaves as punishment (Figure 2.10).

A branch of lace-bark was cut, with a portion of the outer wood being removed, and the bark twisted into a lash called a "Negro-whip." Throughout slavery, whips were commonly made from the tree.[113] Punishment occurred daily on plantations and within urban spaces. Sloane wrote that for "negligence slaves were usually whipped by the overseers."[114] Under the enslavers' whip, neither age nor sex made any difference. Female house slaves were more vulnerable than field slaves as they were in closer proximity to the enslaver, and therefore the frequent victims of sadistic whims. Occasionally, the slave woman might be the target of the mistress's jealous rage.[115] Pregnant slaves were not shielded from the whip either, and were unnecessarily flogged, which jeopardized both the life of the mother and unborn child.[116] Ironically, the same bark used to thrash the slave was also used to heal the tortured black body. In addition, lace-bark whips used in pens to "drive" cattle and horses were called "horse whips." In spite of this, the bark's most common use was in the production of household items and clothing manufacture.

Among the Leeward Maroons, labor was divided by gender in the lace-bark industry. Maroon men were responsible for harvesting the bark, making ropes, and hammocks. Women, on the other hand, dominated the processing of lace-bark for clothing and household use.[117] Unlike bark-cloth production among the Ashanti in West Africa, lace-bark production in Jamaica was gendered female. It is not clear when or how lace-bark became gendered female considering the strong West African cultural characteristics amongst the Maroons and many enslaved Africans in Jamaica. One possible explanation for the switch in gender roles has to do with the Maroon leader, Cudjoe. In the early eighteenth century, Cudjoe became chief of the Leeward Maroons and charged the men with warfare and hunting, and he directed the women in "planting provisions and managing domestic affairs."[118] Possibly the women embraced lace-bark as part of their domestic duty to provide clothing for themselves and their families; however, the evidence is inconclusive.

In contrast to other bark-cloths examined in this study, lace-bark production was very different. The men canvased sections of the rain forest in search of mature lace-bark trees for harvesting. Depending on the amount of lace desired, branches were removed for processing or narrow strips of bark were cut longitudinally from the bole of the tree. More often, wide sections of bark were removed all at once, thus preventing the tree bark from regenerating and eventually killing the tree. Most detrimental was the felling of trees for their entire bark. Once harvested, the inner bark was separated from the corky outer bark. The inner bark had a fine texture, almost elastic, very strong, and consisted of several layers of riticuled fibers. The open spaces within the net-like structure of the fibers was rhombus in shape. The layers could be divided into a number of thin filaments, which, after being soaked in water, could be drawn out or teased out with fingers, thus spreading the lacy fibers five times wider than the original width of the bark strip. The web-like filaments or fiber was rolled into large "puff balls" then left to be dried on the ground (Figures 2.11, 2.12, 2.13).

Edward Long explained that the rolled fiber was then stretched again and, "in order to bleach it, after being drawn out as much as it will bear, they expose it stretched to the sunshine, and sprinkle it frequently with water. . . . It bears washing extremely well . . . with common soap . . . and is equal to the best artificial lace."[119] Dried bark required some effort to remove the fibers due to less moisture. The bark could be boiled or soaked for easy separation. Freshly harvested bark could be separated by hand. Soaking or boiling did not harm the fibers. However, typical of

FIGURE 2.11 Drying the lace-bark puffs. Photo by Ashley E. Smith from the book *Souvenir of Jamaica* circa 1903. Author's private collection.

FIGURE 2.12 Working out the lace-bark. Photo by Ashley E. Smith from the book *Souvenir of Jamaica* circa 1903. Author's private collection.

FIGURE 2.13 A piece of prepared lace-bark, Jamaica. Courtesy of the University of the West Indies Library, Mona.

some vegetable fibers like flax, which is used for linen and has a natural wax that adds stiffness and sheen, the cell makeup of the lace-bark produced a naturally occurring, protective stiffener that could be rinsed out to achieve the desirable softness of lace.[120] The end product resembled fine lace, but could also imitate linen and gauze.

Long observed, "The ladies [slaves and freed women] of the island are extremely dexterous in making caps, ruffles, and complete suits of lace with it ... the wild Negroes [Maroons] have made apparel with it of a very durable nature."[121] Several sources corroborate Long's statements. John Lunan, for instance, in 1814 acknowledged the popularity of lace-bark dress among Jamaican women and the role of the Maroons in the industry. Lunan added, "There is no doubt but very fine clothes might be made with it."[122] These early accounts provide tantalizing clues of clothing made from lace-bark. Long does not provide detailed description of the actual dress styles; however, references to ruffles and suits of lace suggest some European influences in design. The lace was versatile, soft, and malleable to be stitched into diverse styles, including suits of lace, to ruffles, and lace caps. One of the most curious surviving clothing artifacts is a child's night dress and cap from Jamaica (Figures 2.14, 2.15). The dress was

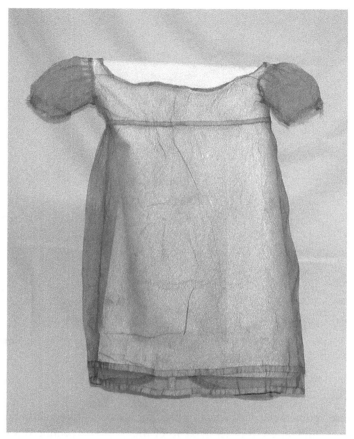

FIGURE 2.14 Lace-bark dress, donated in 1833 by Marchioness Cornwallis. Photograph: © Saffron Walden Museum, Essex.

fashioned into the "empire style" of the 1820s in lace-bark, reflecting a closely fitted torso, high-waist bodice, short sleeves, and a scooped neckline.[123] The dress and cap belonged to the Marchioness Cornwallis, wife of Lord Braybrooke of Audley End, whose father-in-law resided in Jamaica.[124] The simplicity in the dress design reflects a certain degree of elegance and suggests that styles reciprocated between classes as some Europeans found Jamaican lace-bark appealing.[125]

Other types of clothing and accessories made from lace-bark included bonnets, fans, and slippers overlaid with lace-bark (Figure 2.16). Natural lace was used to make fashionable "dress up" clothes for special occasions and, like the Haya people in East Africa where bark-cloth was associated with mortuary rites, both men and

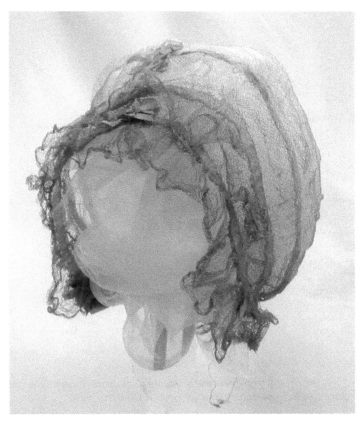

FIGURE 2.15 Lace-bark cap from Jamaica, donated in 1833 by Marchioness Cornwallis. Photograph: © Saffron Walden Museum, Essex.

women in late seventeenth-century Jamaica used the lagetto linen for mourning dress.[126]

Early accounts suggest there was a change in fashion trends over time amongst the subjugated population. In the seventeenth century, Hans Sloane mentioned that lace-bark was used by both men and women in clothing especially for mourning. By the eighteenth century, this seems to have shifted and lace-bark became primarily women's wear. Natural lace was used to make shawls and veils. In 1823, the visitor Cynric Williams recalled he met a girl on the road wearing "a veil over her face, which I [he] thought at first to be lace, but found to be made of the bark of a tree; it is drawn out by the hand while the bark is green, and has a very pretty effect."[127] Maybe the veil was worn to conceal her identity or provide shade from the hot sun while traveling. It could have been used as an expedient article of clothing to cover facial scarring and disfigurement. The veil might have been an

FIGURE 2.16 Slippers of lace-bark with soles made of coconut bark India rubber fiber (1827). Photograph: © Trustees of the Royal Botanic Gardens, Kew.

appropriation of the fashionable Spanish *mantilla* brought to Jamaica by immigrants and visitors from the Spanish colonies. Natural lace was a great substitute when European lace was scarce or too expensive, and it was used for every clothing purpose that manufactured and European handmade lace was used.[128]

Among other functions, lace-bark was used in the home to make doilies or "fern mats" and runners to decorate tables and home furniture (Figure 2.17), and it was used as a sieve during cooking. Lace-bark was ideal for bandages to treat wounds, and as window curtains and space dividers in the home. Veils made from lace-bark were used as protective coverings for the cradle of newborns to shield them from gnats or mosquitos from biting the child lying under it.[129] The multitude of lace-bark uses provides some semblance of a cottage industry in clothing manufacture,[130] and a level of personal freedom and creative impulse among enslaved people.

FIGURE 2.17 Placemat made of lace-bark. Photograph: © Trustees of the Royal Botanic Gardens, Kew.

Situation in Haiti, Cuba, and the question of women's labor

"Árbol que nace torcido, jamás su tronco endereza."—A tree that is born bent cannot be made straight.[131]

CUBAN PROVERB

The situation in Haiti and Cuba was somewhat different from that in Jamaica. The *lagetto* tree was very rare in Haiti and did not have as wide a distribution and abundance as in Jamaica. Consequently, Haitian lace-bark never attained the same level of fame. In Haiti, the lace-bark tree or bwa dantèl[132] was found in Jacmel and on the Island of la Gonãve, off the coast of Western Haiti.[133] In rural areas, the bark was used to make ropes for farm use, and whips to punish disobedient children.[134] Bwa dantèl was among a variety of fibrous plants suitable for making paper and textiles; however, several species of the genus *Daphnopsis* were more popular. Likewise, bwa chandèl [*Pinus occidentalis*] was widely utilized for its fibers. Bast-fibers were woven into cloth for secular and ritual dress, including brightly colored sequined costumes for African influenced celebrations such as Rara.[135] Interestingly, lace-bark was used in Vodou for customary medicine and as spiritual food for loa (spirits) on special occasions and during certain rites. Among some Vodou practitioners, lace-bark was known as *laget* or *ma laget*.[136] Meanwhile, in the Dominican Republic, the lace-bark tree was rare and was not used in clothing manufacture due to the abundance and widespread use of cotton.[137]

The Spaniards in Cuba were long aware of lace-bark and in the late "sixteenth century," sent to the king in Old Spain a splendid collar of lace made of this tree-bark."[138] Several species of the *Lagetta* genus are endemic to Cuba, yet lace-bark or Daguilla[139] did not have a wide distribution as in Jamaica. In Cuba, the tree was found on the *Loma Daguilla* (Lace-bark Hill) an isolated mountain south-west of the San Juan hills, and Isle de Pinos, where it grew high up on cliffs and terraced mountain sides, thus was difficult to access.[140] *Daguilla*, also called *Guana*, was utilized by Spaniards and Afro-Cubans alike. Spanish farmers used it to make ropes, and in the eighteenth century, *daguilla* fibers were sent to the Queen in Spain and other principal ladies at court.[141] Rural farmers meantime used lace-bark scarves to woo young ladies.[142] Lace-bark was used to make aprons, kerchiefs, and overalls for covering while working in the fields and cooking.[143] The principal use of the lace-bark in Cuba was for making ropes. Botanist Baron H. Eggers reported from Cuba in 1889, "Some very interesting bast was obtained from three different trees, the finest of a lace-bark tree, called *Guana* [*Lagetta linteria*] ... the common Cuban bast very much used for ropes."[144] Cuba was actively engaged in ship building; therefore ropes would be needed for the industry. As in Haiti, lace-bark was used in the Afro-Cuban religion of Santeria. *Daguilla* was associated with the god Osun.[145] However, there is no evidence to suggest that lace-bark was used in Afro-Jamaican religions.

Lace-bark was appealing to many colonized people in Jamaica for its beauty, versatility, and resemblance to European manufactured lace. Most interesting, it was strong and durable. It was washable with regular soap, and the fibers could be dyed. Some women wore natural lace as a means of elevating themselves within the colonial society. For centuries, lace represented the social mores and attitude of the wearer in that "the apparent fragility of its delicate design suggested the refinement and gentility of its wearer."[146] However, enslaved people were denigrated and considered by colonists as incapable of refinement. Throughout slavery, comparisons between African women and animals were not infrequent.[147] Sir Hans Sloane compared the breasts of African women who had borne children to the udders of goats, and Edward Long suggested that African women had a natural affinity to the orangutan.[148] Such racist analogies not only allowed for the economic and sexual exploitation of enslaved women, but sought to humiliate and defeminize black women. For enslaved women, who could afford it, lace-bark clothing was a means of reclaiming and asserting their femininity and simultaneously rejecting the stereotypes associated with black women. Some women were lured by the delicate beauty of lace-bark. Like linen, the lightness and airiness of the fabric was attractive as it kept the body cool in the tropical heat. A few may have viewed lace-bark as an opportunity to own something unique and valuable, to reminisce of bark-cloth production in Africa, and at the same time establish a cultural link to their ancestral homelands.

Women as producers and distributors of lace-bark were rewarded with some financial independence for their skills and creative energies by producing exquisite lace materials for colonized consumers. Lace-bark was less strenuous to produce, unlike tapa in Polynesia and bark-cloth in Africa; it did not require special tools, and long hours of continuous, noisy pounding of bark with heavy mallets. Lace-bark could be processed in the quiet of the home after a long day in the fields, in gendered spaces that enabled women to strengthen solidarities. Some colonized women most likely found lace-bark production relaxing while others with industrious fingers were attracted to the entrepreneurial opportunities lace-bark production and sale provided. Enslaved persons, particularly women, were in fact interested in increasing their share of the colonial wealth by engaging in the market economy as "commodity producers and distributors."[149] Eco-botanists Brennan, Harris, and Nesbitt raise the important question about market distribution of lace-bark and reveal that since the area was largely inaccessible to outsiders and the trees grew within Maroon territory, it is likely that "Maroon collectors of bark traded it to the rest of the island."[150] This seems logical and, as we will see, the Maroons of Accompong Town and surrounding areas continued to supply lace-bark into the twentieth century. Although lace-bark was traded across Jamaica and the "ladies were dexterous" in making lace-bark dresses, it should not be assumed that lace-bark was inexpensive and within everyone's reach. On the contrary, lace-bark was not affordable to everyone; in fact it was "valuable when manufactured into articles of dress."[151]

In a series of interviews, several Maroon women recalled their mothers and grandmothers actively processing lace-bark for personal adornment and for trade in local markets. Women dominated the lace-bark industry in Jamaica. The women argued that "lace-bark" was "women's business" and jokingly uttered that "no man dared" to "double-cross" a trader—if not, all the women would "beat him."[152] On another occasion, one of the women remarked, "Women are head of the household; we only let the men think they are in charge!"[153] The ebullience of the women conveyed a sense of solidarity and self-reliance, as well as their ability to supervise their skills. Although women dominated the trade and manufacture of lace-bark, men played a key but peripheral and complementary role to the women as the harvesters of the bark. Individual families were engaged in lace-bark while some women organized themselves around lace-bark production. The men were hired and paid by the women to locate and cut the bark in the forest. Sometimes the women accompanied the men to make sure the men were cutting the bark correctly or to "keep an eye" on the men who might sell to the competition. There are stories of African women, not happy with the services of the men, dismissing the men and cutting the trees themselves.[154] This history raises important questions about male dominance and gender relations within the colonial context. Moreover, lace-bark was often a collective process that involved the skills of several women in the household or from the community working in groups to produce lace-bark for sale in the local markets.[155]

Scholars, such as Claire Robertson, in her analysis of West African women's role as traders and the importance of women's collective bargaining, organizing, and solidarity, have helped shape our understanding of African women's lives and their economic activities and contributions to their households and communities at large.[156] African women brought their trading skills to the Caribbean and put these skills to work in the lace-bark industry and other sectors of the slave economy. Jamaican sources from the period do not mention men's participation in bark clothing production, which suggests that women not only made the lace products but they traded and controlled this sector. This enabled women to provide clothing for themselves, their families, and members of the slave community. Perhaps Jamaican women, slave and freed, found lacemaking more profitable and worthwhile than textile weaving and, therefore, concentrated their efforts in this industry when they could. Slave men who had sufficient clothing saw no need to participate in this type of creative process. Others, perhaps, chose not to be involved because of the stigma associated with bark-cloth. In some West African societies, such as the Asante, bark-cloth over time became the dress of the lower classes and was made and worn by the poorest slaves.[157]

In post-Emancipation Jamaica, lace-bark production declined. As readymade European clothing became more accessible and affordable, the demand for bark clothing waned. Lace-bark was not seen as a viable commercial item and was never embraced by the retail sector that emphasized European imports. Gradually lace-bark became a tourist item of curiosity, an exotic souvenir for the emerging tourist market but, as we will see, there will be challenges for the lace-bark tree. Some freed women perhaps chose not to wear lace-bark because it was associated with slavery, while others were lured and seduced by the numerous refined fabrics once denied them and the ease with which these items could now be purchased. Others embraced European imported fabrics as a means of elevating their position in the new social order.

As slaves, African women's bodies were controlled by their enslavers and, as freed women, they were subjects of the colonial state. Yet, African women were not completely powerless. Women's solidarity and their gendered shaped experiences provided the necessary strength to survive in the colonial economy while women's collective bargaining skills enabled African women to combat male dominance and simultaneously secure their business interests as lace-bark traders. African women's role in the Jamaican lace-bark industry was a great example of grassroots commerce in a unique commodity that provided some wealth and financial independence for women. Hence, women were empowered by their ability to "control their silver" and contribute to their households.

Despite this, African women's desire to create a new world for themselves through entrepreneurial activities such as lace-bark production came under threat. Women's contribution to the colonial economy was dismissed and the imposition of colonial capitalism sought to control women whose labor was essential to the survival of their families. In Jamaica, for example, some colonial settlers called on the government to "take control in the service of Great Britain as a manufacturing Nation," and in 1885 a government committee was established to test the capabilities of certain machines to produce plant fibers on a commercial scale.[158] This action suppressed women's participation in lace-bark, and the colonial state offered no support; women's dominance in lace-bark was seen as a barrier to government plans to diversify the colonial economy that had relied heavily on sugar. The focus was now the development of a cotton and textile industry.

3 VICTORIAN JAMAICA: "FANCY FANS AND DOILIES"

Women's labor, moreover, is absolutely essential to the economy, even though usually unrecorded or underestimated in value. Without it the economy, and the society, could not function.[1]

CLAIRE ROBERTSON, *TROUBLE SHOWED THE WAY*

Post-Emancipation dress in Victorian Jamaica

Queen Victoria's ascension to the British throne in 1837 ushered in a new political and cultural era that impacted the lives of all people throughout the British Empire. The democratization of fashion took shape as the Victorian reign unfolded while important technological advances, such as the development of photography as a visual record and the invention of the sewing machine, occurred during these decades. These innovations were to have an enormous impact on dress customs and transformed the iconography of style throughout the empire, including Jamaica. Beside the developments in fashion, it was also a time when natural wonders were in vogue, and Britain's explorations for wealth epitomized the intersections between colonialism, racism, and science. In 1838, Queen Victoria's coronation year, the Emancipation decree gave rise to a new social order in Jamaica that created new challenges for freed people and established its priorities based on the patriarchal plantocratic traditions of white supremacy. Consequently, large numbers of colonized Jamaicans realized that the only way to escape their subordinate status and uplift themselves in the new social structure was to rid themselves of the "coarseness" of slavery and adopt the imported Victorian etiquette and standards in beauty and dress. The new objective of the British Imperialists was to create a new society based on improved manners, morals, and character; in other words, what became known as the "Civilizing Mission."[2] The period of transition from slavery to freedom brought insecurities and uncertainties for freed people, and those who did not conform to these new standards were deemed as unattractive and stereotyped as "uncivilized." In this chapter I explore several concepts, including how lace-bark was used and what types of clothing were made with lace-bark during the Victorian period. Moreover, how did lace-bark clothing reflect the emergence of a black middle class in post-Emancipation Jamaica? The chapter will address the role of the Women's Self-Help societies in lace-bark art and needlework for the emerging tourist market. A section of the chapter also explores how lace-bark clothing reflected the material environment of Victorian Jamaica and the colonial government's attempts at marketing lace-bark, and their failure at industrializing the lace-bark industry.

Victorian dress in Britain was a combination of social expectations that exemplified the manners and social habits of the time. This meant that emphasis was placed on external forms, rules, propriety, and conventions. Dress was an important symbol in this process. Fashionable ladies and gentlemen went to great extremes to follow the prescribed social behavior while decent and well-dressed Victorian ladies were expected to be genteel and avoided boisterous behavior. The vast difference in comfort and elaborate ornamentation between men's and women's clothes reflected the vast separation in male and female roles of the Victorian period. Throughout the nineteenth century, the use of lace typified elite social standing, gentility, and affluence, as well as the ability of the wearer to consume luxury goods. Among upper class women, lace was lavished on Victorian dress, and accessories were very beautiful and of the finest quality.[3] In the late 1860s and early 1870s dresses were designed with a fichu, often made of lace combined with velvet ribbons or net trimmed with lace to create a charming effect. Perhaps the most significant development of the 1880s was the use of heavy, showier laces. In the 1880s, wide collars and lace jabots and cascades falling from the throat became fashionable. However, by the end of Queen Victoria's reign, lace in women's dresses seemed more fashionable and popular than at any other time in history. The future of the luxury industry was secure and machine-made lace had become most popular.[4] In the late nineteenth century, *Brussels* and *Honiton* lace had become the standards for elite brides, and it was considered proper for the bride's trousseau to include at least one "set" of lace. The Honiton lace for Queen Victoria's wedding dress in 1840 cost £1,000, and by the end of her reign she owned lace worth £76,000. Only the Pope's collection of lace at that time was valued at more at £200,000.[5] The design of European lace was not static, but changed over time based on country, trade, travel, and consumer demand.[6]

Lace of all kinds was in demand for various accessories such as lace-edged handkerchiefs, hat trimmings, which were often combined with ribbons, flowers, and even stuffed birds on top of a small hat.[7] Victorian clothes among the upper and middle classes in Britain became works of art, intended to reflect wealth and social standing. Women's dresses required heavy skirting and corseting that fostered an image of fragility, respectability, and dependence. These styles were often uncomfortable and restricted the movements of the Victorian lady.[8] Victorian fashions in Britain were introduced to the colonies and circulated by various means. In the colonial society, portrait photography after the 1840s, as well as post cards, cartes-de-viste, paintings, magazines, and fashion dolls, depicted the latest fashions and helped popularize Victorian dress. The works of artists, such as Isaac Mendes Belisario and Joseph Bartholomew Kidd, as seen earlier, provided visual commentaries on urban life, dress styles, and social structure in Jamaica during the early years of transition from slavery to freedom.

The liberation of enslaved people gave way to a new social order in Jamaica, which consisted of three socioeconomic groups. The new structure corresponds to the racial division of the plantation economy during slavery. At the top of Jamaican society were the few Europeans who owned most of the land and were accustomed to controlling the Jamaican economy. They were the ones who set all social and cultural standards, and established the acceptable fashion trends in Victorian dress and beauty.[9]

The second group was the large "brown skinned" population called mulattos or coloreds, and they made up the majority of the emerging middle class in Jamaica. This group was not a homogenous body and was divided by profession, education, and economics. Mulattos continued to see themselves as a separate and distinct group and, therefore, disassociated themselves from the lower classes of Jamaicans. Their dress reflected this distinction.[10] Some mulattos who received financial backing from their white parents or white sexual partners got involved in some type of economic activity. Several mulatto women offered health care services to sick travelers and strangers while some were engaged in the hospitality industry where they worked as managers and housekeepers of lodges, inns, and taverns.[11]

The third group comprised those of African descent who made up the majority of Jamaicans and lived in another world rooted in poverty and steeped in African traditions. They were forced to provide for themselves without the advantages of property, enough skills, or education. Some managed to acquire land through the assistance of missionaries who created "Free Villages," and they obtained wages from seasonal work.[12] They became members of the peasant and laboring class.[13] The peasant class was diverse, and not everyone was involved in agricultural labor.[14] Among this class, Victorian dress was not easily affordable, and most members sought alternative dress styles to make themselves presentable.

Amongst the white population, many believed that progress was linked to race; therefore, freed people could not achieve success without the assistance of whites. The large exodus of Europeans from Jamaica after Emancipation and the decline of many estates compelled the few remaining white elite to concern themselves with the "instruction" of the newly emancipated ex-slaves. The Hon. E. Stanley endorsed this idea; he stated, "Where the white proprietor has failed, the negro will not succeed, more especially if deprived of the instruction and example of European."[15] Freed Jamaicans were now considered as "subject" people to be civilized and saved from degradation by means of white paternalism and an intolerant Judea Christian tradition. Freed people had become the "mission frontier."[16] To achieve this aim, some believed that the physical appearance of the emancipated body had to be transformed and reimaged, and dress was an important part of this process. Mrs. Carmichael, a long-time European resident in the Caribbean, remarked that it was "easy to trace the progress of civilization in different Negroes according to their style of everyday dress."[17] Many Europeans regarded their dress customs as a mark of civilization. Yet, as we saw earlier, before Emancipation the number of enslaved people who had access to European dress and refined fabrics such as lace was few as some visitors observed, "All who can afford it appear in very gay apparel. . . . But it is only a small portion who can afford to dress thus finely."[18] The majority of enslaved women and men managed on what was provided for them by their owners.

Economic changes after Emancipation rapidly transformed the social fabric of Jamaican society. The disappearance of many sugar estates and the introduction of wage labor, plus increased urbanization, all contributed to the emergence of a consumer society and a vibrant middle class who demanded more material possessions. This group also wanted greater access to British goods, such as clothing. Consequently, "There was [sic] now springing up everywhere stores stocked with the common necessaries of life. Many provincial merchants began to import their own goods and to open up small branches wherever the opportunity occurred."[19] The commercialization of dress and textiles fostered a new group of consumers, regardless of their class, who became more fascinated with Victorian dress and refined fabrics such as lace.

The new economy was now oriented towards wholesale and retail commerce. Several merchants began to import larger quantities of clothing from major cities in North America to complement their London supplies and offered customers more variety at competitive prices.[20] Most stores were located in Kingston along King Street, Duke Street, and Harbour Street, which became the center for fashion and for buying fashionable ready-made clothes and beautiful Victorian laces. Storeowners enticed and lured potential customers to their businesses with regular advertisements in various local newspapers, such as the *Falmouth Gazette* and *Daily Gleaner*. These advertisements included a detailed list of the latest clothing items for sale and their prices. In 1879 Metropolitan House, renowned for its milliners, tailors, and outfitters, as well as an extensive wholesale department, advertised beautiful lace embroideries and lace trimmings direct from London at 6d per yard.[21]

Most of the famous and fashionable stores, like Metropolitan and Dick and Abbott, catered to members of the upper classes or those who could afford their "fancy prices." Many of those who could not afford these "high end" store prices on a regular basis, except for special occasions, did their shopping for clothes and less expensive lace in "low end" shops and stores in other areas of the city. There were also peddlers who sold ribbons, laces, cloth, and trimmings out of their grips[22] tied to their bicycles, and small cloth traders who traveled the countryside selling textiles obtained from wholesale merchants. In some markets, like the Jubilee, a few vendors sold clothing accessories, such as laces, buttons, squares of tie-heads [scarves], and handkerchiefs.[23] Some members of the white elite viewed the growth of clothing facilities unfavorably. Livingstone, for example, felt that the rise of consumerism among the subaltern could have an adverse effect on social attitudes of the lower classes. He argued, "These facilities [shops] were leading them [freed persons] unconsciously into higher habits . . . to spend a large part of their money on dress."[24] Some freed people were seduced by the material processions once denied to them and the apparent ease with which they could now purchase objects such as handmade Victorian lace. The fact that many ex-slaves now had access to European clothing and refined fabrics meant that the old class distinctions reflected in dress were disrupted and white privilege threatened.

As early as the 1840s, dress in Victorian Jamaica mirrored the summer styles in Britain, especially among the new middle class who had abandoned the old plantation ways of dressing. Among the mulatto women in the emerging middle class, their dress reflected their status and featured a full skirt, long enough to hide their feet and held out by numerous petticoats. As in Britain, bonnets were now popular, which hid the face except from a frontal view, while the neck was covered by a veil made of lace or gauze attached to the bonnet; large shawls covered the shoulders when outdoors, and gloves covered the hands to keep off the sun.[25] Bonnets and hats were small, and dresses were trimmed with lavish lace.[26] Likewise, black clothing became increasingly popular among numerous elite and middle-class women. Black color was more suited to hide the dirt from coal-burning stoves and the blowing dust from crowded busy streets in city centers. Black became popular as it was easily adapted for mourning dress and was made fashionable by Queen Victoria, who wore black accessorized with sumptuous lace for forty years, from the death of her husband in 1861 until her death in 1901.[27]

The period of the 1870s to the 1880s saw elaborate hairstyles bedecked with ornaments and fake hair pieces while hats were splendid in shape and decoration, and jewelry was bold and opulent. Dress designs meantime became flatter in the front and fuller in the back. Simultaneously, tight corseting and lacing distorted the body and at times accentuated soft curves, while extra yardage of skirting was pulled back, causing a bunching of the sides and back, leading to a huge bustle and train laden with trimmings of ruffles, ribbons, and luxurious Mechlin lace.[28] The huge rear extension added little to increase mobility. In some instances, a Victorian dress with trimmings weighed over ten pounds: this reduced walking to mere mincing steps. Even though Victorian dresses in Jamaica were made from lighter and airier fabrics, they were no less layered and embellished with lace. Freed women who wanted to be socially acceptable and "civilized" did not want to be associated with slave dress and, therefore, adopted Victorian-style clothes richly accessorized with imported lace.

The vast numbers of Mulattos who chose to accommodate to Victorian dress at first led to a surge in seamstresses in urban spaces. The number of seamstresses in Jamaica increased from 14,565 in 1871 to 18,966 by 1891; during the early part of the twentieth century the numbers increased to 20,340.[29] The status and prestige of seamstresses within post-Emancipation society changed drastically. Seamstresses and needleworkers who flocked to urban centers after Emancipation sought opportunities other than agricultural wage labor. Some used their skills to establish independent businesses, often working out of their home, while others became domestic workers. These women became members of the respectable lower middle class, but their status was undermined by their growing poverty,[30] and "the importation on a larger scale of ready-made clothing, the introduction of the sewing machine, and the contracted income of better circumstanced families militate seriously against the comforts of this class."[31] Some seamstresses gained employment teaching sewing skills and making lace-bark souvenirs but, more significantly, they provided the foundation of a factory-based industry in the twentieth century that relied on home-based labor.[32]

While the elite and middle class were busy emulating Victorian culture and wearing London dresses of refined fabrics and lace to reflect their social standing, the peasants' dress reflected their status within the broader colonial society. It was amongst this group that Afro-Jamaican religions were nurtured and African characteristics in dress were maintained. Despite their poverty, peasant women and men donned European dress when possible and affordable, but usually for special occasions. In the fields, unlike the urban areas, they continued to wear osnaburg daily, while in some areas the osnaburg was replaced with cotton. The pull-skirt and the tie-head remained popular among peasant and rural laboring class women.[33] For many among the class, the ritual of "dressing up" was important.[34] As the elite and middle classes abandoned lace-bark for European lace with "status labels" to display their new found wealth and accommodation to Victorian dress, it was primarily among the lower classes and the Maroons that bark-cloth and lace-bark production continued for use in clothing.[35]

Jamaicanization of Victorian dress

Perhaps the elite and middle classes shunned lace-bark because they saw it as folk art or could not look beyond its association with slavery. Among lower class women, this was not the case. They appropriated the fashions of the upper classes, copied and modified them to their liking, and used lace-bark to "make fashion" to show that they too could be beautiful—but on their terms. As during slavery, the dress styles that developed among this group reflected a fusion of African and European influences in style, thus giving rise to a "Creole dress" or local fashion that was distinctly Jamaican yet Victorian. Among these women, the Creole dress embodied the process of Jamaicanizing the Victorian dress. A few examples of the Jamaican Victorian dress customs can be seen in Figures 3.1, 3.2, and 3.3. Although the artifacts are from Victorian Jamaica, we know very little about their origin. There is no evidence of the milliner or designer who fashioned these exquisite pieces, nor do we know if the artifacts were actually worn or if they were merely craft items that survived the ravages of time. Nonetheless, they provide some visual representation and tantalizing clues of Victorian Jamaica fashion sensibilities.

The artifact in Figure 3.1 is a child's outdoor cap from the parish of St. Elizabeth in Jamaica and was made between 1850 and 1861. The cap is made from lace-bark

FIGURE 3.1 Cap of lace-bark ornamented with seeds. Photograph: © Trustees of the Royal Botanic Gardens, Kew.

FIGURE 3.2 Lace-bark bonnet, after conservation on a custom-made mount (1865). The bonnet is made of an array of materials including metal, cotton, silk, seeds, moss, and strips of raw plant fiber. The lace-bark is overlaid, ruched, and decorated with stitching. Photograph: © Trustees of the Royal Botanic Gardens, Kew.

which is stained beige with aging, but otherwise would have been white at the time of manufacture. The base of the cap is ornamented with brown acasia seeds strung together to form a unique, cascading geometrical design that circles the crown of the cap and the peaked brim. The high crown suggests the cap was designed to cover much of the head and thus shield the eyes and complexion from the hot sun. The design is in accordance with the Victorian tradition, as white lace caps were part of a Victorian child's wardrobe, and during the early part of the era, both girls and boys between the ages of one and three wore lace caps to complement embroidered outfits trimmed with lace. What is most intriguing is the visual display of effective transplantation of an African aesthetic into an idyllic fashionable Victorian Jamaican dress. The cascading beads are reminiscent of the Yoruba beaded head dress in Nigeria.[36]

FIGURE 3.3 Cap of lace-bark ornamented with seeds. Photograph: © Trustees of the Royal Botanic Gardens, Kew.

Most curious is the second image of Victorian Jamaican dress in Figures 3.2 and 3.3. The object is a lace-bark bonnet of intricate design in the Victorian fashion and embellished with several natural substances from the Jamaican environment. The bonnet mirrors the popular headdresses of the 1840s to early 1850s and, typical of the period, were smaller in size compared with earlier years. The wire frame of the bonnet is covered with pink satin fabric stretched into place to create a wide brim for shielding the face from the sun. The fabric is gathered in the back towards the base of the bonnet to create a flare, which retained the hair at the nape of the neck. The entire crown is covered with layers of lace-bark draped over the fabric and ruffled across the back of the bonnet. Two narrow strips of pink fabric are stitched across the ruffles to create a symmetrical design that reinforces the shape and secures the lace (Figure 3.3). The artifact's designer was inspired by nature and sought to utilize material from their natural environment. The bonnet is bedecked with lace-bark ribbons, seeds, and dried moss formerly of a bright green. Exposed stylized wires were painted with vermillion, and two long silk ribbons are attached for securing the bonnet on the head. The ribbons would be tied under the chin, thus creating a nice frame around the face. In Victorian Jamaica, as in Britain, bonnets embodied a heightened sense of propriety, and it was unthinkable for a lady to leave the house without wearing a hat or bonnet that complemented her hairstyle and harmonized with her outfit.

Both hat designs from Victorian Jamaica suggest their creators sought to have fun with fashion and were skillful with improvisation. These fine examples of

"Creole dress" were the embodiment of the complex process of creolization, not merely a continuous fusion of African and European influences, but also a process of negotiating and battling for cultural space within the colonized society. The Victorian Jamaican dress was an example of fabulous appropriation with which freed Jamaicans sought to preserve themselves, to hold on to their African heritage while creating a space for themselves in the European-dominated society. By refusing to conform to the European aesthetic, they challenged the established fashion sensibilities and embraced a style that was their own and symbolic of freedom. Victorian Jamaican dress was a symbol of resistance, a form of fashionable subversion and adaptation that sought to disrupt and destabilize the deeply imbedded polarities of colonial society—that of black and white, European and African.

Lace-bark and the tourist industry

"Too much si'-dun bruk breeches"—Sitting down too much wears out one's trousers.[37]

JAMAICAN PROVERB

In the early post-Emancipation period, lace-bark continued to be significant in some colonized people's lives. As during slavery, lace-bark was used as a kitchen strainer during food preparation, and it was used to make "dress-up clothes," like evening dresses and ball gowns.[38] By the 1860s, lace-bark was still common and was used to make aprons for protective covering while cooking or working outdoors, as well as collars and caps.[39] Some women took pride in displaying their creative talents by combining lace-bark garments with other types of vegetable fibers. Among the Maroons, some women fashioned "stylish" outfits consisting of a lace-bark blouse and a banana-fiber or caratoe-fiber skirt and matching hat. Others used lace-bark trimmings to accessorize and embellish outfits.[40] While lace-bark was part of the wardrobe for some women, most men donned garments of cotton fabrics. However, as ready-made European apparels and lace became increasingly accessible and affordable, the demand for lace-bark clothing declined. Lace-bark was not considered a viable and profitable commercial item by clothing stores, especially with the influx and popularity of European manufactured lace. Therefore, clothing stores shunned lace-bark and it was never embraced by the retail industry that emphasized and promoted European textiles.[41]

Victorian lace had eclipsed lace-bark as the desired lace of choice of clothing among elite and middle-class Jamaican women. This narrative is a familiar one within colonial discourse. In many cultural contexts, colonial industrial manufacturers have been damaging to hand-crafted items that are similar and to the artisans who produced them. The increased importation of European textiles and clothes into Polynesia and bark-cloth producing areas of Africa led to a decline in tapa and bark-cloth production. In West Africa, Manchester cloth from Britain captured the textile trade on the coast, replacing the more expensive Indian cottons. European textile printers traveled to the West African coast to bring back samples of indigenous cloth, which they copied and later traded with Africans. The introduction of inexpensive Europeanized African fabrics led to a decline in the indigenous textile industry in several areas of West and Central Africa.[42] As with Polynesian tapa, lace-bark gradually evolved into an art form and exotic craft geared towards an emerging tourist market. Nonetheless, the Leeward Maroons in Jamaica continued to make lace-bark fashions for a while, and they supplied lace-bark to craft centers, church groups, and women's societies that produced ornamental souvenirs. The development of a souvenir market based on lace-bark led to a shift in the mode of production. As lace-bark became increasingly commercialized for the tourist sector, more men began to get involved in the production process and trading (see Figures 2.11 and 2.12 in Chapter 2). Consequently, women's collective bargaining strength within the industry was greatly diminished.[43]

By the second half of the nineteenth century, colonial authorities began to promote Jamaica as an attractive tourist destination and the island became the "New Riviera." Promotional materials were directed at potential American tourists. The *Imperial Direct West Indies Mail Service* enticed visitors with picturesque advertisements with reference to "this lost Garden of Eden—this incomparable combination of American comfort, English cleanliness, and Italian climate? And such beauty—such glory of coloring, such opulence of Natures best gifts!"[44] The Jamaican landscape that had been scarred from deforestation and pollution brought on by sugar plantations was now re-conceptualized to reflect a departure from the bucolic to a landscape that was both poetic and exotic. Although the tourist industry formally began in 1891 with the opening of the Jamaica Great Exhibition, there were numerous accounts of early visitors to the island. At the time of the exhibition, persons in convalescence also began to arrive as they were attracted to the island's temperate climate.[45] The advent of tourism led to the development of several hotels in Kingston and other parts of the island to accommodate the wave of guests arriving at the time. A few of the major hotels of the period were the Myrtle Bank and Constant Spring hotels in Kingston, and Titchfield Hotel in Port Antonio. The hotels were built for tropical comfort, and a few, like the Constant Spring Hotel, were especially attractive to invalids and those in feeble health.[46] These hotels were beacons of social activities with the occasional after tea sewing circles on the hotels' verandahs where female guests engaged in polite conversation, embroidery, and various needlework skills. Such activities were usually part of the daily leisurely routine that involved sight seeing, the occasional garden strolls and promenades in the city parks.[47]

The rich variety of Jamaican vegetation, and the often striking forms it took, fascinated visitors. Jamaican landscapes with "exotic" palms and magnificent bamboo and ferns became popular in souvenir photographs.[48] Ferns, easily divided, were often incorporated into collage designs with lace-bark for albums and doilies[49] (Figures 3.4 and 3.5).

A plethora of souvenir and curio shops emerged between the 1880s and the 1920s, selling lace-bark items for tourists. Numerous souvenir shops were opened during the period and their wares for sale were advertised in local papers like the *Gleaner* and in tourist guide books and hotel brochures.[50] Some of the more popular and larger souvenir shops included The Educational Supply Company Tourist Depot and the Lady Musgrave's Women's Self-Help Depository in Kingston. Many shops carried diverse lace-bark souvenirs for tourists, such as doilies, overlaid lampshades, decorated book covers, lace whips, and ladies' accessories

FIGURE 3.4 A doilie on lace-bark ground with decorations of ferns surrounded by seed hairs of French cotton, *Calotropis procera* (*Aiton*). 1926–1931. Diameter 34 cm. Photograph: © Trustees of the Royal Botanic Gardens, Kew.

FIGURE 3.5 Shaving tidy and souvenir book; lace-bark used as base for decorative cover. Photograph: © Trustees of the Royal Botanic Gardens, Kew.

including fans, ties, shawls, and pieces or puffs of actual lace-bark fiber. Fans and doilies were often ornamented with dried Jamaican flora like ferns and edgings of French cotton.[51] Doilies seemed to have been the most popular lace-bark souvenir (see Figures 3.4 and 3.6).[52] Other ornaments for sale included carved coconuts and calabashes, tortoise-shell works, and Jippi-Jappa straw hats (Native Panama hats).

FIGURE 3.6 Fan/mat made of pith of lace-bark and decorated with seed hairs and ferns. Photograph: © Trustees of the Royal Botanic Gardens, Kew.

Besides lace-bark, some bark-cloth souvenirs were also included, such as date bark caps.[53] By far the most appealing souvenirs were those made from lace-bark. Commenting on Jamaican curios at the end of the nineteenth century, Sir Alfred Jones revealed, "A good variety of interesting souvenirs of the island may be collected ... fans and doyleys [doilies] made by natives from lace-bark ... will especially appeal to lady visitors. Many of these are works of art, and exhibit refined tasted and excellent workmanship."[54] Jones goes on to add that some lace-bark fans were of a "very beautiful specimen, showing the greatest skill in its production."[55]

Most souvenir shops were located in the main shopping district of Kingston, along Harbour Street and Church Street, while a few shops were found in several upscale resorts of the period. Curio shops were located in the town of Mandeville, which had become a popular tourist destination, and curios could be purchased in urban markets frequented by tourists. Jamaican lace-bark found new fame in the nineteenth century and many lace-bark curios were exported overseas as gifts and sold in curio shops in London. Branches of lace-bark revealing the lace-like fibers were available at Selfridge's department store on Oxford Street in London and labeled as "Selfridge's White Sale."[56] Lace-bark curios, whether in London or Jamaica, were very appealing and yet expensive. Visitors at first often remarked how "these things cost a great deal of money ... but they are very decorative."[57] Many of these souvenirs were crafted by young women affiliated with church groups and various self-help organizations.

Lace-bark and the Jamaican woman's education

After 1865, a partnership developed between the churches and the colonial authorities of the state to create a new moral order based on Victorian values. Christianity was the foundation of this moral order reinforced by secular middle-class Victorian notions of propriety and etiquette. Churches were granted some financial support to operate elementary schools, and various constituents of the colonial state did their part to fulfill the civilizing mission.[58]

Against this background, and to achieve their goals, missionary societies published church magazines, such as *The Jamaican Moravian: A Christian Monthly Magazine* and *The Moravian Messenger*, that extolled the virtues of the obedient and dutiful wife and offered advice on home care and child rearing. Several missionary societies established self-help organizations and outreach centers operated by missionary wives for women, like the Upward and Onward Society of the Women of Jamaica, founded by the Moravians at the end of the nineteenth century to promote womanly virtue and "pure family." The Upward and Onward organization, as the name implies, sought to "uplift" freed Jamaicans out of a state of degradation by teaching young women domestic skills and crafts. In Upward and Onward classrooms and group meetings across Jamaica, women were taught, among other things, laundry skills, hat making, basket weaving, Victorian dressmaking, and needlework crafts that included intricate stitch designs, baby boots, crochet, embroidery tea cloths, and pantry towels. These skills were considered an essential part of a young woman's education in preparation for her future role as wife and mother.[59]

The Victorian missionization had at its core the desire and goal to construct a "new civilized, consensual society by eradicating beliefs and practices that were deemed barbarous and immoral."[60] White women, particularly missionary wives, shouldered the responsibility to help uplift black Jamaican women out of their state of moral degradation and poverty. The visitor and adventurer Alfred Leader viewed the role of white women in this regard as a "very much praiseworthy effort . . . to improve the home life of the people" and he added, "It should be remembered, also, that the people [Jamaicans] are not yet three generations removed from slavery, and that many of its baneful results will take long to eradicate."[61] Several elite white women established self-help societies across Jamaica to instruct colonized women in needlework skills, beadwork, and making baskets for sale locally and elsewhere.[62] Churches and the colonial authorities believed that these skills would not only make women industrious, but most of all instill a sense of purity, temperance, and righteousness, leading to high thinking and high living within the home. Colonial officials concerned about moral decay hoped that these qualities would eventually spread and influence the entire freed population.

Prominent among the outreach organizations was the Women's Self-Help Society, founded on November 1, 1879, by Lady Jeanie Lucinda Musgrave (1833–1920) (Figure 3.7), wife of the Governor of Jamaica, Sir Anthony Musgrave, who served from 1877 to 1883. The society building was located on Church street in Kingston and became famous for producing some of the most beautiful lace-bark souvenirs for local and foreign guests, dignitaries, and international exhibitions.[63] Lady Musgrave identified three objectives for the organization: first, to enable industrious women of all classes to help themselves and others by producing a sale room for all kinds of work; second, to provide occasional employment to distressed needle women; and, finally, to teach plain needlework, which she believed was not being taught "thoroughly" except for a few places on the island.[64] She believed that by affording the women opportunities for selling their work of all kinds, especially those peculiar to the island such as lace-bark, ferns, calabashes (gourds), and preserves, among others, would develop them into small industries.[65] Although the society was a leisure activity for white women to teach freed women Victorian needlework, decorum, and dressmaking skills,[66] the society played a key role in revitalizing the trade and interest in lace-bark through its promotion and sale of lace-bark products abroad and in influential circles. Several exhibition catalogues and numerous newspaper articles attribute huge sales and countless exhibitions of lace-bark products to the society. In 1882, the amount of £465 was realized by sale of articles placed on deposit and during the Colonial and Indian Exhibition of 1886 in London over forty exhibits at once were sent from the Women's Self-Help Society.[67]

Many of the women who were gainfully employed at the society learned new skills while others perfected their craft of making beautiful lace-bark ornaments.

FIGURE 3.7 *Jeanie Lucinda, Lady Musgrave (1833–1920)*; founded the Lady Musgrave Women's Self-Help Society in 1879. Courtesy of the National Library of Jamaica.

Most ornaments were placed on "deposit" and artisans received a percentage from the sale of their work. In 1883 artisans reported they were "most thankful for the supply of easy work."[68] Those artisans who crafted lace-bark curios produced exquisite works of art that captivated audiences including British royalty. In 1891, Lady Lathom, one of the most prominent figures in London society, and a guest of the new governor's wife, Lady Blake at Kings House, "took considerable interest in Jamaican curios and frequently visited the Women's Self-Help Society."[69] That same year Britain's "Princess Beatrice was presented with a lace-bark fan as a wedding gift, and the Duchess of Fyfe received a similar fan as a gift purchased by the Duchess of St. Albans from the Women's Self-Help Society."[70] Local newspapers regularly reported the praises for Jamaican lace-bark and the beautiful art works dignitaries received from the Women's Self-Help Society.[71] Lady Musgrave's organization attained high levels of achievement and success for its artisans. There is no doubt that some of its successes were due to her privileged status and social connections. Nonetheless, the superb skills and the level of artistry displayed by the women cannot be denied. Before returning to England in 1883, Lady Musgrave passed on the tradition of a "close, practical and sympathetic connection between the ladies of Kings House and the Self-Help."[72] Under new patrons, the society continued to showcase lace-bark ornamentals and fancy needlework talents of Jamaican women on the national and international stage.

Other self-help societies and church groups, such as the Educational Supply Company, produced lace-bark curios and art works for sale.[73] But not all lace-bark products were made by self-help societies. Young women in teachers' training colleges for women learned how to make lace-bark products for their classrooms and school girls made fans and doilies from lace-bark for fundraising benefits to aid the poor and special needs organizations, such as Orphanage for Girls at Half-Way Tree in Kingston. Amidst the Jamaican exhibits at the World's Exposition in New Orleans 1884–1885, several lace-bark ornaments were made by St. Mary's College and St. Mary's Practicing School for Females.[74]

These self-help societies, outreach centers, and missionary schools, all influenced freed women's dress and encouraged them to conform to British cultural standards. They provided basic skills that enabled some freed women to gain employment as seamstresses, a skill that was becoming increasingly redundant. Lady Musgrave's Self-Help Society played a key role in reviving the lace-bark trade for the emerging tourist market and to provide some income for local women in need of financial support. Such patronage and maternalistic attitudes on the part of missionaries and white women were based on their own racist conditioning and a firm belief in British cultural, racial, and religious superiority, enforced upon their "inferiors" by "appropriate" educational efforts. Colonized women of all classes sought this type of education because no one wanted to be stigmatized for ignorance or be left out on the opportunity for social mobility. Freed women were now perceived by missionaries as the beacons of hope, the up-lifters of their race, and the ones who could bring some "salvation" to the freed population. However, African women have long been the up-lifters of their people. Their role in Africa and the Diaspora as guardians, healers, resistors, providers, and conveyors of African cultures were all activities that were meant to better their race.[75]

By the late nineteenth century, Jamaican lace-bark was both popular and desirable once more.[76] Scientists sought specimens for their labs, greenhouses, and botanical gardens, while travelers and collectors alike desired a piece of natural lace. Throughout the Victorian period, specimens were collected and shared with a few botanical gardens and museums, including The Royal Botanic Gardens at Kew and Field Museum in Chicago, but various attempts to distribute the plant to major botanical gardens continued to be a challenge for botanists and scientists.[77] The first attempt to introduce the tree to the gardens at Kew was in 1793 by Rear-Admiral William Bligh, but his attempts failed; he stated, "It appears to have been soon lost, and it had been a desideratum in the garden for many years."[78] In 1844, saplings were obtained, but they grew only four inches.[79] Several attempts to cultivate the tree in marley, sod-like limestone were unsuccessful; while others tried good yellow loam mixed with a little leaf-mold and sand, which gave better results, except the tree grew eight feet and "became an evergreen."[80] It did not yield any blossoms. Lace-bark, like other fibrous trees of the Thymelaeaceae plant family, remains a difficult plant to propagate outside its natural habitat. Today very few people have seen the tree in its habitation or even the flowers and fruit of the plant.

At the height of the Victorian era, lace-bark gained international fame through Jamaica's participation in numerous international expositions. Beginning with the Great Exhibition of 1851 in London, which emphasized Britain's imperial power and celebrated the industrial achievements of all nations, Jamaica made its debut with a small exhibit of plant fibers. The exhibitor, Mrs. Nash from the parish of Manchester, had "ten varieties of tropical flowers, made from the film of the 'yucca' or dagger plant."[81] Jamaican lace-bark was not featured in the exhibition. However, foreign nations were invited to participate in the Great Exhibition, including Spain, which had on display a "[tree] trunk of the plant *Laghetto* [*lagetto*] *lintearia*, showing the fibers of the interior bark."[82] The tree trunk was obtained from the Spanish colony of Cuba and submitted by the Cabinate Botanical Gardens of Madrid.

Most interesting is the mystery surrounding Queen Victoria's lace-bark dress. Some scholars alleged that the queen received an entire dress made from Jamaican lace-bark at the 1851 exhibition. Although an intriguing idea, to date, no primary evidence has been found to substantiate this claim.[83] Perhaps the dress has been overlooked or deteriorated over time and the record lost. We really do not know. Nonetheless, Spain's lace-bark exhibit attracted some attention, but it was not until after 1851 at successive local, state, and international expositions and fairs that Jamaican lace-bark gained international exposure and fame (Figure 3.8). At these international events, Jamaican exhibition spaces and courts were laden with manufactured goods representing the various unique industries in Jamaica, including lace-bark, bast fibers, and leaf fibers suitable for textile production. Participation in international expositions was organized and supervised by a Commissioner for Jamaica, appointed by the Governor who provided reports to the colonial authorities on the successes and rewards of these international events.

The Jamaican exhibition courts were beautifully designed with Jamaican products on display. Consequently, the Jamaican courts were often complimented on their attractive exhibits (Figure 3.9). At the World's Industrial and Cotton Centennial Exposition in New Orleans, 1884–1885, a visitor remarked that "there was scarcely a space ... where a few minutes could be more pleasantly spent ... Jamaica made a splendid exhibit."[84] Lace-bark products were for display, but some products could be purchased. The uniqueness of lace-bark lured huge audiences

FIGURE 3.8 Articles of lace-bark/purses from the Kingston and Paris Exhibitions of 1855. Photograph: © Trustees of the Royal Botanic Gardens, Kew.

FIGURE 3.9 Jamaica: Looking towards the South. Courtesy of the University of the West Indies Library, Mo.

and gave rise to a demand for lace-bark products. At the Paris Exhibition of 1855, lace-bark was noticed as "very valuable ... and orders were received from M. Fremont, the agent for supplying large quantities for the Paris [Fashion] market."[85] Earlier in the period, lace-bark cloth was imported into Liverpool under the name "guana,"[86] and some retailers prepared to meet customer demand by stacking enough lace-bark curios ahead of time as was the case with one business owner, who had 400 dozen lace-bark puffs and 250 dozen whips ready for sale at the World's Fair.[87]

Lace-bark products for exhibition and sale were made predominantly by female artisans. Several women became well known for their artistic talents and specialized skill in working with lace-bark. Mrs. J. Nash from Kingston developed fame for wafting bonnets made from the cuticle of the leaves of the dagger plant [*Yucca aloifolia*], lace-bark, and the spathe of the Cabbage Palm. She also made bonnets from the leaf of the banana plant.[88] Her lace-bark exhibits were often objects of "special admiration," and she received numerous awards, including a written commendation from the House of Commons in Britain on the "remarkably beautiful baskets of flowers . . . made of the dagger plant and lace-bark."[89] Likewise, the women of Lady Musgrave's Self-Help Society attracted considerable attention in 1886 for their bonnets, fans, and baskets made of lace-bark during the Colonial and Indian Exhibition in London.[90]

The popularity of Jamaican lace-bark souvenirs during the second half of the Victorian era coincided with major economic challenges for the island colony. In the wake of the Industrial Revolution and the age of machinery, Britain continued to engage in bio-prospecting and sought to expand colonial agriculture with a renewed interest in plant fibers suitable for industry. Meanwhile, by the 1880s the Jamaican economy was far from flourishing due to the dire economic conditions brought about by the decline of the sugar industry that had based its successes on the profits of slave labor. Consequently, cotton cultivation was once again promoted in Jamaica,[91] and the colonial administrators turned their attention to economic plants.[92]

Concerned about the Jamaican economy, Daniel Morris, the Director of Public Gardens and Plantations in Jamaica, explained in 1881 the urgent need for development of an industry based on bark-fiber for textiles. He wrote, "We [Jamaica] have no large stores of timber, we have no minerals, we have no manufacturing industries and we cannot hope to struggle successfully with other countries in the more advanced arts and sciences."[93] Morris was appointed Director by the Governor of the Jamaica and served in the role from 1879–1886. He had attended several international exhibitions as commissioner of the Jamaica court and had every opportunity to see the latest innovations and technology in industry. Morris may have been influenced by his experiences at the exhibitions.[94] Nonetheless, he was determined that Jamaica had to build its natural resources to survive and compete economically. Morris added, "It is evident that Jamaica must depend for its prosperity and success, almost entirely on the resources and products of an agriculture character."[95]

To achieve this, Morris and his supporters in the colonial administration proposed several steps, including the "maintenance and improvement of several establishments [gardens] entrusted to its care,"[96] and "the importation and distribution of valuable economic plants calculated to promote the agricultural interests of the colony."[97] The colonial trade and distribution of seeds and economic plants was not new. As we saw earlier, Captain Bligh had introduced the bread fruit to Jamaica in the eighteenth century, and West Indian firs and pines were transferred to the Princess of Wales's garden at Kew, thus creating the foundation for most of the royal botanical gardens.[98] Kew Gardens in London had been at the center of a network of pilot gardens in many British territories to be used as nurseries for the cultivation of plants economically useful to the expansion of colonial agriculture. As a result, in the eighteenth century, botanical gardens proliferated throughout many British territories, including Jamaica.[99]

The first botanic gardens in Jamaica were founded in the late seventeenth century.[100] Although for centuries plants have been studied, transplanted, and swapped for more species, in the nineteenth century, it had become a major colonial enterprise to expand valuable resources such as plants. Castleton Botanical Garden (Figure 3.10) was founded in 1862 on the site of a plantation in Jamaica, followed by Hope Botanical Garden established in 1873 as a major experimental station for economic plants.[101]

FIGURE 3.10 Castleton Gardens, St. Andrew Jamaica. A Duperly and Sons Photograph. Courtesy of the National Library of Jamaica.

Hope Gardens was intended to form the chief garden instead of Castleton, which became the major Jamaican center for tree sale and distribution. Between 1888 and 1890, for instance, some "22,500 plants [were] sold, and 1,731 plants distributed free."[102] Furthermore, "active steps" were taken during the year to promote the cultivation of fiber plants.[103] Fiber specimens included pineapple [*Ananas sativa*], banana [*Musa sapientum*], dagger [*Yucca aloifolia*], and silk grass or ramie [*Boehmeria nivea*].[104] Unlike lace-bark, some of these fibers were extracted by means of scutching, a mechanical process to release the soft inner fibers of the plant. In other situations, fibers were obtained by retting (actually rotting) the hard outer shell of the bast fiber plant to separate the fibers from the stalks as in the case of flax, hemp, and ramie.[105] Interestingly, to appeal to the scientific minds of the day, Jamaican plant and vegetable fibers along with tree specimens from the Botanical Department of Jamaica were often exhibited at international expositions with lace-bark products from the Women's Self-Help Society.[106]

The impetus for promoting economic plants was the hope that it would lead to the establishment of a fiber industry that produced fibers on a commercial scale. Kew Gardens played an integral role in providing seeds and plants for one of the most successful botanical enterprises in Jamaica's history. This gave way to new plantations and nurseries for varieties of economic plants, like Cinchona, coffee, various fruit trees, and more.[107] At the same time, the collaboration between Kew and Jamaican botanists led to a sweeping re-landscaping in some places through the transplanting of new plants and exchanging old ones and distributing seeds. The cumulative impact of these conditions resulted in a government committee to test the capabilities of certain machines driven by steam power for the purpose of producing mass quantities of fibers.[108] Vegetable fibers had received considerable attention during the late Victorian years, and scores of fiber machines were invented and exhibited at industrial expositions.[109]

Fiber machines of the period reflected achievements in engineering and innovation. Most significant to the Jamaican context was the Kennedy Eureka Machine (Figures 3.11, 3.12, 3.13), invented by the engineer James Kennedy in Jamaica to extract fibers from plants. Unfortunately, we know little of Kennedy, the American who resided on Duke Street in the island's capital. The machine weighed 210 lbs. and was 25 inches long, 25 and a half inches broad, and 12 inches deep. It took up very little space. The machine was used to extract fibers from several plants, including silk grass [*Furcraea cubensis*] and *Agave keratto* [*common Keratto*]. The machine appears to have been successful for some customers and was highly recommended by planters. Despite this, the fiber machine failed to yield the results the government committee had hoped for. James Cecil Phillippo, chairman of the committee overseeing the experiments, remarked, "During the experiments, certain obvious defects in the machine were noted."[110] Based on the findings, he revealed, "If the efforts of the ingenious inventor, to discover some method whereby the machine can be fed faster ... there is no doubt that the

FIGURE 3.11 J. Kennedy machine for obtaining fiber. Courtesy of the University of the West Indies Library, Mona.

machine will prove most valuable."[111] A debate ensued as to whether the machine was fast enough to yield quality fibers per hour or per day. This was not resolved. Still, Kennedy's machine won several awards for his innovation, including a silver medal at the Amsterdam Exhibition, and he received a prize of £50 offered by the Institute of Jamaica. Kennedy did update his invention the following year, but his fate or that of the machine is unknown.[112] Other experiments followed with the "Smiths Patent Machine," manufactured by Death and Ellwood in Britain, but this also failed.[113]

The experiments on various economic plants for commercial fiber did not include lace-bark for several reasons. First, for a fiber industry to be successful, it would require cultivation of the plants on a large scale or "sufficiently abundant to supply plants to establish large areas [plantations] at once."[114] The unique soil and environment necessary for lace-bark trees to grow made this impossible. Furthermore, any type of mechanized scutching would damage the natural netting of the lace-bark fibers. Nor was there an abundance of trees as in earlier decades.

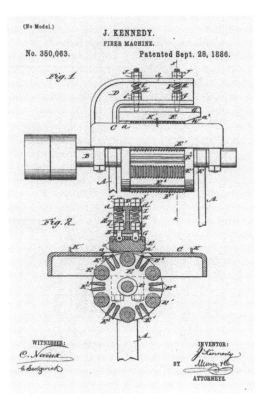

FIGURE 3.12 J. Kennedy Fiber machine, patented September 18, 1886. United States Patent Office.

Eventually, in 1885 the Institute of Jamaica that supervised the experiments concluded, "The celebrated lace-bark of Jamaica . . . formerly more abundant than it is now it is manufactured into ropes, whips and other articles. It can however, even at its best, be hardly included amongst fiber plants likely to be useful on a commercial scale."[115] The celebrated exotic tree, though not suitable for large commercial use, remained a popular ornamental souvenir among tourists who could afford it. However, by the late nineteenth century, at the height of its fame, the lace-bark industry had begun to decline as the tree was threatened with extinction.

By 1884, the decline in lace-bark was noticeable and a crisis developed in the souvenir business. The Women's Self-Help Society that relied on the natural lace expressed their concern; the society's leadership stated, "The growing scarcity of the lace has been arousing the serious attention of the committee, as this bark is extensively used in articles sold by the society."[116] Clearly, many souvenir shops that depended on lace-bark were worried about going out of business and the

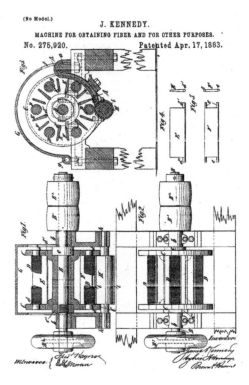

J. KENNEDY.

MACHINE FOR OBTAINING FIBER AND FOR OTHER PURPOSES.

No. 275,920. Patented Apr. 17, 1883.

FIGURE 3.13 J. Kennedy machine for obtaining fiber and other purposes, patented April 17, 1883. United States Patent Office.

impact on their production line. The situation was dire and further compounded by fears of the tree becoming extinct, which led to a public plea from the Botanical Department of Jamaica. In 1890, the department issued an urgent statement: "The lace-bark tree provides a very beautiful natural lace, the bark of the tree which is used in large quantities by ladies for 'fern work,' a characteristic art product of Jamaica. It is feared that this tree will soon become extinct."[117] The public notice further stated that "The Director of Public Gardens and Plantations will be thankful if anyone will send him seeds of this tree, in order that a small plantation may be formed for the purpose of providing seeds in the future for those who may wish to grow this valuable and interesting tree."[118] The appeals for help went unheeded, and by 1900 there was no mention of the lace-bark tree in the Government's annual report on Plantations and Gardens. Most shocking, by 1906 several reports issued estimated "only about half a dozen lace-bark left in existence."[119] And two years later, the number of trees remained the same.[120] The lace-bark tree that was once "in great plenty" in the seventeenth century had dwindled to almost none!

Basically, the lace-bark industry collapsed due to overuse, but the story of this remarkable tree is not yet over. In fact, the data of six trees remaining might have been overstated, but it does not diminish the fact that the tree was almost completely eradicated and already disappeared from many regions. The high demand for ropes and ornamentals for both the tourist market and exhibitions led to the depletion of the *lagetto* trees from Jamaican forests. To make the situation worse, "lace-bark trees are [were] being constantly cut down for fencing purposes as well as for bark, and there is nothing to indicate that new trees are being planted."[121] This suggests there was no oversight of the lace-bark production and harvesting process and the colonial government either underestimated the tree population or lapsed in its duty to protect the tree, especially at a time of considerable interest in economic plants. Perhaps the call for seeds by the Director of Public Gardens and Plantations as a last-minute effort to save the trees may seem a good intention, but it came rather too late. Furthermore, many peasant and rural farmers in close proximity to the lace-bark trees' habitat regularly cut down *lagetto* trees for their slender branches to be used as vine sticks for yam hills on their farms.[122] Urban sprawl and deforestation for farm lands and logging of saleable tree species created environmental degradation that further deprived the tree of its natural habitat.[123] Concerned about deforestation, in 1886, the Department of Public Gardens and Plantations reported to the governor of Jamaica:

> It is undoubtedly the fact that the indigenous plants of the West Indies are fast decreasing in numbers from a variety of causes, but chiefly among them is that of careless destruction by fire when burning spaces for cultivation, and it is important therefore that early steps should be taken to secure full sets of the original flora of the island.[124]

Despite the blatant destruction at human hands, there were natural factors that played a role. Towards the ending of the Victorian period, there was great concern for several tree species that were affected and damaged by beetles and various diseases, particularly scaly blight.[125]

Meanwhile, the lace-bark tree in Haiti and Cuba did not fare well either, especially towards the end of this period. The tree, already rare, had greatly diminished particularly in Haiti due to deforestation. Possibilities for gaining seeds or new plants from these regions seemed unlikely, and no attempts were made in that regard.[126]

The question arises, what about the Maroons, and did they notice that the tree population was declining? As late as the twentieth century, souvenir retailers of lace-bark ornamentations continued to voice their frustration over the scarcity of lace-bark products while newspaper columnists such as Inez Sibley admitted, "The days of selling this wonder product in much large quantities is long past. Lace-bark is now difficult to obtain,"[127] and further added an explanation for the decline: "the families who traded [lace-bark] in it had died."[128] For retailers of lace-bark products, the loss of the traders greatly impacted the industry, but there was also a gender component. According to Sibley, "The men of the present generation think it too much trouble to go into the hills to find the trees."[129] The assumption here is that the trees were still in existence, thus the men were to be blamed for the collapse of the trade. It is not surprising that some retailers and members of the tourist industry who benefited from the sale of lace-bark souvenirs would be concerned. Maybe, a few were more anxious about their profit margin than the destruction of the tree population.

During the early decades of the twentieth century, there were some attempts to protect Jamaican trees that were valuable for their bark. In 1929, the local Assembly passed the *Bark of Trees (Sale Prevention) Act*[130] to both protect certain trees and prevent the sale of tree bark without the consent of the owner or risk a citation. The law was applied to three trees, Mahogany, Mahoe, and Dogwood.[131] Lace-bark was not included. Perhaps the colonial authorities saw no need, since lace-bark was not valued for its lumber, nor was it necessary to include lace-bark on the list if the tree had already become scarce or was no longer in existence as so many thought. No explanation was given. The declining lace-bark industry continued to hold on for a while longer, but the souvenirs gradually disappeared. A few post cards overlaid with lace-bark were sold in souvenir shops in 1906, and several small lace-bark items were made in 1938.[132] A limited number of ropes were made for commercial purposes from the tree as late as 1941. By then Jamaica's famous lace-bark tree had become a distant memory amongst the wider population Sadly, today the knowledge of lace-bark has been forgotten, and overuse of the tree has made it scarce, bringing the industry to an end.[133]

The role of Jamaican women as creators of unique art works in lace-bark was very significant. Not only did their participation and exhibits bring some prestige to Jamaica and to Britain as the "mother country," but it enabled numerous women to attain some level of achievement and fame on the national and international stage. The mode of production and consumption of lace-bark had shifted drastically during the period. Prior to Emancipation, women dominated the production and distribution of lace-bark. However, now their situation was mitigated by different circumstances. During slavery, many women desired sufficient clothing and financial independence; after slavery, several women maintained some financial independence, but were no longer independent producers of lace-bark. Consequently, the "push" for more lace-bark to meet the demand of the souvenir business and international fairs "sidelined" women, as more men saw lace-bark as a lucrative business and government authorities became increasingly interested in its commercial and economic viability. Furthermore, the commercialization of lace-bark not only gave way to increased male participation, but also the emergence of family monopolies in the lace-bark tree territories. These families became the "new" producers of lace-bark fibers.[134]

Freed Africans kept the customary practices of African bark-cloth production alive. Their innovation and experimentation in dress was a response to their oppressed state and a desire to create their own economic sphere. As during slavery, some colonized women continued to work in the lace-bark industry where they produced souvenirs for sale on the tourist market. This enabled several women to be financially independent of freed men. The survival of African customs in dress, and the use of plant substances in the care and production of bark-cloth and lace-bark, required creativity and ingenuity, and the principal transmitters of these customs in dress were African women.

CONCLUSION

"Fanm se kajou; plis li vye, plis li bon."—Woman is mahogany—the older she gets, the better she is.[1]

HAITIAN PROVERB

Throughout this study, I emphasized the significance of bark-cloth in several cultures and its impact on the lives of enslaved and freed people in Jamaica. Bark-cloth as a form of dress was not a mere whim, but an important and valuable commodity in several cultures, including Jamaican slave society and beyond. Apart from protecting and adorning the body, bark-cloth was used by enslaved Africans to showcase their creative talents, symbolically resist stereotypes associated with their race, be culturally expressive, and at the same time convey that they too could be as beautiful and refined as their European colonizers. Jamaican lace-bark was a form of bark-cloth as it was produced from the inner bark of the fibrous *lagetto* tree. Globally, bark-cloth has a long and varied history dating back to pre-historic times, while across many bark-cloth producing regions the production techniques consisted of stripping the bark off the source tree followed by a process of "thinning" and softening the moistened inner bark by pounding it with a mallet to transform it into malleable, smooth cloth.[2]

West and Central Africa have been among some of the world's great producers of textiles and bark-cloth. The most prevalent source for bark-cloth in many areas of Africa was the tropical fig or Ficus tree. Across the continent of Africa where bark-cloth was produced, the basic technique of beating bark was evident. As we saw earlier, among the Ashanti people, long pieces of bark were stripped off the *Kyenkyen* tree [*Antian's toxicaria*], soaked in water, and beaten with wooden mallets called *abore ayifore* in Guang and *ayitin* in Twi. The result was a soft piece of cloth much wider than the original cut from the bark.[3] In Ashanti culture, these techniques were often passed down from father to son and artist to apprentice. Thus, within this cultural context, men were the transmitters of bark-cloth knowledge from one generation to the next. Be that as it may, women's importance as traders of cloth cannot be denied. In West Africa, for instance, where trading was a significant part of the socioeconomic culture of African women, many traded in local markets as wholesalers and retailers, and in some cases women held a monopoly over trade in several coastal ports.[4] Women's activities as traders were essential to the local economies of the region and to the very survival of the bark-cloth industry.

In this study, I have tried to provide some ideas of how bark-cloth was obtained from several tree species in Polynesia and Africa. By following the process and the artists who transformed bark into meaningful things that influenced and shaped people's lives and society, we learn how identities were constructed within the confines of gender display and how material objects became meaningful things. Material objects such as bark-cloth by itself rarely ever has one single or fixed, unchanging meaning; instead, the objects acquire meaning by how they were used and integrated into everyday practices.[5] Indeed, bark-cloth acquired different meanings within societies based on how it was used and represented. Bark-cloth was a functional object, a sacred cloth, valued trade commodity, and a decorative art within specific cultural contexts. It is in the representation of bark-cloth that we see important connections and intersections across various social groups and between generations over time.

During the pre-colonial era, the Taínos were among the earliest people of the Caribbean to use bark-cloth and lace-bark in their daily activities. From the perspective of Taíno gender ideology, cloth was symbolic of social relations, and the way people adorned themselves provided some clues as to their identity in terms of gender, ethnicity, and class. Within the Taíno cultural context, cloth was gendered in that Taíno women were the ones engaged in spinning and weaving cotton into cloth. Women's empowerment through the matrilineal system of descent and their economic role as producers and distributors of valuable commodities were displaced by Spanish hegemonic masculinity embodied in patriarchal institutions and capitalist commercial enterprises seeking wealth and profit.[6] Despite the genocide unleashed on the Taínos by their Spanish conquerors, some aspects of Taíno culture survived and knowledge of local plants was transmitted to enslaved Africans.[7]

Deconstructing cloth within its cultural context, and examining how it was used and produced, enables us to fully comprehend the gendered roles of men and women in Taíno and colonial Jamaican society, especially in shaping identities. Henry Glassie emphasized this point; he argued, "All objects exist in context."[8] Within Taíno culture, cloth and lace-bark were intertwined with Taíno women's daily lives in both a functional and spiritual manner. Just as cloth was significant in the lives of Taíno women, so too did lace-bark become an important vehicle for personal and social transformation in the lives of enslaved African women.

The rise of natural history in the Caribbean was an important phenomenon that greatly impacted the metropolitan's view of the colonial world and its inhabitants. Sir Hans Sloane, who played a significant role in introducing Jamaican lace-bark to the scientific and the European communities at large, published colorful works of art and detailed narratives of the flora and fauna of the colonies; these depictions captivated the imagination of the readers back in Europe. Although the works of artists such as Brunias provided some semblance of the complexity and contradictions inherent in West Indian slave society, natural history publications enhanced Europeans' knowledge of the Caribbean. Sloane's publications illuminated the hidden treasures, wonders, and fascinating objects of the Caribbean's natural world and an awareness of the potential commercial enterprises for profit. For Sloane and his contemporaries, the region had become part of the imperial fantasy, a Garden of Eden within which the voice of the subjugated is muted.

Sloane's involvement in bio-prospecting was not new. In fact, bio-prospecting has existed throughout human history ever since humans looked to nature for sources of food, clothing, fuel, and medicine.[9] In this regard, African slaves were also engaged in bio-prospecting as they too searched the local forests and their alien environment for plant sources to use in clothing and medicine, and for food. Through the process of experimentation, trial, and error, along with information acquired from the Amerindians, enslaved Africans developed an extensive pharmacopeia of medicinal plants. In the seventeenth century, bio-prospecting in the Caribbean took on a new feature and chief amongst prospectors were European botanists who served the colonial enterprise by cataloguing and identifying exotic plants in new colonies thus allowing their governments to procure inexpensive medicinal plants, food and luxury items for the domestic markets.[10] Today, bio-prospecting is big news, particularly in the form of drug prospecting, medical research, and the quest for genetic resources possessed by indigenous people and nations in the tropical zones.[11] Such activities continue to fuel old debates and draw attention to age old questions such as who owns nature and if bio-prospecting actually is bio-piracy with a pedigree? Furthermore, greater awareness of bio-diversity and the heightened global concern for the environment have created interest in the use of natural dyes for coloring fabrics leading to bio-prospecting for dye yielding plants. The search for plant species with economic potential due to valuable properties such as fibers and oil is an increasingly popular activity.[12]

Throughout the period of enslavement, proslavery practitioners sought not only to exploit their African slaves for their labor but intentionally tried to deculturate Africans through a process of dehumanization and psychological conditioning, hence fostering a powerless and submissive class that was easily controllable. Despite European attempts at cultural annihilation, cultural characteristics were retained and nurtured in Jamaica and numerous parts of the African Diaspora because they guaranteed the survival of African people and their descendants. Enslaved people from West and Central Africa who possessed the knowledge and expertise in weaving textiles, bark-cloth production, beading, dyeing, and tailoring, brought these skills with them to the Caribbean and other parts of the African Diaspora. Slave women who could sew became seamstresses and played important roles both in the informal slave economy by sewing for their family, friends, and members of the slave community. Africans also brought their skills in trading to the Caribbean and incorporated them into the local informal produce and fabric markets. As in many areas of West Africa, women dominated Caribbean markets as traders and consumers.[13]

Slavery impacted slave men and women in different ways. Slave women were expected to be creative and flexible. They worked in the fields during the day and continued to work in the slave household at night. Yet they kept the customary practices of African bark-cloth production alive. Their innovation and experimentation in dress was a response to their oppressed state and a desire to create their own economic sphere. This enabled some to trade and be financially independent of slave men. African slaves' responses to enslavement were greatly influenced by African cultural patterns. Historian Walter Rodney has argued that the culture of Africans was the "shield which frustrated the efforts of the Europeans to dehumanise Africans through servitude, and was an indicator of the tenacity, and ability of the subordinate to survive, and resist the cultural imposition of their white masters by maintaining their unique identity."[14] The preservation of this cultural identity was essential to their survival, and lace-bark was a principal exponent of this process.

In Jamaica, enslaved African women utilized the skills they had acquired in West Africa to obtain suitable raw materials for dress from their environment. The African arrivants acquired some knowledge of native plants from indigenous Caribbean people, and they built on this knowledge, and developed it further. They also passed this knowledge on to their descendants.[15] The survival of African customs in dress, and the use of plant substances in the care and production of bark-cloth and lace-bark, required creativity and ingenuity, and the principal transmitters of these customs in dress were African women. Slave women's essential roles as mothers, healers, teachers, and even spiritual leaders within the slave community made them ideal conduits for the transmission of African customs in dress. Melville Herskovits argued that a distinctive characteristic of African societies in the New World was the role women played as the principal exponents and protectors of African culture.[16] Slave owners were not concerned when enslaved people retained certain aspects of their African culture, such as dress, because it emphasized the differences between Africans and whites; they also did not wish to provide more expensive clothing. Nevertheless, the continuation and nurturing of these African customs in dress such as bark-cloth and lace-bark not only reflected Africans' harmonious relationship with their environment, but it also enabled slave women to maintain a vital link with their ancestral homeland and simultaneously resist cultural annihilation.[17]

The gender ideology of the plantation complex perceived women's labor as not as valuable as men's labor even though women worked side by side in the fields with their male counterparts. Therefore, enslaved women were often denied the same rights and privileges associated with dress and received smaller clothing rations. Consequently, women had a greater need than slave men for sufficient clothing. Thus many Africans looked for plants in the forest that could be used to make bark-cloth and produce dye pigments to color the fabrics they received from their enslavers.[18] For enslaved African women, the nurturing of an African aesthetic in their dress allowed them to "dress up" or "nice up" the drab and plain clothing they received from their enslavers, to transform their appearance from a slave aesthetic to a more pleasing and familiar African mode in dress.[19]

Most enslaved people in Jamaica did not have access to refined fabrics such as lace. Rather, European manufactured lace was limited, expensive, and considered a highly prized commodity out of the reach of most slaves and even some poor whites. In Jamaican colonial society, as in Europe, lace was a signifier of elite status; hence, the few slaves who had access to European lace clothing increased their social standing within the slave community. Thus, many enslaved persons resorted to lace-bark or natural lace as a substitute for European manufactured lace. In Jamaica, lace-bark was used to make a multitude of clothing and decorative objects, including cravats, collars, cuffs, window curtains, basically for every purpose that manufactured lace was used. It was also used to make shawls and even wedding veils. The widespread use of lace-bark among slaves, freed persons, and Maroons in Jamaica gave rise to a thriving cottage industry based on lace-bark. The Leeward Maroons were at the center of this vibrant industry, and lace-bark production was gendered female. In Cuba and Haiti, a vibrant industry in lace-bark did not develop as in Jamaica due to the rarity of the lace-bark trees in those territories.

The rapid transformations in Victorian Jamaican society gave way to the democratization of fashion that coincided with Europeanization and missionization. Luxury goods, including lace by means of importation, were more accessible and the upper classes preferred Victorian lace to lace-bark. The period saw the rise of self-help organizations such as the Lady Musgrave Self-Help Society[20] that promoted lace-bark crafts and souvenirs for the emerging tourist market and international fairs. Jamaican women as creators of unique art works in lace-bark were very significant. Their extraordinary talents were a source of empowerment that made it possible for many women to have a livelihood, and at the same time make a contribution to the colonial economy. Not only did the women's participation and exhibits boost Jamaica's image abroad, they also brought some prestige to the Self-Help Society, to Jamaica, and to Britain as the "mother country." By the same token, exhibitions and industrial fairs provided the opportunity for a few Jamaican women to attain some level of achievement and fame on the national and international stage. Women engaged in the souvenir business making lace-bark ornamentals were propelled into the working class and secured some financial gains for themselves and their family. However, mission schools and women's self-help societies often taught embroidery, sewing, knitting, and lace-making to colonized women and young girls—textile arts that were becoming increasingly unnecessary and simultaneously made extensive use of industrial materials that undermined the transmission of indigenous skills.[21]

The heightened excitement surrounding lace-bark as an exotic object desirable by tourists and collectors of curiosities was reminiscent of the prospectors of the seventeenth century who often failed to see the humanity behind the object of their fascination. Artisans in the wake of such capitalists' expansion nonetheless responded to the emergent market for hand-crafted lace-bark products by tourists, travelers, and others nostalgic for exotic objects. Some perhaps were attracted to the "ethnic art" as a gesture of imperialist pity or solidarity with oppressed colonized women.[22] At the same time, women traders and distributors of lace-bark were gradually displaced as more men and the local authorities became increasingly interested in lace-bark's commercial and economic viability. Furthermore, the commercialization of lace-bark not only gave way to increased male participation, but also the emergence of family monopolies in the lace-bark tree territories. These families became the "new" producers of lace-bark fibers.[23] At any rate, freed African women kept the customary practices of African bark-cloth production alive.

Lace-bark today: a tree in crisis

I have always loved the mechanics of nature and to a greater or lesser extent my work is always informed by that.[24]

ALEXANDER MCQUEEN, FASHION DESIGNER

Trees are among the most essential features of nature. They are beautiful and life sustaining. Without their role in the biodiversity and ecosystem of the planet, life as we know it here on earth would be nonexistent. It is no wonder that some of the oldest living things on earth are in fact trees.[25] I would like to think that Alexander McQueen felt the same, and just as his professional work was informed by nature, so too were the many African women, both slave and freed, whose beautiful creations of lace-bark products from bonnets and caps to gowns and curios were informed by nature. They worked with nature and allowed it to shape their creative energies.

At the end of the nineteenth century, the lace-bark industry had collapsed due to the scarcity of the tree, and the glorious days of Jamaica's lace-bark tree were long gone. The industry remained dormant for a while but in the 1950s new trees were spotted deep in the rain forest, and soon interest in lace-bark was reignited, but only for a brief period, and never to its former glory. A few Maroons continued to produce some puffs of lace-bark fibers for sale in regional markets in the towns of Black River and New Market, thus providing an income for several families in the Cockpit Country. A few residents of the Cockpit Country used lace-bark for making mats, baskets, and ropes for home use. This continued for a while, but eventually the Maroons stopped producing lace-bark for household purposes.[26] Some clothing was made for home consumption, such as marina tee shirts (under shirts) for men, and a few Maroon women continued to use lace-bark to make curtains and accessories for their dresses. In the 1960s the new generation of Maroon men was not interested in keeping the old art of lace-bark production alive and had grown weary and reluctant to harvest lace-bark trees. Young men complained about spending too many days in the forest in search of trees while others considered it too much work for men.[27] Others left the community in search of better job opportunities in the big cities of Kingston and Montego Bay.[28]

The period also saw a decline in certain traditional handicrafts, such as furniture making, that brought some well-needed revenue to the colonial economy. By the mid-twentieth century, the largest handicraft industry in Jamaica was based on straws and fibers. In 1953, export sales of straw and fiber handicrafts had increased from £5,000 annually a decade earlier to nearly £90,000. It was believed that visitors to Jamaica that year bought at least another £100,000 worth of straw and fiber products.[29] During the same period, government officials promoted hand loom weaving, a comparatively new craft to Jamaica that produced fabrics for local demand. These hand loom projects were sponsored by local corporations, such as Reynolds Jamaica mines. The fiber, straw, and needlework handicraft industries employed numerous skilled and semi-skilled Jamaican women who dominated the sector and produced exquisite works of art.[30] Surprisingly enough, the industry based on embroidery, fine linens, and dresses struggled due to competition from low wage earning countries, such as China, Madeira, and the Philippines.[31] Apart from the low cost of labor, these countries have a long history of leaf and bast fiber textile production. Hence, dissemination of lace-bark during this period was very limited as the demand was low.

Against this background, the Jamaican government developed a renewed interest in lace-bark and by the early post-independence period,[32] some lace-bark was traded between the 1960s to the 1980s, in part due to the efforts of Edward Seaga (1930–), former prime minister of Jamaica from 1980 to 1989. Seaga, a long-time advocate for the preservation and promotion of Jamaican arts and culture, found Jamaican lace-bark most intriguing and sought to promote it in industry.[33] The resulting situation fostered a close relationship between lace-bark suppliers in the Cockpit Country and the government agency called Things Jamaica Limited that was responsible for reorganizing craft development in Jamaica and promoting the craft sector to produce excellent and high quality Jamaican hand-made products for both the local and tourist markets. The agency provided administrative services, manuals, support networks, and trade opportunities for handicraft workers. Sonia Gallimore, Product Development and Promotional Manager at Things Jamaica Limited, became an advocate for high quality crafts including lace-bark products for the tourist market.[34] A few families in the Cockpit region, such as the Lennon family, took occasional leave from their farming to produce lace-bark, which was sold for $Ja40–$Ja60 per pound, a very lucrative sum by local standards, to Things Jamaica Limited for use in craft production. Similar to earlier decades, highly skilled women were recruited by the agency to make beautiful handicrafts with lace-bark such as greeting cards and doilies.[35]

Meanwhile, the techniques in lace-bark production had changed very little over the years. As during slavery, the men harvested the bark and the women of the household processed the lace-bark fibers for sale. For the families engaged in lace-bark, the new trade was essential to their livelihood. Needless to say, the amount of lace-bark harvested was limited and trade was sporadic due to the scarcity of the trees, but enough lace-bark was produced to supply Things Jamaica Limited for several years. In general, lace-bark was no longer a popular item for domestic consumption and most lace-bark curios were destined for the tourist market and as gifts for visiting dignitaries and royalty. Queen Elizabeth II was presented with a lace-bark souvenir during her state visit in 1983.[36]

By 1981 the trade had taken its toll on the remaining tree population and there were numerous calls from local residents to protect the few surviving lace-bark trees.[37] Finally, the scarcity of the tree along with changes in the political arena led to an end in government interest and the final demise of the lace-bark industry. Today, the production of Jamaican lace-bark into beautiful things with meaning is a lost art form and the small number of trees are faced with imminent danger of extinction. Brennan, Harris, and Nesbitt (2013) have rightly argued that the decline of the lace-bark industry is rather complex and is due to several factors, ranging from the wider decline in interest of traditional crafts in Jamaica to difficulties in harvesting and finding required labor for the task, as well as the scarcity of the trees and the low prices fetched for the raw materials. There was also the impact of Hurricane Gilbert in 1988 that left many people homeless, thus impacting the business.[38] Indeed the industry has declined, but today the habitat of the lace-bark trees is threatened. Although there is plenty of blame to go around, from lack of regulation and protection to overuse of the tree, the central questions are what can be done now to save the few remaining trees, how do we protect them, can they be saved?

Lace-bark: the imminent threat

There are two major threats to the conservation of the lace-bark tree. First, deforestation continues to be an ongoing problem, as well as the cutting down of branches for fencing and for sticks (poles) to be used on farms as a brace for yam vines.[39] But perhaps the greatest threat to the lace-bark trees is that of mining for bauxite and limestone in Cockpit Country, in the very habitat of the *lagetto* tree. Jamaican resident and columnist, Peter Espeut, argues that "although the law requires mining companies to restore mined out lands, it is impossible to restore a natural forest. Simply planting trees," according to Espeut, "will not restore the complex interactions between flora and fauna nor will it allow all functions of the ecosystem of the forest to be adequately performed."[40] In 2007, Colonel Sydney Peddie, leader of the Maroons, declared that mining "will not happen or else there will be war."[41] Hence, the Jamaican government was compelled to withdraw a license for the US-based aluminum producer Alcoa Inc. and the state-owned Clarendon Aluminum Production Ltd. to begin mining in the northwestern region of the Cockpit Country due to threats of street protests by environmental activists.[42] Jamaica is the world's fifth largest producer of bauxite, the raw material for aluminum. Most recently, more attempts have been made to grant licenses for mining prospecting in the Cockpit Country. Any mining of the region for limestone or bauxite would be fatal to the lace-bark trees due to the nature of its habitat and its roots embedded into the crevices of limestone. In addition, twenty-seven of the twenty-eight endemic species of butterflies and the largest butterfly in the Americas, the giant swallow tail, would be endangered.[43]

On Friday, July 3, 2015, it was announced by the Jamaican government that the Blue and John Crow Mountains were inscribed to UNESCO's prestigious World Heritage list. This was exciting news as this represented the first World Heritage Site for Jamaica. The region inscribed is a National Park, the largest contiguous area of natural forests in Jamaica, protecting 193 acres of forest on mountain slopes, comprising ten watershed management units spanning four parishes.[44] While this is indeed exciting news for Jamaica, the question arises, why not do the same for the Cockpit Country? The issue is about border rights. The border of the Cockpit Country must be clearly defined to be considered for the honor. The ongoing dispute over boundary lines between government, the Maroons, and the mining sector makes this an issue unlikely to be resolved anytime soon.

Apart from the obvious collaboration with conservationists, scientists, Maroons, and local officials on protecting the lace-bark tree, there are several other suggestions to conserve and promote greater awareness of the lace-bark. Perhaps by using seed banks and cloning the *lagetto* tree, it can be protected from extinction, while some have proposed stereolithography or 3D-printing technologies to create replicas of the few remaining and very fragile lace-bark artifacts. The replicas would facilitate the opportunity for lace-bark artifacts to be widely circulated among museums and institutions of learning for greater public access. Possibly, we could keep the knowledge of lace-bark alive by including the subject in school curriculums, thus increasing awareness of lace-bark among young Jamaicans who have never heard of natural lace. Although the focus here is on a tree, maybe there are lessons to be learned from fiber conservation efforts analogous to the lace-bark in Jamaica: for example, the Peruvian government's attempt to protect the endangered vicuña (South American camelids) and restore a very limited commercial market for vicuña fiber, which is similar to llama wool, but even more luxurious. These efforts have been a success story.[45] Of incredible importance is the need to engage Jamaican fashion designers and textile makers in the conversation about lace-bark.

The lack of recent data, scarcity of sources, and the loss of lace-bark knowledge makes it extremely difficult to assess or comprehend the current state of the *lagetto* tree population in Haiti and Cuba. In Haiti, most people have never heard of the tree, and scientists and government officials at the Ministry of Forestry and the Botanical Gardens were convinced that the tree no longer exists on La Gonâve and is extremely rare elsewhere in the country. Others argued that the *lagetto* tree has completely disappeared from Haiti. Luckily I persisted and, while my colleagues were traveling in a remote part of Haiti, they enquired about the tree from an elderly man who in turn directed them to a small lagetto plant. This reflects the conundrum inherent in this research. Officials could not confirm, whether the tree exists or not. The sapling represented hope that the tree still grows in Haiti, but how many lace-bark trees are left is a mystery, and how to conserve the remaining trees in Haiti is also a challenge. In a country racked by recent political turmoil and natural disasters, arguably there are far more pressing issues on the Haitian government's agenda than worrying about saving a tree. I would disagree— tree conservation is a priority for sustaining the environment and perhaps the tree can be mass cultivated and regulated for commercial use to enhance the lives of Haitians and other Caribbean people.[46]

Likewise in Cuba, no recent data has been collected and, even though the tree is still in existence, no one knows for sure the extent of its distribution across Cuba or if it is threatened by further deforestation. Again, most Cuban scholars and scientists, except for a few botanists, were unfamiliar with the tree. There is a great need for more field research to assess the current health and growth of the lace-bark tree population. More collaboration between Cuban, Jamaican, and Haitian botanists would be useful. Perhaps, as Cuba and the United States thaw their Cold War era tensions, more funding for research and scholarship will emerge to enhance our understanding of the lace-bark tree in all territories. When I began this research, I had no idea where it would lead. As a historian of dress and costume, I was compelled to depart from familiar methodologies to learn new concepts and theories in the botanical field. I began to learn about tree anatomy and plant conservation and diseases affecting Caribbean trees. This is the great promise of interdisciplinary research, to be able to draw on diverse fields of disciplines to fully comprehend a complex problem.

In 1990, when I began looking for the lace-bark trees in Jamaica, I was told the tree no longer existed and the overall view was that the tree had become extinct from overuse during the previous centuries. I am delighted this was proven wrong. During my first visit into the rain forest in 2001 with representatives from the Forestry Head Office of Jamaica, we were overjoyed to locate small trees under the forest canopy. More recently, in the summer of 2014, this time with representatives from The Natural History Museum at the Institute of Jamaica, several young lace-bark trees were spotted with blossoms and fruits in the forest surrounding Accompong Town. I was jubilant with this revelation as this leads to two conclusions. First, that the presence of so many small trees suggests the *lagetto* tree has "come back" and there must be large parent trees deep in the Cockpit Country. Second, the resurgence in the tree population suggests that the barks of the *lagetto* trees have not been harvested for the purpose of making ropes, vine sticks, and hammocks in recent years. Regardless, more in-depth study and research is needed to determine what types of conservation efforts can be implemented to ensure the survival of the lace-bark trees.

One of the questions posed by Brennan, Harris, and Nesbitt (2013) is whether or not lace-bark can be revived as a viable economic activity and livelihood for many people. Is it sustainable? As Brennan, Harris, and Nesbitt revealed, lace-bark thrived and was sustainable for centuries before being overused in the nineteenth and early twentieth centuries.[47] This requires further investigation. At a time when their is much interest in environmental responsibility and sustainable harvesting, could lace-bark be revived for the tourist industry and handicraft sector, and could it be of use in the Caribbean fashion industry? Within the past decade, the Caribbean fashion industry has become world renowned for its innovative styles and talented designers who have made an imprint on the international fashion scene. The annual Caribbean Fashion Week (CFW) with collections from at least fifty designers represents a regional fashion industry worth more than J$10 billion per annum.[48] In years gone by, Things Jamaica Limited organized craft exhibitions including lace-bark, and leaf and bast fiber materials from local plants for possible commercial use, but there have been no recent interests or attempts to use lace-bark in the fashion sector. Several cultures have successfully incorporated sustainable fibers in their fashion industries, such as ramie in South Korea, and piña (pineapple) fiber in the Philippines for high-end fashion markets.[49]

Despite this, the demise of the lace-bark industry did not diminish Jamaicans' fascination with lace. On the contrary, manufactured lace remains an important aspect of contemporary dress customs in Jamaica and throughout the Caribbean. Moreover, it is conceivable that Jamaicans' love for lace and linen fabrics today has its roots in the bark-cloth industry. Lace-bark was not a frivolous material item on the periphery of women's lives, but a central and significant cultural object that shaped identities, cultural taste, and values. From this point of view, lace-bark is an important part of our history, a rich legacy and the embodiment of a cultural link with West Africa. I have posed several questions in this study; admittedly I have no answers, but I hope this study will spark a conversation about lace-bark and the fate of the *lagetto* tree. I began this text by reminiscing about my childhood and the needleworkers of my family who taught me so much about Jamaican dress and the plants that have sustained us. I celebrate them and all Jamaican women who have and continue to transform our lives with beautiful and meaningful things.

APPENDIX

Plant fibers and natural substances used in the making of textiles and the care of clothes in Jamaica. Common or popular and botanical names listed

Common name	Botanical name
Sources for perfume:	
Musk wood	*Trichilia moschata* Sw. [Native]
Rose wood	*Zanthoxylum rhodoxylon* (Urb.) P. Wilson [Endemic]
Musk okra	*Abelmoschus moschatus* Medik. [Introduced]
Prince wood	*Hamelia ventricosa* Sw. [Native]
Plants for vegetable soaps:	
Coratoe	*Agave morrisii* Baker [Native]
Broad-Leafed broom-weed	*Sida acuta* Burm. [Native]
Soap-tree/bush	*Clidemia hirta* (L.) D. Don. [Native]
Lignum Vitae leaves	*Guaiacum officinale* L. [Native]
Soap wood	*Clethra occidentalis* (L.) Kuntse [Native]
Soapberry bush/tree	*Sapindus saponaria* L. [Native]
Ackee pods	*Blighia sapida* K. D. Koenig [Introduced]
Sources for dyes and pigments:	
Indigo	*Indigofera tinctoria* L. [Introduced]
Scarlet seed	*Laetia thamnia* L. [Native]
Anatto	*Bixa orellana* L. [Introduced]

Common name	Botanical name
Prickly pear	*Opuntia dillenii* (Ker Gawl.) Haw. [Native]
Logwood	*Haematoxylum campechianum* L. [Introduced]
Morinda root or Yaw-weed	*Morinda* sp. (probably *Morinda royoc* L. [Native])
Fustic tree	Maclura *tinctoria* (L.) D. Don. ex Steud subsp. *tinctoria* [Native]
Prickly yellow pear	Zanthoxylum *martinicense* (Lam.) DC. [Native]
Indigo berry	*Randia aculeata* L. var. *aculeata* [Native]
Shrubby goat-rue	(Scientific name unidentifiable)
Bastard saffron	(Scientific name unidentifiable)
Lignum vitae leaves; for refreshing flowers	*Guaiacum officinale* L. [Native]
Vine sorrel	*Cissus trifoliata* (L.) L. [Native]
Mountain or Surinam calalue	(Scientific name unidentifiable)
Yellow wood	(Scientific name unidentifiable)
Cashaw, bark and root	*Prosopis juliflora* (Sw.) DC. [Introduced]
Flower fence	(Scientific name unidentifiable)
Cashew and cashew tree	*Anacardium occidentale* L. [Introduced]

Plant fibers for textiles and clothing:

Cotton wood	(Scientific name unidentifiable)
Laghetto bark	*Lagetta lagetto* (Sw.) Nash [Native]
Down-tree-down	*Ochroma pyramidale* (Cav. ex Lam.) Urb. [Native]
Bon-ace bark	(Scientific name unidentifiable)
Carotoe leaf	*Agave morrisii* Baker [Native]
Mountain Cabbage	*Roystonea altissima* (Mill.) H. E. Moore [Endemic]
Silk Grass	(Scientific name unidentifiable)
Cocoa-husk	*Theobroma cacao* L. [Introduced]
Mahoe-bark	*Hibiscus elatus* Sw. [Native]
Red sorrel bush	*Hibiscus sabdariffa* L. [Introduced]

Common name	Botanical name
Plant substances for tanning leather:	
Mahoe-bark	*Hibiscus elatus* Sw. [Native]
White bully bark	*Sideroxylon salicifolium* (L.) Lam. [Native]
Black olive bark	*Terminalia arbuscula* Sw. [Endemic]
Red mangrove	*Rhizophora mangle* L. [Native]
Button tree	*Conocarpus erectus* L. var. *erectus* [Native]
Dogwood	*Piscidia piscipula* (L.) Sarg. [Native]

Source: Information from Edward Long, *The History of Jamaica or General Survey*, 3 vols., 1774; C.D. Adams, *Flowering Plants of Jamaica*, 1972; Steeve O. Buckridge, *The Language of Dress*, 2004.

Botanical nomenclature: an explanation

Carolus (Carl) Linnaeus (1707–1778): Botanist responsible for establishing a binomial system of plant nomenclature. Prior to his work, plants had lengthy and descriptive terms in the name. Linnaeus standardized botanical nomenclature by creating a genus and species name for each plant, followed by its designator.

Botanical name: Clinical reports and studies involving a plant must always include the plant's botanical (binomial) name, which consists of both the genus and the species. Both terms are usually italicized or underlined. The first letter of the genus is always capitalized (for example, *Lagetta*).

Genus (plural, genera): may consist of a single or several hundred species (for example, genus *Lagetta*; genus and species *Lagetta lagetto*, *Lagetta wrightiana*, *Lagetta venezuelana*).

Repens: the particular species within the genus, and is always lower cased letters. It is best to include the names of the person (usually abbreviated) who named the particular species as part of the scientific name to avoid confusion between similar or related plants (for example, *Lagetta lagetto (sw.) Nash*; genus—*Lagetta*, repens/species—*lagetto*).

Classification of plant: Botanists continue to revise the classification system of specific plant families or groups to reflect additional knowledge and a more natural, evolutionary-based system. Plants are frequently moved into different genera; to limit confusion when previously employed names are changed, they become recognized synonyms.

Family: The genera are placed in a family. The family name is not italicized, but the initial letter is always capitalized (for example, Thymelaeaceae—family for *Lagetta*; genus—*Lagetta*; repens/species—*lagetto*). When the name of the genus is followed by the word "species" (spp.), it means there are numerous species in this particular genus.

Common names: There are no rules for establishing common names of plants.

GLOSSARY

Selected textiles, clothing, and plant fibers from this study[1]

Adinkra Cloth fabric from Ghana covered in symbolic designs printed using stamps carved from calabash shell and wood.

Aso oke Yoruba strip woven cloth that symbolizes high status. The component strips are often designed with weft-float work.

Baise, Baize coarsely woven woolen or cotton fabric napped to imitate felt and dyed in solid colors. This was distributed to slaves on many plantations.

Bandana or bandanna from the Hindi word bandhnu, which refers to a method of dyeing where the cloth is tied in places to prevent it from receiving the dye. This produces a dark red or blue ground, and white as well as yellow spots left by this process. In the nineteenth century cotton bandanas were produced by chemical means producing a type of check pattern of the same colors. In the Caribbean the term bandana was coined or merged with the term Madras to refer to popular tie-heads worn by many women. Bandana became very popular in post-emancipation Jamaica. This fabric was used as neck cloth or tie-heads. Bandana is also part of the Jamaican national costume/dress.

Barege gauze-like, semi-transparent fabric originally made at Bareges in the French Pyrenees in the 1850s.

Bark-cloth generic term for cloth produced or obtained from the bark of trees.

Bast fibers fibers obtained from the phloem or inner skin of a plant that are separated from the xylem or woody core of the plant for processing and textile production.

Batik a vibrant, colorfully patterned fabric that has wax applied prior to dyeing to produce a pattern that resists the dyeing process. The word is of Indonesian origin, but resist dyeing is done in many parts of the world.

Bib a type of apron worn by many female traders in Jamaican markets consisting of two large pockets, one for silver coins and the other for copper coins.

Bobbin lace a generic term for all lace made by twisting and plaiting threads wound on bobbins. The bobbins hold the threads, which are laced together and held down onto a pillow with pins. There are numerous types of bobbin lace, including Chantilly, Genoese, Bruges, and Brussels.

Bogolanfini mud-dyed ritual cloths of the Bamana and other ethnic groups of Mali.

Bois dentelle common French term for lace-bark in Haiti. *Dentelle* is also the French word for lace, and the term was popular in the nineteenth century. Other French terms in Haiti include *laget à dentelle, arbè a dentelle,* and *daguille.*

Bombasine, Bombazine a fine, English fabric and one of the oldest materials known. It comes from the Latin term *Bombycinum,* meaning "silk in texture" and was originally all silk. Later twilled or corded dress material composed of silk, or rayon, worsted and sometimes cotton or worsted alone. The fabric in the black was worn in mourning.

Bombyx mori the cultivated silk moth that feeds on the leaves of the mulberry tree. It is both blind and flightless.

Bwa dentèl Creole term for lace-bark in Haiti. Other Haitian Creole words include *dagwi, lagèt,* and *ma-lagèt* in Vodou rituals.

Calamanco glazed woolen fabric made in Flanders in the sixteenth century. Often checked in the warp so that the checks are visible on one side of the material. By the nineteenth century, highly glazed and made of a mixture of cotton and wool. Some enslaved women wore dresses made from this fabric on special occasions.

Calico, Calycot cotton cloth originally imported from India and named after its city of origin, Calicut, on the Malabar Coast. In England the name refers to a plain white cotton cloth; in the Americas, a printed cotton. Calico was popular during and after slavery and is used in Jamaican national dress or costume along with bandanna or madras fabric.

Cambay, Cambaye coarse cotton cloth made in India.

Chemise a woman's loose fitting, shirt like under-garment or type of dress with an unfitted waist. A smaller version was also made for young babies, and in some Afro-Jamaican religions, a red chemise is believed to keep evil spirits away.

Cotta, Catta a piece of cloth or dried banana leaves rolled and shaped like a donut and placed on the head to aid in the balancing of heavy loads. During slavery in Jamaica, some women signaled the end of a relationship by cutting their cotta into two and giving their estranged partner a half as an eternal end to the union. This is no longer done, but the cotta is still used when carrying heavy loads.

Crinoline originally from the Latin *-crinis* and the French *-crin* for hair, the material used in the 1840s for making stiffened petticoats worn by women to support the weight of other petticoats. Later this type was replaced with the cage-crinoline of quilted materials with whalebone and in 1857 flexible with steel hoop, which provided the requisite shape.

Crotchet an interlooped structure created with a hook.

Cut-pile embroidery a form of embroidery practised by the Kuba in the Congo. Women stitch softened raphia fibers through the surface of raphia cloth and then trim them with a short blade at an equivalent height above the surface of the textile, leaving a small u-shaped piece of embroidery in place. Also called *kasai* velvets.

Cutwork originally an appliqué of cut-out shapes, the name was transferred to embroidery in which parts of the background material are cut away. After the sixteenth century, it became a generic name for all forms of needle lace based on a woven ground.

Cutwork lace a form of lace constructed by the removal of threads from a woven background fabric. The threads left over are then manipulated with embroidery to enhance open spaces.

Daccasses calamanco woolen coats worn by some slave and freed women during Carnival and festive occasions in Jamaica. The style or design of these coats is not known.

Dagúilla Spanish term for lace-bark in the Dominican Republic. The term is also used in Cuba.

Damask term used in the Middle Ages to describe silk fabrics of elaborate designs worn in Damascus. Later the word was applied to fabrics made of wool, linen, or cotton, which displayed light and shade effects by use of contrasting shiny and matte surfaces. The shiny/matte appearance is created by jacquard weaving. Damask dresses were popular with some slave women and were worn during holidays and special occasions, such as carnivals and masquerades.

Delaine an abbreviation of the French, *mousseline de laine*, which is a lightweight dress fabric resembling woolen muslin. Originally of wool, later of wool and cotton.

Ells or Ell an old European measure of length, used for cloth, which varied from one country to another. For example, the British ell was 45 inches, but in Scotland it was 37 inches.

Fairtrade the concept developed in the Netherlands, where "Fairtrade" labels assure customers that the clothing product has met international Fairtrade standards and farmers were paid a premium above market value for their commodity.

Felt a non-woven fabric made by matting and condensing fibers together.

Fiber a long, thin, flexible object obtained from plants and animals. These fibers are spun to create a yarn.

Filament: a single continuous strand of fiber.

Flounce strips of material gathered or pleated, one edge of which was applied to the garment with the other left to flare. This was very fashionable on women's garments of the mid-eighteenth century.

Gauze a sheer, transparent fabric of cotton, silk, linen, or rayon. This was used as early as the Middle Ages. The fabric is often used for veils, hat, and clothing accessories and over dresses.

Green Chemistry concepts or principles that define the true ecological, ethical, and sustainable credentials of a raw material or object.

Guanilla another Spanish name for lace-bark in Cuba. Other Cuban terms include *dagüilla*, *dagüilla de loma*, *común*, and *palo de encaje*.

Guipure another name for the gimp or an open bobbin lace. The term came to mean laces with a tape foundation made without a ground mesh; the parts either touching or linked by occasional bars. In the nineteenth century, the term was used broadly for many types of laces with large patterns.

Hackling a process of combing out the short broken fibers or linters, as well as untangling the bundles for further processing and final spinning. This is done only with bast fibers, however, with cotton the process is called "combing" or "carding."

Hemp the generic name for the Cannabis family of plants. Hemp does make for a very good blend when woven together with cotton. Hemp can be made into fabrics as diverse as the finest lace to heavy industrial canvas.

Holland a type of linen from the Dutch province of Holland, which when bleached is called brown Holland and is to be distinguished from the "Holland cloth" or the "real wax" Dutch manufactured imitations of Indonesian batiks. Batiks were introduced into West Africa by the Dutch and today are very popular in many areas of Africa. The term Holland cloth was also used broadly to include manufactured cotton fabrics in Holland. Plain and striped Holland cloth was also distributed to some slaves on several plantations.

Jute also called *hessian*, one of the cheapest natural fibers to produce and the second most important vegetable fiber after cotton in terms of usage, global consumption production, and availability. Jute is long, shiny vegetable fiber and is not appropriate for garments. The plant is of the *Corchorus* genus and is native to tropical and sub-tropical regions.

Kemis embroidered, shirt-like smock worn by the Amhara or other Christian highland women of Ethiopia.

Kendal green woolen cloth named after its town of origin in Northwest England. This was also distributed to several slaves on a few Jamaican plantations.

Kente cloth ceremonial, strip-woven cloth of the Ashanti people in Ghana.

Kilmarnock woolen serge named after the town of its origin, Kilmarnock in Scotland. This type of fabric was used to make Kilmarnock caps, which were distributed to enslaved people on a few plantations in Jamaica. The style of these caps is not known.

Kimate deep-red bark-cloth highly desired in Buganda and obtained from the *Ficus natalensis* tree, commonly called natal fig.

Kyen kyen *Antiaris africana* tree, also called tsobo, from which bark-cloth was produced in Ghana amongst the Ashanti people.

Lace a fabric made of yarn or thread with ornamental open work, similar to web-like patterns. The fabric is often used for a variety of accessories to clothing and is often made with threads of flax, cotton, silk, gold, or silver and occasionally of hair or aloe fiber. The open work patterns or spaces in the fabric can be hand or machine made. There are three basic ways to make lace—with a needle called *Needle Point lace*, with bobbins to create *Bobbin lace* and by machinery or *Machine lace*, which can be imitations of both bobbin and needle point lace. There are numerous types of hand and machine made lace fabrics. Lace was first used by priests, then popularized in the late fifteenth and early sixteenth centuries when it was highly valued as a symbol of affluence and status. The origin of lace is an on-going topic of debate among scholars. The concept of lace or lacing evolved out of braiding.

Lace-bark or bark-lace A form of natural lace or linen obtained from the *lagetto* tree's bark. The bark was cut, soaked, and the thin plant fiber between the outer and inner core of the bark was then pulled out with the fingers. The material was dried in puffballs and then stretched in the sun to be naturally bleached white. The material was used as a substitute for manufactured lace and linen. Slaves, Maroons, and freed persons in Jamaica used the bark material to make clothes for daily attire. Both men and women also used it as mourning linen. The bark of the tree also had medicinal properties. Bark cloth industry was vibrant in Jamaica from the seventeenth century onwards and lasted in Jamaica until the early twentieth century. The industry eventually died, primarily due to overuse. Unfortunately, The Bark of Trees (sale prevention) Act of 1929, offered very little protection at the time. New evidence suggests that the tree once thought to be scarce is in fact thriving and on the verge of a comeback.

Lace knitting knitting with many holes or spaces in the design that leaves a lace-like effect. This is often considered the highest form of knitting.

Lace-mantilla a kind of shawl worn by women in Spain and later introduced into colonial Latin America. Many women used it to cover their head during religious services.

Lacis an ancient technique in which hand-made, knotted net is decorated with embroidery.

Lagetta lagetto the current botanical name of the lace-bark tree from which natural lace is obtained. Earlier botanical names were *Daphne lagetto*, *Lagetta lintearia*. Some of the common names for the tree in Jamaica include *alligator bark, sweet scented spurge laurel*, and *white bark*.

Leaf fibers produced from the strands of fibers that run through the leaf and are often considered a "hard fiber" as compared with bast fibers, which are soft. Not all leaf-fibers are "hard" such as piña fiber, which looks and feels like linen.

Linen a yarn and fabric considered the oldest textile in the world, made from the fibers of the stem of the flax plant (flax is also referred to as linseed). Linen can also be made from any bast fiber including hemp, ramie, and cannabis. Flax fibers are considered the strongest of all vegetable fibers and much stronger than cotton. The plant produces flowers, and the fruit capsules contain seeds, which are converted to linseed oil.

Machine-made Leavers lace lace made by mechanical methods rather than by hand. The earliest machine-made net was produced on knitting frames during the 1760s. This was followed by Heathcote's invention of the bobbin-machine in 1808. Machine-made patterned nets evolved, and from the 1840s onwards elaborate machine laces were made.

Madras a yarn-dyed plaid in red, blue, and white colors without borders. Different colors were preferred in different areas by consumers. Originally made in Madras and other parts of South India, the Portuguese were the first Europeans to trade this Indian fabric for more than 400 years and it became popular on several continents and by different names. It is called "Real Madras handkerchief" in India; "Indian Madras" in the United States and Britain; and in West Africa it is called *George* among the Igbo, and *Injiri* among the Kalabari of Nigeria, meaning "Real India" in their language. British textile manufacturers eventually copied this fabric and mass-produced several cheaper grades of Madras for the colonial markets. Plaid was very

fashionable during the Victorian era due to the royal family's Scottish heritage. Madras was imported into the Caribbean and other parts of the empire. There is no evidence to suggest that this fabric was popular among slaves in Jamaica but this is quite possible since several sources refer to the importation of Indian cottons. However, after slavery was abolished, Madras became very popular in Jamaica among freed women, especially those of the laboring and peasant classes. In the nineteenth century, striped or checked muslin, also named Madras, appeared. In the Caribbean, the term Madras cloth was merged with the term bandana to mean tie-head or head wrap, and was used by Jamaican women primarily as a form of tie-head.

Milliner and Millinery a place that makes hats, and the hat maker is called a milliner. Both terms come from the word *milaner*, an inhabitant of Milan, Italy; someone who traded articles of apparel, especially for bonnets made in Milan. Later the term came to be applied to the designer and decorator of ladies' hats and bonnets.

Mituba Bagandan term for the tropical fig tree.

Moraceae large plant family composed of fibrous trees and shrubs ideal for obtaining fibers for cloth production.

Mulberry one of the largest tree and shrub species suitable for bark-cloth; belongs to the *Moraceae* family of plants. The famous bark-cloth of the pacific is made most frequently from the paper mulberry [*Broussonetia papyrifera*]. The same plant family also includes many fig species.

Mundillo a popular form of handmade bobbin lace made in the small town of Moca, Puerto Rico.

Muslin named after the city of Mosul on the river Tigris in Iraq, where the fabric was made. Later, muslin became a general term covering a broad spectrum of fine cotton imported into Western Europe from India. Slave and freed women who could afford it or had access to refined fabrics did wear muslin dresses on holidays and special occasions.

Needle lace lace made using a needle and thread and the most flexible of the lace-making techniques. The technique can be very time consuming and refers to all laces made by the needle, not with bobbins.

Nyanda (also known as Chiwondo) bark-cloth processed from the *Brachystegia longifolia* tree in parts of southern Africa, such as Malawi and Zambia.

Ochre mud mixed with animal fat or water.

Olubugo bark-cloth in the Buganda Kingdom in Uganda.

Oznaburg, Osnaburgh, Oznaberg coarse, durable cotton in the plain weaves of flax and originally made in Osnabruck, Germany. This was considered the cheapest grade of cotton and was used in the gray for bagging and industrial purposes. This was the main or most common fabric distributed to enslaved Africans throughout the British Caribbean and parts of the US Antebellum South. The very poor and some peasants in some regions continued to wear Osnaburgh long after emancipation.

Penniston, Pennystone coarse, heavy woolen cloth originating at Penistone in Yorkshire and made into outdoor wear in the sixteenth to eighteenth centuries. This fabric was also distributed to slaves on several Jamaican estates, and by the late eighteenth century, it became as popular as Osnaburgh on some plantations.

Perpetuana, Perpets, Petuna a very durable, glossy surfaced woolen cloth made in England after the late sixteenth century. It was worn especially by the Puritans of the seventeenth century in England and later in the American colonies. Some Jamaican slaves received this fabric as part of their clothing rations.

Piña fibers obtained from the leaves of the pineapple plant. It is used primarily in the Philippines as a fabric. Strands are hand scraped from the leaves of the plant then hand knotted to form a continuous filament.

Raffia (*Raphia*) a leaf fiber obtained from the Raffia Palms native to the tropical regions of Africa, Madagascar, and Central and South America. The fibers are long and thin, and they absorb dye very well. Raffia has a stiff texture and is rarely used in clothing.

Ramie a very old fiber used for textiles dating back some 7,000 years. The fiber is very strong, but often blended with cotton and wool. Ramie has also been used as a substitute for linen. China is the largest producer.

Regis, John Francis Catholic Saint, born 1597 and died 1640, an ordained priest and a member of the Society of Jesus. He worked tirelessly for the poor, but is remembered primarily for his work with at-risk women and orphans. He helped many become trained lace-makers. St. John Francis Regis was canonized in 1738 and became known as the patron saint of lace-makers.

Renda di bilros bobbin lace introduced into Brazil by Portuguese colonists in the 1600s. Bobbin lace is the predominant type of lace made on Brazil's northeast coast. A homemade pillow stuffed with grass or even banana leaves forms the work place for lace makers. A collection of pins or cactus thorns holds the design in place on the pillow. Condomblé priestesses in the northeast coast of Brazil don elaborately made lace-blouses and hooped lace skirts on feast days and major religious festivals and rituals.

Satin a silk or rayon fabric of close texture with a glossy face and dull back. It has been worn for hundreds of years. The glossy texture is made by the long floats in the woven structure (satin weave) then pressing it between heated rollers enhances the sheen.

Scutching the process used for all bast vegetable fibers to separate the fiber from the stalk.

Spanish lace technique of weaving together groups of warps to create a pattern of holes.

Tapa, Kapa means "the beaten thing" in Hawaiian and is a common term for bark-cloth made across the Pacific from islands south east of Asia to Hawaii and Rapanui or Easter Island. It is not produced in all communities, but is widely made in Melanesia as well as in most parts of Polynesia. There are various types of tapa, some thick in texture, some varnished, and others fine and lightweight. In some cases, tapa is decorated, but can also be plain. The uses of tapa are culturally defined across the region from rituals to ceremonial exchanges and as symbols of wealth and status.

Tatting a lace-making process done with a tiny shuttle instead of a hook as in crochet or needles in knitting to create a form of lace. This type of lace is usually used in edging, collars, and doilies.

Threshing the process of beating or threshing the material in turbines to extract the long flax fibers from the epidermis, shive, and short fibers known as tow.

Tie-head a popular term used in Jamaica to describe a woman's headwrap.

Yarn count a form of measurement used in grading all woven fabrics according to the fineness of the fiber. In the United States, linen yarn is measured in LEA. The finer the yarn, the higher the LEA number.

Yoruba large ethnic group in Southwest Nigeria.

Yoruba lace a common form of decoration in Yoruba strip-woven cloth to introduce rows of holes along the length of the strip. The technique is akin to the Spanish lace. In Yoruba lace, lateral rows of four to six tiny holes are spaced every 5 cm (2 in.) or so down the strip. A supplementary warp thread is drawn from hole to hole down the length of the strip, thus creating an almost lacy effect.

NOTES

Introduction

1   Anne Hollander, *Seeing through Clothes* (Berkeley: University of California Press, 1978), xiii.

2   Guy Trebay, "Admit It. You Love It. It Matters." *New York Times*, Sept. 2, 2007.

3   Mary Ellen Roach and Joanne Bubolz Eicher, "The Language of Personal Adornment" in *The Fabrics of Culture: The Anthropology of Clothing and Adornment*, ed. Justine M. Cordwell and Ronald A. Schwarz (New York: Mouton Publishers, 1979), 7–21. See also Mary Ellen Roach-Higgins, Joanne B. Eicher, and Kim K.P. Johnson, eds, *Dress and Identity* (New York: Fairchild, 1995), 1–18.

4   Steeve O. Buckridge, *The Language of Dress, Resistance and Accommodation in Jamaica, 1760–1890* (Kingston: The University of the West Indies Press, 2004), 3–9 for some analysis of the function of dress. See also Roach-Higgins, Eicher, and Johnson, *Dress and Identity*, 1–18.

5   Virginia Woolf, *Orlando* (London: Wordsworth Edition, 2003), 91–92. See also the introduction in Hildi Hendrickson, ed., *Clothing and Difference: Embodied Identities in Colonial and Post-Colonial Africa* (Durham, NC: Duke University Press, 1996).

6   Barbara Burman, ed., *The Culture of Sewing: Gender, Consumption and Home Dressmaking* (New York: Berg, 1999), 3.

7   Londa Schiebinger, *Plants and Empire: Colonial Bioprospecting in the Atlantic World* (Cambridge, MA: Harvard University Press, 2004), 7, 73–91.

8   Anna-Karina Hermkens, *Engendering Objects: Dynamics of Barkcloth and Gender among the Maisin of Papua New Guinea* (Leiden: Sidestone Press, 2013), 25.

9   Steven Lubar and W. David Kingery, eds, *History from Things: Essays on Material Culture* (Washington, DC: Smithsonian Institution Press, 1993), xiii.

10   Jennie Batchelor and Cora Kaplan, eds, *Women and Material Culture, 1660–1830* (New York: Palgrave Macmillan, 2007), 1–2.

11   Hermkens, *Engendering Objects*, see the introduction, 17–25.

12   Ibid.

13   Maureen Daly Goggin and Beth Fowkes Tobin, eds, *Women and the Material Culture of Needlework and Textiles, 1750–1950* (Farnham, Surrey: Ashgate, 2009), 2–3.

14   Quoted in Hermkens, *Engendering Objects*, 25.

15 Henry Glassie, "Studying Material Culture Today" in *Living in a Material World: Canadian and American Approaches to Material Culture,* ed. Gerald L. Pocius (St. John's, Newfoundland: Institute of Social and Economic Research, 1991), 256.

16 Susan McClure, *The Midwest Gardener's Book of Lists* (New York: Taylor Trade Publishing, 1998), 30–31.

17 Margot M. Wright, *Barkcloth: Aspects of Preparation, Use, Deterioration, Conservation and Display* (London: Archetype Pub., 2001), 4.

18 Ibid.

19 Jennifer Newell, *Trading Nature: Tahitians, Europeans and Ecological Exchange,* (Honolulu: University of Hawaii Press, 2010), 2.

20 Ibid., 3.

21 Buckridge, *The Language of Dress*, 11–12.

22 Mrs. F. Nevill Jackson, *A History of Hand-Made Lace* (1900; reprint, Detroit: Tower Books, 1971), 1–21.

23 Clive Hallett and Amanda Johnston, *Fabric for Fashion: A Comprehensive Guide to Natural Fibres* (London: Lawrence King, 2010), 28–29.

24 Ibid., 128–32.

25 Roach-Higgins, Eicher, and Johnson, *Dress and Identity*, 7–8; Buckridge, *The Language of Dress*, 3.

26 Roach-Higgins, Eicher, and Johnson, *Dress and Identity*, 12, 19, 134–35.

27 Glassie, "Studying Material Culture Today," 256.

28 Stuart Hall, ed. *Representation: Cultural Representations and Signifying Practices* (London: Open University, 1997), 3.

29 Ibid.

30 Jennifer DeVere Brody, *Impossible Purities: Blackness, Femininity, and Victorian Culture* (Durham, NC: Duke University Press, 1998), 8–11, for a discussion on the importance of Black Feminist theory. See also Hazel Carby, *Reconstructing Womanhood* (Oxford: Oxford University Press, 1987), and Valerie Smith, *Self-Discovery and Authority in Afro-American Narrative* (Cambridge, MA: Harvard University Press, 1987).

31 Franklin W. Knight and Colin A. Palmer, eds, *The Modern Caribbean* (Chapel Hill: The University of North Carolina Press, 1989), 1–19.

Chapter 1

1 Popular proverb used by Gang-Gong.

2 Michael Howard, ed., *Bark-cloth in Southeast Asia* (Bangkok: White Lotus, 2006), 1.

3 Anne Leonard and John Terrel, *Patterns of Paradise: The Styles and Significance of Bark Cloth Around the World* (Chicago: Field Museum of Natural History, 1980), 10–14, for a discussion of bark-cloth around the world.

4 Ibid., 10–11. See also Mary J. Pritchard, *Siapo: Bark-cloth Art of Samoa* (Honolulu: Edward Enterprises, 1984), 1–10.

5 See also Colleen E. Kriger, *Cloth in West African History* (New York: AltaMira Press, 2013), 8–9.

6 Kriger, *Cloth in West African History*, 9.

7 Ibid., 53–74. See also Howard, *Bark-cloth in Southeast Asia*, chap. 1.

8 Ibid.

9 Ibid.

10 Serge Tcherkézoff, *"First Contacts" in Polynesia: The Samoan Case (1722–1884) Western Misunderstandings about Sexuality and Divinity* (Canberra: The Australian National University Press, 2004), 159–62.

11 Hall, *Representation*, 249.

12 George Yancey, *Black Bodies, White Gazes: The Continuing Significance of Race* (Lanham: Rowman & Littlefield, 2008), xii.

13 Yancey, *Black Bodies*, xii.

14 Brad Weiss, "Dressing at Death: Clothing, Time, and Memory in Buhaya, Tanzaia" in Hendrickson, *Clothing and Difference*, 133–40.

15 Diana Crane, *Fashion and Its Social Agendas: Class, Gender, and Identity in Clothing* (Chicago: University of Chicago Press, 2000), 1–5.

16 Leonard and Terrell, *Patterns of Paradise*, 10–15.

17 Brigham, *Ka Hana Kapa*, 1–3. The broad use of the term tapa can be misleading as many Polynesian islands had their own indigenous name for bark-cloth. In Tahiti, bark-cloth was commonly called "ahu" while in Tonga, it was referred to as "hiapo," and in Samoa as "siapo," and "masi" in Fiji.

18 Margot Wright, *Barkcloth*, 29.

19 Ibid.

20 Howard, *Bark-cloth in Southeast Asia*, 1.

21 Rober Neich and Mick Pendergrast, *Pacific Tapa* (Albany, Auckland: David Bateman Ltd., 1997), chap. 1.

22 Brigham, *Ka Hana Kapa,* 6–7.

23 Ibid. Banks had accompanied Captain Cook on his first voyage to Polynesia in 1768–1771.

24 Douglas Oliver, *Return to Tahiti: Bligh's Second Breadfruit Voyage* (Melbourne: Melbourne University Press, 1988), 112–13.

25 Ibid., 12.

26 Tcherkézoff, *"First Contacts" in Polynesia*, 161; Leonard and Terrell, *Patterns of Paradise*, 17.

27 Ghanaian proverb in Twi: The person closest to you is the one who can hurt you most.

28 Buckridge, *The Language of Dress*, 19–20; Duncan Clarke, *The Art of African Textiles* (San Diego, Thunder Bay, 1997), 8.

29 Rev. R.H. Stone, *In Africa's Forest and Jungle: Or Six Years Among the Yorubans* (New York: Fleming H. Revell, 1899), 20–21, 23.

30 Juliet E.K. Walker, *The History of Black Business in America*, Vol. 1 to 1865 (Chapel Hill: The University of North Carolina, 2009), 11–12.

31 Ibid.

32 Ibid.

33 Kriger, *Cloth in West African History*, 1–3.

34 Ibid., 1.

35 Ibid.

36 Clarke, *The Art of African Textiles,* 8–45. See also Gillow, *African Textiles* for more descriptive details. Metal thread embroidery is popular throughout Ethiopia and used to decorate kemis and trousers.

37 Margot Wright, *Barkcloth.*

38 Kriger, *Cloth in West African History*, 4–6, 34–51; Gillow, *African Textiles*, 19, 181; Clarke, *The Art of African Textiles*, 8–15.

39 Roy Seiber, "African Textiles," *Handweaver and Craftsman* 23, 4 (November/December 1972), 9–14.

40 Ibid.

41 Venny Nakazibwe, *Bark-cloth of the Baganda People of Southern Uganda: A Record of Continuity and Change from the Late Eighteenth Century to the Early Twenty-First Century*, PhD. Thesis, School of the Arts, Middlesex University, 2005, 38. See also Martin, Claude. *The Rainforests of West Africa: Ecology, Threats, Conservation* (Basel; Boston: Birkhäuser Verglag, 1991), 12–16.

42 Margot Wright, *Barkcloth*, 1; Martin, *The Rainforests of West Africa*, 12–16.

43 Brink, *Fibres*, 65–66.

44 Douglas Oliver, ed., *Return to Tahiti: Bligh's Second Breadfruit Voyage*, 4.

45 Gayle Caldwell, "Breadfruit: Captain Bligh's Bounty," in Special Section: Insiders' Guide to the Caribbean Islands. *An International Magazine* (December 1988), 33.

46 Roy Seiber, "African Textiles," in *Handweaver and Craftman*, 10–11.

47 Gillow, *African Textiles*, 181–82.

48 Akosua Adorna Perbi, *A History of Indigenous Slavery in Ghana from the 15th Century to the 19th Century* (Legon-Accra, Ghana: Sub-Saharan Pub. & Traders, 2004), 92.

49 John Beecham, *Asantee and the Gold Coast* (1841; reprint, New York: Johnson Reprint Corporation, 1970), 147.

50 Kwamina B. Dickson, *A Historical Geography of Ghana* (Cambridge: Cambridge University Press, 1969), 93–95.

51 Ibid.

52 Brink, *Fibres,* 65–66; Margot Wright, *Bark Cloth*, 2.

53 Dickson, *A Historical Geography of Ghana*, 93–95.

54 Albert J. Constantine, Jr., and Harry J. Hobbs, *Know your Woods: A Complete Guide to Trees, Woods, and Veneers* (New York: Lyons Press, 2005), 144.

55 Margot Wright, *Barkcloth*, 6–8.

56 Ibid.

57 Dickson, *A Historical Geography of Ghana*, 94; Margot Wright, *Barkcloth*, 6–8; John Picton and J. Mack, *African Textiles* (London: British Museum Publication, 1979), 43.

58 Nakazibwe, *Bark-cloth Baganda People*, 80–83; Wright, *Barkcloth*, 1.

59 Peter Haggett, *Encyclopedia of World Geography* (Singapore: Marshall Cavendish, 2001), vol. 17, 2375; David Conrad, *Empires of Medieval West Africa: Ghana, Mali, and Songhay* (London: Chelsea House Pub., 2009), 79.

60 Margot Wright, *Barkcloth*, 8.

61 Margot Wright, *Barkcloth*, 2.

62 Nakazibwe, *Bark-cloth Baganda People*, 85–96.

63 Jerom Merolla da Sorrento, "A Voyage to Congo and Several Other Countries Chiefly in Southern Africk," in *A General Collection of the Best and Most Interesting Voyages and Travels in All Parts of the World*, ed. John Pickerton (London: Longman, Hurst, Rees, and Brown Pub., 1814), vol. 16, 195–236, 316.

64 Margot Wright, *Barkcloth*, 2.

65 Bep Oliver-Bever, *Medicinal Plants in Tropical West Africa* (Cambridge: Cambridge University Press, 1988), 27, 356. See also E.G. Achigan-Dako and M. Brink, eds, *Fibres (Plant Resource of Tropical Africa 16)* (London: Earthprint, 2012), 65–66.

66 Brien A. Meilleur, Richard R. Jones, C. Alan Titchenal, and Alvin S. Huang, *Hawaiian Breadfruit; Ethnobotany, Nutrition and Human Ecology* (Honolulu: CTAHR Publication, 2004), 4–5; see also Irene J. Taafaki, *Traditional Medicine of the Marshall Islands, the Women, the Plants, the Treatments* (Colombo, Sri Lanka; IPS Publications, 2006), 167.

67 Oliver-Bever, *Medicinal Plants*, 4–5.

68 Hermkens, *Engendered Objects*, 107.

69 Patricia L. Howard and Gorettie Nabanoga, "'Are there Customary Rights to Plants?' An Inquiry among Baganda, (Uganda) with Special Attention to Gender," *World Development* 35, 9 (2007), 1542–63.

70 Ibid.

71 R.S. Rattray, *Religion and Art in Ashanti* (Oxford: Oxford University Press, 1927), 220.

72 S.R. Mishra, *Morphology of Plants* (Delhi: Discovery Publishing Pvt. Ltd., 2004), 180.

73 Claire Robertson, "Ga Women and Socioeconomic Change in Accra, Ghana," in *Women in Africa: Studies in Social and Economic Change*, ed. Nancy J. Hafkin and Edna Bay (Stanford: Stanford University Press, 1976), 111–35.

74 Hall, *Representation*, 3.

75 Quoted in David Watts, *The West Indies: Patterns of Development, Culture and Environmental Change since 1492* (Cambridge: University of Cambridge, 1987), 1.

76 Atkinson, Lesley-Gail, ed., *The Earliest Inhabitants: The Dynamics of the Jamaican Taíno* (Kingston: University of the West Indies Press, 2006), 7.

77 Fatima Bercht, Estrellita Brodsky, John Alan Farmer, and Dicey Taylor, *Taíno: Pre-Columbian Art and Culture from the Caribbean* (New York: Monacelli Press, 1997), 34–35.

78 Ibid., 18.

79 Ibid.

80 Ibid.

81 Kathleen A. Deagan and José María Cruxent, *Columbus's Outpost among the Taínos: Spain and America at La Isabela, 1493–1498* (New Haven: Yale University Press, 2013), 27.

82   Ibid.

83   Ibid., 27.

84   Ibid., 27.

85   Sonya Lipsett-Rivera, "Clothing in Colonial Spanish America," in *Iberia and the Americas: Culture, Politics, and History (Transatlantic Relations)*, ed. John Michael Francis (Santa Barbara: ABC-CLIO, 2005), 240.

86   Deagan and Cruxent, *Columbus's Outpost,* 27.

87   Bercht et al., *Taíno*, 18.

88   Deagan and Cruxent, *Columbus's Outpost*, 25.

89   Ibid.

90   Atkinson, *The Earliest Inhabitants*, 6.

91   Ibid., 2.

92   William F. Keegan, "No Man (or Woman) Is an Island: Elements of Taíno Social Organization," in *The Indigenous People of the Caribbean*, ed. Samuel Wilson (Gainesville, FL: University Press of Florida, 1998), 113.

93   Bercht et al., *Taíno*, 20.

94   Keegan, "No Man . . .," 113.

95   Ibid.

96   Ibid.

97   Deagan and Cruxent, *Columbus's Outpost*, 32.

98   Ignacio Olazagasti, "The Material Culture of the Taíno Indians," in Wilson, *The Indigenous People*, 136.

99   Beth Fowkes Tobin, *Picturing Imperial Power: Colonial Subjects in Eighteenth-Century British Painting* (Durham, NC: Duke University Press, 1999), 139–45.

100 Ibid.

101 Lipsett-Rivera, "Clothing in Colonial Spanish America," 240.

102 Bercht et al., *Taíno*, 29.

103 Roach-Higgins, Eicher, and Johnson, *Dress and Identity*, 13.

104 Lipsett-Rivera, "Clothing in Colonial Spanish America," 240.

105 Perhaps the Taínos used cotton, but it is not a good material for this use. Hemp is far better in salt water as it does not mold or rot as fast as cotton.

106 Olazagasti, "The Material Culture of the Taíno," 135–37.

107 Inga Clendinnen, "Yucatec Maya Women and the Spanish Conquest: Role and Ritual in Historical Reconstruction," *Journal of Social History* 15, 3, Special Issue on the History of Love (Spring 1982), 429.

108 Bartolomé De Las Casas, *An Account, Much Abbreviated, of the Destruction of the Indies*, ed. Franklin W. Knight, trans. Andrew Hurley (Indianapolis: Hackett, 2003), 5.

109 Irving Rouse, *The Taínos: Rise and Decline of the People Who Greeted Columbus.* (New Haven: Yale University Press, 1992), 17.

110 Leonard and Terrell, *Patterns of Paradise*, 44.

111 Zachary S. Rogers, "Nomenclatural Notes on American Thymelaeaceae," *Novon: A Journal of Botanical Nomenclature* 20, 4 (2010), 448–62; see also Richard Evans

Schultes and Robert F. Raffauf, *The Healing Forest: Medicinal and Toxic Plants of the Northwest Amazonia* (Portland, OR: Dioscorides Press, 1990), 9–37.

112 Leonard and Terrell, *Patterns of Paradise*, 42.

113 Rouse, *The Taínos: Rise and Decline*, 17.

114 Ibid.

115 Bercht et al., *Taíno*, 23, 24, 31. See images of wood carvings.

116 Ibid., 170.

117 Ibid.

118 Ibid.

119 Ibid., 3.

120 Atkinson, *The Earliest Inhabitants*, 105.

121 Ibid.

122 Ibid., 105–108.

123 Schiebinger, *Plants and Empire*, 75–76.

124 Ibid., 104.

125 Atkinson, *The Earliest Inhabitants*, 50.

126 Olazagasti, "The Material Culture of the Taíno," 133.

127 Sven Lovén, *Origins of the Tainan Culture, West Indies* (Göteborg: Elanders, 1935), 402.

128 Sir Hans Sloane, *A Voyage to the Island of Madera, Barbados, Nieves, St. Christopher and Jamaica, with the Natural History of the Herbs and Trees, Four-Footed Beasts, Fishes, Birds, Insects, Reptiles, Etc. of the Last of Those Islands.* 2 vols. London: B.M., 1707–25, vol. 1, 131.

129 Edward Long. *The History of Jamaica or General Survey of the Ancient and Modern State of the Island: with Reflections on Its Situation Settlements, Inhabitants, Climate, Products, Commerce, Laws and Government.* vol. 3 (London: T. Lownudes, 1774), 748.

130 "Scenes of Hispaniola," James Hamilton, ed., *Excelsior: Helps to Progress in Religion, Science, and Literature* (London: James Nisbet and Co. Berners St., 1856), 31–38. The author is not known; the Indian retreat was among a few that survived.

131 Ibid.

132 Ibid.

133 Ibid.

134 De Las Casas, *Destruction of the Indies*, portrays the horrifying experience of Taíno men and women under Spanish colonial rule and how Taíno culture was destroyed.

135 Rouse, *The Taínos: Rise and Decline*, 162, 138–68. The author provides an analysis of the Spanish conquest and the re-peopling of former Taíno habitats by enslaved Africans.

136 Rex Nettleford, *Caribbean Cultural Identity: The Case of Jamaica* (Kingston: Ian Randle, 2003), 2–3.

137 Verene A. Shepherd, Ahmed Reid, Cavell Francis, and Kameika Murphy, *Jamaica and the Debate over Reparation for Slavery: A Discussion Paper Prepared by the Jamaica*

National Bicentenary Committee (Kingston: Pelican Publishers, 2012), 1–10; Barry Higman, *Slave Populations of the British Caribbean 1807–1834* (Kingston: The Press, University of the West Indies, 1995), 128.

138 Edward Brathwaite, *Contradictory Omens: Cultural Diversity and Integration in the Caribbean* (Kingston: Savacou, 1985), 13.

139 Buckridge, *The Language of Dress*, 26–27.

140 Buckridge, *The Language of Dress*, 26. See also Robin Law and Paul E. Lovejoy, eds, *The Biography of Mohommah Garbo Baquaqua: His Passage from Slavery to Freedom in Africa and America* (Princeton: Markus Weiner, 2001), 153.

141 Buckridge, *The Language of Dress*, 26–27.

142 C.L.R. James, *The Black Jacobins* (New York: Vintage Books, 1989), 8.

143 Brathwaite, *Contradictory Omens*, 13; see also Franklin W. Knight and Colin A. Palmer, *The Modern Caribbean* (Chapel Hill: The University of North Carolina Press, 1989), 6–8, for more on the slave trade and demographics.

144 Philip Sherlock and Hazel Bennett, *The Story of the Jamaican People* (Kingston: Ian Randle Publishers, 1998), 133–49.

145 Buckridge, *The Language of Dress*, 26–27.

146 Quoted in Edward Brathwaite, "Jamaican Slave Society, A Review," *Race & Class* 9, 3 (1968), 331–42.

147 Buckridge, *The Language of Dress*, 26–27.

148 Ibid., 9.

149 Higman, *Slave Populations of the British Caribbean*, 128; Brathwaite, "Jamaican Slave Society," 331–42.

150 Buckridge, *The Language of Dress*, 49.

151 Ibid.

152 Barry Higman, *Slave Population and Economy in Jamaica, 1807–1834* (Cambridge: Cambridge University Press, 1976), 18, 36–41.

153 Barbara Bush, *Slave Women in Caribbean Society, 1650–1838* (Kingston: Heinemann, 1990), 33–40.

154 Ibid.

155 Douglas V. Armstrong, *The Old Village and Great House: An Archaeological and Historical Examination of Drax Hall, St Ann's Bay, Jamaica* (Urbana: University of Illinois Press, 1990), 178.

156 Robert Farris Thompson, *Flash of the Spirit: African and Afro-American Art and Philosophy* (New York: Vintage Books, 1983), 216.

157 Ibid.

158 Matthew Gregory Lewis, *Journal of a West-Indian Proprietor: Kept During a Residence on the Island of Jamaica* (London: John Murray, 1834), 35–36.

159 Bryan Edwards, *The History, Civil and Commercial, of the British Colonies in the West Indies. 3 vols. 2nd ed.* (London: J. Stockdale, 1796–1801), 2, 152.

160 Buckridge, *The Language of Dress*, 86–87

161 Bush, *Slave Women in Caribbean Society*, 47.

162 Jill H. Casid, *Sowing Empire: Landscape and Colonization* (Minneapolis: University of Minnesota Press, 2005), 199.

163 Lorna Elaine Simmonds, "The Afro-Jamaican and the Internal Marketing System: Kingston, 1780–1834," in *Jamaica in Slavery and Freedom: History, Heritage and Culture*, eds Kathleen E.A. Monteith and Glen Richards (Kingston: The University of the West Indies Press, 2002), 275.

164 Jillian E. Galle, "Assessing the Impacts of Time, Agricultural Cycles, and Demography on the Consumer Activities of Enslaved Men and Women in Eighteenth Century Jamaica and Virginia," in *Out of Many One People: The Historical Archaeology of Colonial Jamaica*, James A. Delle, Mark W. Hauser, and Douglas V. Armstrong, eds, (Tuscaloosa: The University of Alabama Press, 2011), 213; Bush, *Slave Women in Caribbean Society*, 47.

165 *Out of Many, One People: The Historical Archaeology of Colonial Jamaica (Caribbean Archaeology and Ethnohistory)*, James A. Delle, Mark W. Hauser, and Douglas V. Armstrong, eds (Tuscaloosa: The University of Alabama Press, 2011), 12–13.

166 Simmonds, "The Afro-Jamaican and the Internal Marketing," 276.

167 Ibid.

168 Bush, *Slave Women in Caribbean Society*, 49.

169 Ibid.

170 Edwards, *The History of the West Indies*, 2: 162.

171 John Stewart, *An Account of Jamaica and its Inhabitants* (London: Longman, 1808), 207.

172 Buckridge, *The Language of Dress*, 129.

173 Ibid.

174 Long, *The History of Jamaica*, 2, 493.

175 *Invoices, Accounts, Sales of Sugar etc. Jamaica Windsor Lodge and Paisley Estates (1833–37)*, Manuscript collection, 32 NLJ.

176 Neville Hall, *Slave Society in the Danish West Indies: St Thomas, St John, and St. Croix*, ed. B.W. Higman (Baltimore: Johns Hopkins University Press, 1992), 116, 149.

177 Ibid.

178 Edwards, *The History of the West Indies*, 602–16. Official imports do not include lace.

179 Buckridge, *The Language of Dress*, 30.

180 Ibid., 31.

181 Long, *The History of Jamaica*, 2: 280.

182 Bernard Martin Senior, *Jamaica, As It Was, As It Is, and As It May Be* (New York: Negro Universities Press, 1969), 29.

183 Buckridge, *The Language of Dress*, 46.

184 Ibid.

185 Ibid., 46.

186 Ibid.

187 Buckridge, *The Language of Dress*, 47.

188 Ibid.

189 Ibid.

190 Edner A. Jeanty and O. Carl Brown, *Paròl Granmoun: Haitian Popular Wisdom* (Port-au-Prince: Editions Learning Center, 1976). Quote in Joel Timyan, *Bwa Yo: Important Trees of Haiti* (Washington, DC: South-East Consortium for International Development, 1996), 335.

191 C.D. Adams, *Flowering Plant of Jamaica* (Kingston: The University of the West Indies Press, 1972), 484. There are three species of the *Lagetta* genus. Some scientists list a sub-specie of the group as a fourth. The other two species are *Lagetta wrightiana* and *Lagetta valenzuelana*, both are endemic to Cuba.

192 Ibid., 484.

193 Dr. Juan Tomás Roig y Mesa, *Diccionario Botanico de Nombres Vulgares Cubanos* (La Habana; Editorial Cientifico—Tecnica, 1988), 363–64; Correspondence, Sergio Valdés Bernal, July 29, 2014.

194 The term *guanilla* is often confused or used erroneously to identify lace-bark. *Guanilla*, also called *guana*, is the common name for the *Lagetta valenzuelana* species in the *Lagetta* genus. This species is endemic to Cuba.

195 Alain Henri Liogier, *La Flora de la Española*, 1 (San Pedro de Macorís: Universidad Central Del Este, 1982), 215–16; Liogier provides the names of the tree in Haiti and Cuba. Common names in Jamaica obtained during interviews, Accompong Town, July 2003 and July 2014.

196 W.R. Gerard, "Origin of the Word Lagetto," *American Anthropologist, New Series* 14, 2 (April–June 1912), 404.

197 Sergio Valdes Bernal, Cuban Linguists, correspondence, July 29, 2014.

198 Georgina Pearman and Hans D.V. Prendergast, "Items from the Lacebark Tree [Lagetta lagetto (W. Wright), Nash: Thymelaeaceae] from the Caribbean," *Economic Botany* 54, 1 (January–March 2000), 4–6.

199 Long, *The History of Jamaica*, 3, 747.

200 Adams, *Flowering Plants of Jamaica*, 454.

201 Long, *The History of Jamaica*, 3, 747. Long states where the tree was found; however, it grew in a much wider range along the central axis of the island, including areas such as the Vale in St. Catherine. Figure 1.6 shows where specimens were found in recent years.

202 G.F. Asprey and R.G. Robbins, "The Vegetation of Jamaica," *Ecological Monographs* 23, 4 (October 1953), 384–85.

203 Asprey and Robbins, "Vegetation of Jamaica," 384.

204 Ibid.

205 Sir William Jackson Hooker, David Prain, Otto Stapf, *Curtis's Botanical Magazine*, vol. 76 (London: Reeve & Benham, 1850), 4503.

206 Ibid.

207 Sherlock and Bennett, *The Story of the Jamaican People*, 133–49.

208 See Long, *The History of Jamaica*, B: 747–48. Long refers to the "wild negroes" making lace-bark; "wild negroes" were the Maroons.

209 Hooker et al., "*Lagetto lintearis*; Jamaica Lace-bark," *Curtis's Botanical Magazine* 76, 4502. See also Asprey and Robbins, "Vegetation of Jamaica," 383.

210 Field research in Cuba, summers of 2003 and 2014 at the Instituto de Ecologia y
     Sistematica. See also Victor R. Fuentes Fiallo, "Apuntes para la Flora Economica de
     Cuba 1: Especies Productoras de Fibra," *Revista del Jardin Botanico Nacional* (*La
     Habana*) XX (1999), 57–81.
211 Asprey and Robbins, "Vegetation of Jamaica," 369.

Chapter 2

1 See Arthur MacGregor, ed., *Sir Hans Sloane: Collector, Scientist, Antiquary, Founding
   Father of the British Museum* (London: British Museum Press, 1994), 47.
2 Geoff Quilley and Kay Dian Kriz, eds, *An Economy of Colour: Visual Culture and
   the Atlantic World, 1660–1830* (Manchester: Manchester University Press, 2003),
   87–89.
3 Christopher P. Iannini, *Fatal Revolutions: Natural History, West Indian Slavery and
   the Routes of American Literature* (Durham, NC: The University of North Carolina
   Press, 2012), 9.
4 Ibid., 9.
5 Ibid., 19–21.
6 Schiebinger, *Plants and Empire*, 7, 15, 75.
7 Ibid., 75–80.
8 Ibid., 76.
9 Pratik Chakrabarti, "Sloane's Travels: A Colonial History of Gentlemanly Science," in
   From Books to Bezoars: Sir Hans Sloane and His Collections, eds Alison Walker, Arthur
   MacGregor, and Michael Cyril William Hunter (London: British Library, 2012), 76.
10 Watts, *Patterns of Development, Cultures and Environmental Change*, 219–32.
11 Susan Scott Parrish, *American Curiosity: Culture of Natural History in the Colonial
   British Atlantic World* (Durham, NC: University of North Carolina Press, 2006), 7–9.
12 Ibid.
13 Ibid.
14 Ibid.
15 Kay Dian Kriz, *Slavery, Sugar, and the Culture of Refinement* (New Haven: Yale
   University Press, 2008), 4–5.
16 Fowkes Tobin, *Picturing Imperial Power*, 1–3.
17 Ibid.
18 Ibid.
19 Brochures, Royal College of Physicians; "A Programme of Events Celebrating the 350th
   Anniversary of the Birth of Sir Hans Sloane and the Founding of the Royal Society,"
   7 June–30 September 2010; "Trail around the Medicinal Garden of the Royal College
   of Physicians," Trail 1 and 2, 2010.
20 Ibid.
21 The term has been used in several early sources and as late as 1968. See Inez K. Sibley,
   "Jamaica's Wonder Tree," *Jamaican Gleaner*, June 6, 1968.

22 Sloane, *Voyage to the Islands*, II, 32. Sloane was familiar with bark-cloth and made reference to a mangrove tree in the Congo whose bark, when beaten and stretched, was used for clothing like the Jamaican lace-bark.

23 Early historians commented on the abundance of the tree. See Sloane, *Voyage to the Islands*, II, 22; Long, *The History of Jamaica*, III, 748; Brown, *The Civil and Natural History of Jamaica*, 371.

24 Mary Mapes Dodge, *St. Nicholas: an Illustrated Magazine for Young Folks* 13, part 3 (May 1886–Oct. 1886), New York: Century, 1886.

25 William Wright, MD, *Memoir of the Late William Wright, MD with Extracts from His Correspondence and Selection of His Papers on Medical and Botanical Subjects* (Edinburgh: William Blackwood, 1787), 207.

26 Sloane, *Voyage to the Islands*, II, 22.

27 Hollander, *Seeing through Clothes*, 23, 29, 30–31.

28 Chakrabarti, "Sloane's Travels," 76–77.

29 Albert Memmi, *The Colonizer and the Colonized* (Boston: Beacon Press, 1965), 90–93.

30 James Robertson, "Knowledgeable Readers: Jamaican Critiques of Sloane's Botany," in *From Books to Bezoars: Sir Hans Sloane and His Collection,* edited by Alison Walker, Arthur MacGregor and Michael Hunter (London: British Library, 2012), 80–89.

31 Sloane, *Voyage to the Islands*, II, 22.

32 Wright, *Memoir*, 207.

33 "Our Local Hero," pamphlet of *The Royal College of Physicians*, 2010.

34 Ibid.

35 Long, *History of Jamaica*, 2010.

36 F. Nevill Jackson, *Old Handmade Lace: A Dictionary of Lace* (New York: Dover, 1987), 2; the author's real name is Emily Nevill Jackson.

37 Ibid., 2–3.

38 Ibid.

39 Jackson, *Old Handmade Lace*, 2–3.

40 Ibid.

41 Eleanor Page. *Lace Making: The Home Craft of All Ages* (New York: Hewlett Press, 2011), 1–4.

42 Ibid.

43 Ibid., 5.

44 Jackson, *Old Handmade Lace*, 2–3.

45 Ibid.

46 Ibid.; "In Fine Style: The Art of Tudor and Stuart Fashion," Exhibit at Queens Gallery, in Ingrid Seward, ed., *Majesty* 34, 5, 21–25; Charles Kendall Adams, L.L.D. *Johnson's Universal Cyclopaedia*, vol. 5 (New York: A.J. Johnson Company, 1895), 9, 45.

47 Aileen Ribeiro, "Dress in the Early Modern Period, c. 1500–1780," in *The Cambridge History of Western Textiles,* vol. 1, ed. David Jenkins (Cambridge: Cambridge University Press, 2003), 661. Discussion about the beginning of fashion.

48 Jackson, *Old Handmade Lace*, 78–80.

49 Ibid.

50 Ibid.

51 Ibid.

52 Marian Powys, *Lace and Lace-making* (New York: Dover, 1953), 10.

53 Seward, *Majesty*, 21–25.

54 Patricia Wardle, *Victorian Lace* (New York: Frederick A. Praeger, 1969), 26–32.

55 Ibid.

56 Katrina Honeyman, *Women, Gender, and Industrialization in England, 1700–1870* (New York: Palgrave Macmillan, 2000), 21–29.

57 Hollander, *Seeing through Clothes*, 213.

58 Kathryn A. Sloan, *Women's Role in Latin America and the Caribbean* (Santa Barbara: Greenwood, 2011), 5.

59 Sr. Stephen Maria Miles, FMS, *History of the Franciscan Missionary Sisters of Our Lady of Perpetual Help of Jamaica* (Kingston: The Franciscan Missionary Sisters, 1996), 91.

60 Susan Migden Sucolow, *Women of Colonial Latin America* (Cambridge: Cambridge University Press, 2000), 106.

61 Laura Morelli, "The Art of Brazilian Lace," *National Geographic*, Traveler, Feb. 2008.

62 Henry John Drewal, *Beads, Body, and Soul: Art and Light in The Yoruba Universe* (Los Angeles: UCLA Fowler Museum of Cultural History, 1998), 188.

63 Kimberly Randall, "The Traveler's Eye: Chinas Poblanas and European-inspired Costume in Postcolonial Mexico," in *The Latin American Fashion Reader*, ed. Regina A. Root (London: Berg, 2005), 44–51.

64 Ellen Fernandez-Sacco, "Mundillo and Identity: The Revival and Transformation of Handmade Lace in Puerto Rico" in *Women and the Material Culture of Needlework and Textiles*, 149–54.

65 Harvey M. Feinberg, *Africans and Europeans in West Africa: Elminans and Dutchmen on Gold Coast During the Eighteenth Century* (Philadelphia: The American Philosophical Society, 1989), 135.

66 Jacqueline A. Gibbons, "Ladies, Lace-making and Imprisonment," *Visual Sociology* 13, 2 (1998), 91–103.

67 H.J. Cadbury, "Conditions in Jamaica in 1687," *Jamaica Historical Review*, 3, 2 (March 1959), 54.

68 Joan Dayan, *Haiti, History and the Gods* (Berkeley: University of California Press, 1995), 64.

69 Philip Wright, *Lady Nugent's Journal of Her Residence in Jamaica from 1801 to 1805* (Kingston: The University of the West Indies, 2002), 17–20.

70 Wright, *Lady Nugent's Journal*, 21 October, 1801, 48.

71 Cynric R. Williams, *A Tour Through the Island of Jamaica from the Western to the Eastern End in the Year 1823* (London: Hunt and Clark, 1826), 3.

72 Buckridge, *The Language of Dress*, 124–25.

73 Ibid.

74 Mary Ellen Roach and Joanne Bubolz Eicher, "The Language of Personal Adornment" in *The Fabrics of Culture*, 9.

75 Richard L. Bushman, *The Refinement of America: Persons, Houses, Cities* (New York: Vintage Books, 1993), 70.

76 Jackson, *Old Handmade Lace*, 69–70.

77 Buckridge, *The Language of Dress*, 101–104.

78 Ibid.

79 Historical sources discuss the extravagant headdress of women in the Eastern Caribbean, but were these images exaggerated?; Buckridge, *The Language of Dress*, 84–96.

80 Fowkes Tobin, *Picturing Imperial Power*, 138–73 for a discussion on the work of Brunias' work.

81 Tim Barringer, Gillian Forrester, and Barbaro Martinez-Ruiz, *Art and Emancipation in Jamaica: Isaac Mendes Belisario and his World* (New Haven: Yale University Press, 2007).

82 Hilary Beckles, "Crop Over Fetes and Festivals in Caribbean Slavery." In *In the Shadow of the Plantation* ed. Alvin O. Thompson, 246–63. Kingston: Ian Randle, 2002, 248–52; See also Richard Burton, *Afro-Creole: Power, Opposition, and Play in the Caribbean.* Ithaca: Cornell University Press, 1997, 169.

83 Lewis, *Journal of a West-Indian Proprietor*, 53.

84 Buckridge, *The Language of Dress*, 91–102; Judith Bettelheim, "The Afro-Jamaican Jonkonnu Festival: Playing the Forces and Operating the Cloth" (PhD. Diss., Yale University, 1979), 2–10.

85 Lewis, *Journal of a West-Indian Proprietor*, 53.

86 NLJ, explanation: It is ridiculous to contemplate an adult fitting comfortably into a child's shirt. One can understand that when we are in trouble, we appreciate whatever help we can get to extricate ourselves, even if under normal circumstances we would have thought such help woefully inadequate.

87 J. Stewart, *A View of The Past and Present State of the Island of Jamaica with Remarks on the Moral and Physical Condition of the Slaves and the Abolition of Slavery in the Colonies* (Edinburgh: Oliver and Boyd, 1823), 269.

88 Barry Higman, *Slave Populations of the British Caribbean*, 224–25.

89 A. C. Carmichael, *Domestic Manners and Social Conditions of the White, Colored and Negro Population of the West Indies.* 2 vols (London: Whittaker, Treacher, 1833), 155.

90 McDonald, Roderick A. *The Economy and Material Culture of Slaves: Goods and On the Slave Plantations of Jamaica and Louisiana* (Baton Rouge: Louisiana State University Press, 1993), 113–19. See also *Harmony Hall Estate Account Book*, MS 1652, vol. 1, NLJ.

91 Bush, *Slave Women in Caribbean Society*, 61.

92 Douglas Hall, *In Miserable Slavery: Thomas Thistlewood in Jamaica, 1750–80* (London: Macmillan, 1989), 231.

93 Theodore Foulks, *Eighteen Months in Jamaica with Recollections of the Late Rebellion* (London: Whittaker, Treacher and Arnott, 1833), 107.

94 Hall, *In Miserable Slavery*, 231.

95 Bush, *Slave Women in Caribbean Society*, 17.

96 Lewis, *Journal of a West-Indian Proprietor*, 125.

97 Ibid., 343.

98 Hilary Beckles, "Sex and Gender in the Historiography of Caribbean Slavery," in *Engendering History: Caribbean Women in Historical Perspective* eds. Verene Shepherd, Bridget Brereton, and Barbara Bailey (Kingston: Ian Randle Publishers, 1995), 137.

99 The knowledge of making hammocks was a skill that was passed on to Africans by the early inhabitants.

100 Long, *The History of Jamaica*, 3, 736–858.

101 See Long, *The History of Jamaica*, 693–95.

102 Sloane, *A Voyage to the Island of Madera*, vol. 2, 22–23. Sloane does not state the date of the governor's presentation of the cravat to the king.

103 Long, *History of Jamaica*, 3, 858; see also Sloane, *A Voyage to the Island of Madera*, 2, 22–23. Long and several early sources makes reference to the Spaniards using lace-bark for ropes.

104 Ibid. Long makes reference to Maroon's involvement. They were also called "wild negroes."

105 Long, *History of Jamaica*, 3, 858; see also Sloane, *A Voyage to the Island of Madera*, 2, 22–23, and the Appendix.

106 Information obtained during field research in Accompong Town. Some of this research was published in *The Language of Dress*, 49–57. Interviews were conducted with members of the Herbal Council and elderly Maroons on November 11, 2002. Permission was granted by the Maroon Colonel Sydney Peddie at the time and the trip was organized by Shirley Lindo-Pennant. Second field research was conducted on April 26, 2014 to Accompong Town, surrounding areas and the village of Quick Step. Permission was granted by Colonel Ferron Williams. The trip was organized by the Natural History Museum at the Institute of Jamaica led by botanist Keron Campbell. Several of the Maroons interviewed in 2002 had passed away and a few had migrated. At the time of the second field trip, the Herbal Council had been disbanded. Names of interviewees have been omitted or a pseudonym used to protect their identity.

107 Long, *The History of Jamaica*, 3, 858; see also Georgina Pearman, "Plant Portraits," *Economic Botany* 54, 1 (2000), 4–6.

108 Lorna Goodison, *Controlling the Silver: Poems* (Urbana: University of Illinois Press, 2005), 65.

109 Wright, *Memoir*, 208. Yaws is a tropical disease caused by bacteria; lues is the sexually transmitted disease Syphilis. For Cuba see Lydia Cabrera, *La Medicina Popular De Cuba* (Barcelona: Ediciones, 1996), 46; for Haiti, Timyan, *Bwa Yo*, 305.

110 Adams, *Flowering Plants of Jamaica*. Contributions by G.R. Proctor and R.W. Reed, 484.

111 Ibid.; see also Bush, *Slave Women in Caribbean Society*, 137–39; Londa Schiebinger, "Agnotology and Exotic Abortifacients: The Cultural Production of Ignorance in the Eighteenth-Century Atlantic World," *American Philosophical Society* 149, 3

(September 2005), 316–43. Sloane and his contemporaries avoided details on abortifacients. Several sources refer to lace-bark as having the "same properties or greater" as that of the plant Mezereon, which was well known in Europe as an abortifacient. See Wright, *Memoir*, 207–8.

112 Verene Shepherd and Carleen Payne, "Comparisons: The Caribbean," in *A Companion to Colonial America*, ed. Daniel Vickers (Oxford: Blackwell, 2003), 431–32.

113 Hooker et al., *Curtis's Botanical Magazine* 76, 4503.

114 John Lindley, *The Vegetable Kingdom: The Structure, Classification, and Use of Plants* (London: Bradbury and Evans, 1853), 531.

115 Bush, *Slave Women in Caribbean Society*, 41–45.

116 Ibid.

117 Based on interviews with Maroon elders in summer of 2002 and 2014. See also Edward Long, *The History of Jamaica*, 3, 747–48.

118 Sherlock and Bennett, *The Story of the Jamaican People*, 136.

119 Edward Long, *The History of Jamaica*, 3, 747–48; J. Lunan, *Hortus Jamicensis*, 1 (St Jago de la Vega Gazette, 1814), 436.

120 Emily Brennan, Lori-Ann Harris, and Mark Nesbitt. "Object Lesson: Jamaican Lace-Bark: Its History and Uncertain Future," *Textile History* 44, 2 (November 2013), 235–53, 242; conversations with Maroons and former traders of lace-bark in Quick Step, Cockpit Country, April 26, 2014.

121 Sloane, *Voyage to the Islands*, II, 22. Pearman, "Plant Portraits," 4–6; Long, *The History of Jamaica*, 3, 747–48.

122 Lunan, *Hortus Jamicensis*, 436.

123 The dress is 560 mm long and the lace cap is 18 cm wide; Saffron Walden Museum Catalogue.

124 Marchioness Cornwallis donated the garments to the museum in 1833. Her father-in-law had been Provost-Marshal of Jamaica in the late eighteenth century and probably the avenue through which the dress was received by her and arrived in England. Saffron Walden Museum Catalogue; correspondence, Carla Purdue, Museum Exhibition Officer, November 24, 2011.

125 There is no evidence as to who made the dress. It could have been made by enslaved or freed seamstresses.

126 Sloane, *Voyage to the Islands*, II, 22.

127 Williams, *A Tour Through the Island of Jamaica*, 83.

128 Buckridge, *The Language of Dress*, 52–57.

129 Interviews conducted with Maroons, November 11, 2002; In Jamaica gauze, lace, or fine netting is still used as protective covering for babies from insects similar to mosquito nets.

130 Armstrong, *The Old Village*, 178.

131 Popular Afro-Cuban Proberb. For more proverbs see Lydia Cabrera, *Refranes de Negros Viejos. Recogidos por Lydia Cabrera* (Miami: Ediciones C.R., 1970).

132 Liogier, *La Flora de la Española 1*, 217; Henry D. Baker and William S. Dardeau, *Flore D'Haiti Clé et Description des Ordres – Familles et Genres des Spermatophytes d'Haiti avec la liste de la plupart des espèces*. Service Technique de Department de

l'Agriculture et de l'Enseignement Professional (Port-Au-Prince, Haiti, 1930), 249; Alain Henri Liogier, *Diccionario Botanico De Nombres Vulgares De La Espanola* (Santo Domingo: Jardin Botanico Nacional, 2000), 188.

133 Ibid.

134 Timyan, *Bwa Yo*, 305. See also E.P. Pawley, *Livre Bleu D'Haiti/Blue Book of Haiti, 1919–1920* (New York: Klebold Press, 1919), 52.

135 Susan Elizabeth Tselos, "Threads of Reflection: Costumes of Haitian Rara," *African Arts* (Spring 1996) 59–65. Tselos provides an analysis of Rara costumes.

136 Conversation and interviews, Vodou practitioners, and high priests, Haiti, May 6 and 9, 2014.

137 Conversations and interviews with botanists at Botanista at Jardín Botánico Nacional de Santo Domingo, July 26, 2013. This is debatable, as some botanists think the lace-bark did not exist in the Dominican Republic. Some argue the tree in Haiti is too far south so the seeds did not spread to the other side of the island. Cotton was used for clothing.

138 Harold T. Wilkins, *Secret Cities of Old South America* (Kempton: Adventures Unlimited Press, 1998), 345.

139 *Lagetta lagetto* has several names in Cuba, *Daguilla, Guana*, among others.

140 Wilkins, *Secret Cities of Old South America*, 345. The Isle of Pines is called today Isle de la Juventud (the Isle of Youth).

141 Alfred Noa Monzón, "Thymelaeaceae," *Flora de Cuba* 15(13), 2009, 4–37.

142 Victor R. Fuentes Fiallo, "Apuates para la Hora económica de Cuba 1. Especies productoras de fibros," *Revista del Jardín Botánico Nacional* Vol. XX (1999), 57–81; Monzón, "Thymelaeaceae," 4–37.

143 Cabrera, *La Medicina*, 46.

144 "Botanical Exploration of Cuba," *Bulletin of Miscellaneous Information* (Royal Gardens, Kew), vol. 1890, 38 (1890), 37–38.

145 Lydia Cabrera, *El Monte* (Havana; Edeboral Letras Cubanas, 1993), 398.

146 Catherine Richardson, *Shakespeare and Material Culture* (Oxford: Oxford University Press, 2011), 67.

147 Bush, *Slave Women in Caribbean Society*, 15.

148 Ibid.

149 Hilary Beckles, *Centering Woman: Gender Discourses in Caribbean Slave Society* (Kingston: Ian Randle, 1999), 140.

150 Brennan, Harris, and Nesbitt, "Object Lesson: Jamaican Lace-Bark," 238.

151 Correspondence, Carla Purdue, Museum Exhibition Officer, November 26, 2011.

152 Interview with elderly Maroon women, members of the Herbal Council, 2002.

153 Interview with Ms. Mavis, Maroon woman, April 26, 2014.

154 Ibid.

155 Ibid.

156 Gracia Clark, *Onions are my Husband: Survival and Accumulation by West African Market Women* (Chicago: The University of Chicago Press, 1994), 284; Cheryl Johnson-

Odim, "Women and Gender in Sub-Saharan Africa," in *Women's History in a Global Perspective*, vol 2–3, ed. Bonnie G. Smith (Urbana: University of Illinois Press, 2005), 37–39; Robertson, "Ga Women and Socioeconomic Change in Accra, Ghana," 111–35.

157 M.D. McLeod, *The Asante* (London: British Museum, 1981), 148–49.

158 *Jamaica Gazette*, Thursday, January 8, 1885.

Chapter 3

1 Claire Robertson, *Trouble Showed the Way: Women, Men, and Trade in the Nairobi Area, 1890–1990*. Bloomington: Indiana University Press, 1997, 5–10.

2 Brian L. Moore and Michelle A. Johnson, *Neither Led nor Driven, Contesting British Cultural Imperialism in Jamaica, 1865–1920* (Kingston: University of the West Indies Press, 2004), 137.

3 Stella Blum, ed., *Victorian Fashions and Costumes from Harper's Bazar, 1867–1898* (New York: Dover Publications, 1974), 3.

4 Wardle, *Victorian Lace*, 32–41.

5 Ibid. See also Alison Gernsheim, *Victorian and Edwardian Fashion* (New York: Dover Publication, 1981), 29.

6 Fernandez-Sacco, "Mundillo and Identity," 152.

7 Ibid.

8 Kathryn Weibel, *Mirror Mirror: Images of Women Reflected in Popular Culture* (New York: Anchor, 1977), 176–77. See also *Fashioning the Future: Our Future from Our Past*, 12–24. Published in conjunction with the exhibition of the same name held in the Snowden Gallery, April 1997, The Ohio State University.

9 Katrin Norris, *Jamaica: The Search for an Identity* (Oxford: Oxford University Press, 1962), 9–13.

10 Ibid.

11 James M. Phillippo, *Jamaica: Its Past and Present State* (London: J. Snow, 1843), 150.

12 J.H. Parry, Phillip Sherlock, and Anthony Mingot, *A Short History of the West Indies* (Revised; London: Macmillan, 1987), 169–70. See also the works of Swithin Wilmot, such as *Plantation Economy, Land Reform and the Peasantry in a Historical Perspective: Jamaica 1838–1980* (Kingston: Friedrich Ebert Stiftung, 1992) (with Claus Stolberg).

13 Ibid., 9–13.

14 Sheena Boa, "Urban Free Black and Coloured Women: Jamaica 1760–1834," *The Jamaica Historical Review* XVIII (1993), 4.

15 John Bigelow, *Jamaica in 1850* (New York: George P. Putman, 1851), 144.

16 Patrick Bryan, *The Jamaican People 1880–1902: Race, Class and Social Control* (London: Macmillan, 1991), introduction, x.

17 Carmichael, *Domestic Manners*, 1, 150.

18 Stewart, *A View of the Past and Present State*, 269.

19 W.P. Livingstone, *Black Jamaica, A Study in Evolution* (London: William Clowes and Sons, 1899), 106.

20 *Falmouth Gazette,* May 23, 1879, UWI Library. This newspaper includes numerous store advertisements of clothes for sale direct from New York and a few other places.

21 Ibid. See also the *Daily Gleaner,* December 1899, The West Indies Collection.

22 A grip was an old fashioned suitcase used for storage or to carry clothes.

23 Based on conversation with representatives of the Market Department KSAC on March 10, 2003 and several market traders, June 1996. Some traders were retired third-generation market women who remembered seeing some clothing in the markets, especially madras cloth tie-heads. One trader's great-grandmother sold ribbons and hair accessories in the market. Jubilee Market was previously named Sollas Market. It was destroyed by hurricane in 1886 and then rebuilt and renamed in honor of Queen Victoria's golden jubilee the following year. The new structure had thirty covered stalls and was lit by ten powerful gas lamps. Space was provided for 1,000 persons. The market was enlarged in 1894; from *Squalid Kingston, 1890–1920: How the Poor Lived, Moved and Had Their Being,* Brian L. Moore and Michelle A. Johnson, eds (Mona: The Social History Project, The University of the West Indies, 2000), 172, 8.

24 Livingstone, *Black Jamaica,* 106.

25 Phillippo, *Jamaica: Its Past and Present State,* 151. See also Glory Robertson, "Pictorial Sources for Nineteenth Century Women's History: Dress as a Mirror of Attitudes to Women," in V. Shepard, B. Brereton and B. Bailey (eds), *Engendering History* (Kingston: Ian Randle, 1995), 111–22.

26 Linda Welters and Abby Lillethun, eds, *The Fashion Reader* (New York: Berg, 2009), 36–45.

27 Ibid.

28 Phillippo, *Jamaica: Its Past and Present State,* 151. See also Robertson, "Pictorial Sources for Nineteenth Century Women's History," 111–22.

29 Quoted in Joan French and Honor Ford-Smith, *Women, Work and Organization in Jamaica, 1900–1944* (Kingston: Sistren Research, 1986), 145.

30 Douglas Hall, *Free Jamaica, 1838–1865: An Economic History* (New Haven: Yale University Press, 1959), 232–33.

31 CO. 137/391 20 April 1865, UWI.

32 French and Ford-Smith, *Women, Work and Organization,* 145–46.

33 Buckridge, *The Language of Dress,* 158.

34 Ibid.

35 Ibid.

36 Blum, *Victorian Fashions & Costumes,* 3–75 for illustrations and images of Victorian fashions.

37 Translation: Sitting down too much wears out one's trousers (Anderson, Cundall), National Library of Jamaica.

38 F.A. Pouchet, *The Universe; or the Wonders of Creation. The Infinitely Great and the Infinitely Little* (Portland: H. Hallet & Co., 1883), 123, 350–51; W. Clute, ed., *The American Botanist, Devoted to Economic and Ecological Botany,* X (Joliet, Ill; Willard N. Clue & Co., 1906); *The Gleaner,* 17 October, 1958; Buckridge, *The Language of Dress,* 52, 158.

39 E.G. Squire, *Tropical Fibres: their Production and Economic Extraction* (New York: Scribner and Co., 1861), 18.

40 Interview with elderly Maroon women recalling what their mothers and grandmothers wore. November 11–13, 2002. Buckridge, *The Language of Dress*, 158.

41 Ibid.

42 Hendrickson, *Clothing and Difference*, 1–8.

43 Interviews, Maroon women, November 11–12, 2002.

44 Jas Johnston, *Jamaica: The New Riviera* (London: Cassell and Company, 1903), 17.

45 Anon., *Hospitality Jamaica,* April 25, 2007. The Great Exhibition of 1891 did not live up to its expectations and the tourists expected did not materialize. It would be years before a major tourist sector developed. The failure of the exhibition and lack of guests led to the bankruptcy of several hotels.

46 Anon., *Souvenir of Jamaica* (London: C.W. Faulkner and Co. 1903), 11; book contains images of hotels and advertisements of the services and amenities available in the facilities.

47 David Boxer and Edward Lacie-Smith, *Jamaica in Black and White: Photography in Jamaica c. 1845–1920: The David Boxer Collection* (Oxford: Macmillan, 2013), 190–96, for pictures of hotels of the time and Europeans strolling through gardens. There are a few photographs from the period of sewing circles on hotel verandahs in the NLJ collection, but not of printing quality.

48 Ibid., 196.

49 Ibid.

50 Johnston, *Jamaica: The New Riviera* (see advertisements).

51 Alfred L. Jones, *Through Jamaica with a Kodak: with Introductory notes by His Grace the Arch Bishop of the West Indies [Enos NuHall]* (London: John Wright & Company, 1907), 12, 178–79.

52 Brennan, Harris, and Nesbitt, "Object Lesson: Jamaican Lace-Bark," 244.

53 Johnston, *Jamaica: The New Riviera* (see advertisements).

54 Jones, *Through Jamaica with a Kodak*, 12.

55 Ibid.

56 Based on observation of lace-bark branch specimen, The Field Museum of Natural History Collection, Chicago.

57 J. Henderson, *Jamaica* (London: A. & C. Black, 1906), 29–30.

58 Moore and Johnson, *Neither Led nor Driven: Contesting British Cultural Imperialism in Jamaica, 1865–1920*, 167, 317.

59 See the "Rules for Teachers Employed in the Schools of the United Brethren in Jamaica, 1880" and the Upward and Onward Society magazines, reports and minutes of several meetings in *The Moravian Collection,* The National Archive of Jamaica. The Upward and Onward Society for young ladies still exists in Jamaica. Many of the nineteenth-century activities have been maintained and are still taught, including sewing and needlework in the British fashion, making pantry towels, and baking scones. Some Jamaican cooking is also taught; however, some people consider many of these activities as not practical.

60 Moore and Johnson, *Neither Led nor Driven,* 174.

61 Jones, *Through Jamaica with a Kodak*, 128.

62 Ibid., 9.

63 Augustus Constantine Sinclair, Lawrence R. Fyfe, and Samuel Paynter Musson, *The Handbook of Jamaica* (London: Edward Stafford, 1886), 433.

64 Ibid.

65 Ibid.

66 Bryan, *The Jamaican People*, 165, 205. See also Clinton Black, *History of Jamaica* (London: Collins Clear-Type Press, 1965), 225; *Daily Gleaner*, 13 January 1886, "Women's Self Help Society."

67 Sinclair et al., *Handbook of Jamaica*, 433.

68 Ibid.

69 *The Daily Gleaner*, August 29, 1891.

70 Ibid.

71 Ibid.

72 Musgrave Collection, HN: Historical Notes, National Library of Jamaica.

73 *The Daily Gleaner*, February 5, 1889; Johnson, *Jamaica: The New Riviera* (see advertisements).

74 Catalogue on the British Colonies by Great Britain, Royal Commission for Paris Exhibition (1878), 40; Daniel Morris, *Jamaica at the World's Exposition: Catalogue of Articles from the Island of Jamaica*, New Orleans, 1884–85, 24.

75 Buckridge, *The Language of Dress*, 129.

76 Hooker et al., *Curtis's Botanical Magazine*, 4503.

77 Ibid.

78 Ibid.

79 Ibid.

80 Ibid.

81 Anonymous, *Official Catalogue of the Great Exhibition of Works of Industry of all Nations, 1851* (corrected edition), Cambridge: Cambridge University Press [1851]2011, 305.

82 Ibid., 166.

83 A few early secondary sources mention that Queen Victoria was presented with a lace-bark dress. To date no evidence or record of this has been found in the Royal Collection or Archive. See Mrs. Bury Palliser, *A History of Lace* (London: Sampson Low, Son & Marston, 1865), 395.

84 Herbert Fairall, *The World's Industrial and Cotton Centennial Exposition, New Orleans, 1884–1885* (Iowa City: Herbert S. Fairall, 1885), 403.

85 Anon., *Transactions of the Institute of Jamaica, 1885* (Kingston: Mortimer C.D. Souza printer, 1885), 46–48.

86 Robert Bentley, *A Manual of Botany: Including the Structure, Functions, Classification, Properties, and Uses of Plants* (London: Spottiswood and Co., 1873), 609.

87 Inez K. Sibley, "Jamaica's Wonder Tree," *The Gleaner*, December 8, 1968.

88 *Catalogue of the British Colonies by Great Britain: Royal Commission for Paris Exhibition* (1878), 40.

89 *House of Commons Papers* Vol. 35 by Great Britain, Parliament (1877), 440.

90 Sinclair et al., *Handbook of Jamaica* (1886), 412.

91 Robert Haut, *Companion to the Official Catalogue Synopses of A Complete Guide to the Contents of the International Exhibition of 1862* (London: Edward Stanford, 1852), 379–385.

92 Anonymous. *Annual Report of the Public Gardens and Plantations for the year ending 30 September 1881*, 1.

93 Ibid.

94 Ibid.

95 Ibid.

96 Ibid.

97 Ibid.

98 Casid, *Sowing Empire*, 51.

99 Ibid., 52.

100 William Fawcett, "Public Gardens and Plantations of Jamaica," *Botanical Gazette*, 24, 5 (Nov. 1897), 345–69.

101 *Jamaica Gleaner,* May 5, 2012; *Observer,* September 11, 2012.

102 *The Governor's Report on the Jamaica Blue Book and Departmental Reports,* 1888–1890, XII.

103 Ibid.

104 Ibid.

105 Hallet and Johnston, *Fabric for Fashion*, 139–41, 169–71.

106 Daniel Morris, *Jamaica at World's Exposition*, 23.

107 D. Morris, *Jamaica Annual Report on the Public Gardens and Plantation,* 1885, 1–31.

108 Ibid., 14.

109 D. Morris, Cantor Lecture on "Commercial Fibres: Their History and Origin, with special reference to the Fiber industries connected with Her Majesty's Colonial and Indian possessions." Foreign and Commonwealth Office Collection (1895), 2, 12.

110 *Jamaica Gazette*, January 8, 1885, see the US Patent for details on design and operation of the fiber machines. US Patent 350, 920 – 1883; US Patent 350, 063 – 1886 accessible online at http://patentimages.storage.googleapis.com

111 *Jamaica Gazette*, May 22, 1884.

112 The advertisement and image of the Kennedy Eureka is very rare. The image was published in the *Colonial and Indian Exhibition* 1886 catalogue but in limited editions, hence not all catalogues have the image. This is also a lost knowledge and no one at the NLJ or the Institute of Jamaica (including the museums) are familiar with the machine, nor could we locate one of the machines.

113 Ibid.

114 Daniel Morris, *Jamaica at the World's Exposition*, 14.

115 Anon., *Transactions of the Institute of Jamaica 1885*, 45–48. The most promising fiber yielding plants were the Agave and China grass. See Morris, *Public Gardens and Plantations*, 1883. Nor did lace-bark become a viable source for paper making.

116 Quoted in V. Morson, "Women's Self-Help Society; End of an Era of Devoted Service," *The Gleaner*, November 10, 1961.

117 Ibid.

118 Ibid.

119 Anon., "*The Lace Bark*", excerpt from Royal Magazine for June, *Jamaica Gleaner,* June 16, 1906.

120 George B. Utter, *The Sabath Recorder*, 64, 1 (Plainfield, NJ: The American Sabath Tract Society, 1908).

121 Quoted in Brennan, Harris, and Nesbitt, "Object Lesson: Jamaican Lace-Bark," 238.

122 Based on observation during field research in the Accompong Town area.

123 *Governor's Report on the Jamaica Blue Book and Departmental Records* (1885–86), 13.

124 Ibid.

125 *Governor's Report on the Jamaica Blue Book and Departmental Records* (1884–85). It is not clear from the report whether lace-bark trees were impacted.

126 Assessment based on interviews with scientists in Cuba and Haiti due to absence of data about the tree population during this period. See also Reinaldo Funes Monzote, *From Rainforest to Cane Field in Cuba: An Environmental History since 1492* (Chapel Hill: University of North Carolina Press, 2008), 84.

127 Inez K. Sibley, "Jamaica's Wonder Tree," *The Gleaner,* December 8, 1968.

128 Ibid.

129 Ibid.

130 R.E. Stubbs, Governor, *The Sale of the Bark of Trees (Prevention) Law*, 1929 (June 13, 1929).

131 Ibid.

132 Overview of final years of the industry, see Buckridge, *The Language of Dress*, 210; Brennan, Harris, Nesbitt, "Object Lesson: Jamaican Lace-Bark," 247–48.

133 Sibley, "Trees Mean Much To Mankind," *The Gleaner*, 2 July 1960; "Women's Self-Help Society; End of an Eva of Devoted Service," *The Gleaner,* 10 November 1961.

134 Interview with Maroons, and individuals whose family had been engaged in lace-bark production for several generations. 2002, 2014. The Lennon family of Quickstep in the Cockpit Country was very involved in lace-bark production. A few men in the lace-bark industry became known for their craft work such as Robert Nunes. His work was on exhibition in Philadelphia in 1876.

Conclusion

1 Timyan, *Bwa Yo: Important Trees of Haiti*, 335.

2 Leonard and Terrel, *Patterns of Paradise*, 10–14, for a discussion of bark-cloth around the world.

3 Brian Mervis and Jerome D. Msonthi, *Chewa Medical Botany: A Study of Herbalism in Southern Malawi* (Berlin: Lit Verlag, 1996), 336–37.

4 Robertson, "Ga Women and Socioeconomic Change in Accra, Ghana," 111–35.

5 Hall, *Representation*, 3.

6 De Las Casas, *Destruction of the Indies*, 2003, portrays the horrifying experience of Taíno men and women under Spanish colonial rule and how the fabric of Taíno culture was destroyed, the population enslaved, and vast numbers of people slaughtered—the exact number not being known.

7 Rouse, *The Taínos: Rise and Decline*, 162, 138–68. The author provides an analysis of the Spanish conquest and the re-peopling of former Taíno habitats by enslaved Africans.

8 Glassie, "Studying Material Culture Today," 257.

9 Ignacio Chapela, "Bioprospecting: Myth, Realities, and Potential Impact on Sustainable Development" in *Mycology in Sustainable Development: Expanding Concepts, Vanishing Borders,* eds. Mary E. Palm and Ignacio H. Chapela (Boone, North Carolina: Parkway Publishers, 1997), 238–39.

10 Schiebinger, *Plants and Empire*, 10–12.

11 Ibid., 16.

12 Ibid., 15–18, on the role of the International Conventions and Plant Patent Act to safeguard plants where they grow.

13 Barbara Lewis, "The Limitations of Group Action among Entrepreneurs: The Market Women of Abidjan, Ivory Coast" in *Women in Africa*, Nancy J. Hafkin and Edna Bay, eds (Stanford: Stanford University Press, 1976), 135–58.

14 Walter Rodney, "Upper Guinea and the Significance of the Origins of Africans Enslaved in the New World," *Journal of Negro History* (LIV: 4 October 1969), p. 327.

15 We do not know exactly what Africans learned from indigenous people in regards to clothing materials and natural dye pigments.

16 Quoted in Barbara Bush, *Slave Women in Caribbean Society*, 153.

17 Buckridge, *The Language of Dress*, 175.

18 Long, *The History of Jamaica*, 3, 736–858.

19 Buckridge, *The Language of Dress*, 47.

20 The Lady Musgrave Self-Help Society opened on Church Street in Kingston in 1879. The original building was destroyed in the fire of 1882 and new premises were erected in 1890, but later destroyed by the 1907 earthquake. The final building was opened on Harbour Street in 1911. The society continued into the mid-twentieth century producing curios for the tourist market. By the 1950s the organization had lost its prestige and faced much competition from other curio shops and organizations.

21 Tilley, Webb Keane, Küchler, Rowlands, and Spyer (eds), *Handbook of Material Culture* (London: Sage, 2006), 203–6.

22 Ibid.

23 Interview with Maroons, and family members whose family had been engaged in lace-bark production for several generations. November 11, 2002; April 26, 2014; For more clarification see Chapter 2, note 106.

24 Alexander McQueen, Savage Beauty Exhibition, Iris and B. Gerald Cantor Exhibition Hall, Metropolitan Museum of Art, 2011.

25 Anon. Natural History Notes, New Issue, vol. 1 no. 8 of the *Natural History Society of Jamaica* (October 19, 1982), 18.

26 Interview with Maroons, November 11, 2002; April 26, 2014. See also Brennan, Harris and Nesbit "Object Lesson: Jamaican Lace-Bark," 248.

27 Interview with Maroons, November 11, 2002.

28 Interviews with Maroons, November 11, 2002; April 26, 2014; See also, Brennan, Harris and Nesbit, "Object Lesson: Jamaican Lace-Bark," 248.

29 H/H. (Historical Notes) Trade Fairs Exhibitions, July 28-August 7, 1954. Souvenir. NLJ. For more on the straw and craft industry in Jamaica see Suzette Wolfe Wilson, "Towards Sustainable Craft Production in Jamaica," *The Journal of Modern Craft*, 3 (July 2010), 191–208; Althea M. Johnson, "The Basket Weaving Tradition in the Communities of the Black River Lower Morass, Jamaica," *Caribbean Geography* (1997), 66–80.

30 Ibid.

31 Ibid.

32 Jamaica gained its independence on August 6, 1962. The new government sought to promote the handicraft sector as a means of boosting revenue for the new economy.

33 Interview with Maroons, November 11, 2002. Interview, family members who supplied lace-bark fibers to Things Jamaica Limited, Quick Step, Accompong Town region, April 26, 2014. Family members remarked they received a letter from Mr. Seaga confirming his support for the industry, but no one knew where the letter was. This claim by the family could not be corroborated by Mr. Seaga, who is currently 85 years old. It is believed that Mr. Seaga developed an interest in lace-bark as early as the 1960s when he served as a cabinet minister. At the time, culture was among the minister's portfolio. The library of the original Things Jamaica Limited is currently missing and nothing related to lace-bark has been found so far in Mr. Seaga's library/papers recently donated to the UWI West Indies collection.

34 *National Cultural Policy of Jamaica: Towards Jamaica the Cultural Superstate, Culture Division*, Ministry of Education, Youth and Culture, December 2003, 54, NLJ. *Daily Gleaner*, Monday June 13, 1988. Things Jamaica Limited tried to promote lace-making. See the story of Olive Rennals, *Craft Worker: Things Jamaican*, 2 (1987), 1–23.

35 Interview with Maroons and family members formerly engaged in lace-bark trade, April 26, 2014.

36 Brennan, Harris, and Nesbitt, "Object Lesson: Jamaican Lace-Bark," note 71, 252.

37 "Lace Bark Legatta Needs Protection," *The Sunday Gleaner Magazine*, May 17, 1981.

38 Brennan, Harris, and Nesbitt, "Object Lesson: Jamaican Lace-Bark," 249.

39 Owen B. Evelyn and Roland Camirand, "Forest Cover and Deforestation in Jamaica: An Analysis of Forest Cover Estimates Over Time," *International Forestry Review* 5 (2003), 354–63.

40 Peter Espeut, "Let us Protect our Forests," *The Gleaner*, November 12, 2015.

41 Anon., "Jamaica Maroons Vow to Fight Mining," *Washington Post*, Sunday, January 7, 2007.

42 Ibid.

43 Petare William Raynor, *The Gleaner*, Monday, August 17, 2015. "Inside the Cockpit Country—Maroons Conservationists say No to Bauxite, Limestone Mining."

44 "Blue and John Crow Mountains Inscribed to UNESCO's Prestigious World Heritage List," *Jamaica Observer*, Friday, July 3, 2015.

45 Jane C. Wheeler and Domingo Hoces R., "Community Participation, Sustainable Use, and Vicuña Conservation in Peru," *Mountain Research Development* 17, 3 (August 1997), 283–87.

46 Data on the current state of Haiti's forest and rate of deforestation is an ongoing debate among scholars and scientists. See Christopher E. Churches, Peter J. Wampler, Wanxiao Sun, and Andrew Smith, "Evaluation of forest cover estimates for Haiti using supervised classification of Landsat data," *International Journal of Applied Earth Observation and Geoinformation* 30 (2014), 203–16.

47 Brennan, Harris, and Nesbitt, "Object Lesson: Jamaican Lace-Bark," 249.

48 "Regional Fashion Industry Worth 10 Billion Per Year," *Jamaica Observer*, Friday, June 22, 2012. Caribbean Fashion week is June 8–11 in Kingston and includes designers from the English, French, Spanish and Dutch Caribbean. It cost J$60 million to stage the show. Chairman of the Caribbean Fashion Industry Association (CAFIA) is Kingsley Cooper, the head of Pulse Modeling Agency. It is debatable whether a fashion industry truly exists in the Caribbean when compared with other fashion industries. See Keith Nurse, *The Cultural Industries* in CARICOM: *Trade and Development Challenges*, EU PROINVEST CAR/5170 (November 2006), 156–84.

49 Hallett and Johnston, *Fabric for Fashion*, 169, 178; Eric Wilson, "Doing their part to Help Save the planet in High Style," *The New York Times*, February 1, 2008; Mina Roces, "Dress, Status, and Identity in the Philippines: Pineapple Fiber Cloth and Ilustrado Fashion," *Fashion Theory*, vol. 17, 3 (2013), 341–72. More designers today are incorporating organic materials, natural vegetable dyes, and technically advanced fibers including soybeans, bamboo, banana, and hemp in their fashions.

Glossary

1 Information from: Adams, Charles Dennis, *Flowering Plants of Jamaica* (Kingston: University of the West Indies Press, 1972); Buckridge, Steeve O., *The Language of Dress, Resistance and Accommodation in Jamaica, 1760–1890* (Kingston: University of the West Indies Press, 2004); Hallett, Clive, and Amanda Johnston, *Fabric for Fashion: A Comprehensive Guide to Natural Fibres* (London: Lawrence King, 2010); Harris, Jennifer (ed.), *5000 Years of Textiles* (Washington, DC: Smithsonian Books, 1993); Long, Edward, *The History of Jamaica or General Survey*. 3 vols. 1774; Yarwood, Doreen. *The Encyclopedia of World Costume* (New York: Bonanza Books, 1978).

SELECT BIBLIOGRAPHY AND FURTHER READING

Abbreviations

MS Manuscript
NLJ National Library of Jamaica/Institute of Jamaica
UWI University of the West Indies, Mona, West Indies Collection
CO Public Record Office, London, Colonial Office
JA Jamaica Archives and Records Department

Manuscripts

Dickenson Collection, Vestry Proceedings, MS 2952, UWI
Harmony Hall Estate Account Book, vol. 1, MS 1652, NLJ
Invoices, Accounts, Sale of Sugar etc. Jamaica Windsor Lodge and Paisley Estates
(1833–1837), MS 32, NLJ
The Moravian Collection and Archives, Good Housekeeping (March 1888), MS 5/5
The Moravian Collection and Archives, Upward and Onward Society, MS 5/5, JA
Public Record Office, London, Colonial Office, C.O., 137 vols. *Governor's Dispatches* (1865),
UWI
Radner Coffee Plantation Journal, 1822–1826, MS 180 NLJ
Smithfield Estate Records and Business, MS 806, NLJ
Worthy Park Plantation Books 4/23, 1 (1783–87), 4/23, 2 (1787–91), JA

Official publications

Brochures of the Royal College of Physicians, London, 2010.
Governor's Report on the Jamaica Blue Book and Departmental Records, 1884–1885,
1885–1886, 1888–1890.
Hand Book of Jamaica, 1884–1885, 1894.
Jamaica Annual Report of the Public Gardens and Plantations, 1881, 1883, 1884.
Journal of The Assembly of Jamaica, vol. 4, 1745–1746.
Laws of Jamaica, 1696, 1929.
Laws of Jamaica, 1831.

Proceedings of the Legislative Council, 1898.
Program Bulletins of the World Fairs, Expositions and International Exhibitions, United
    States Patent Office, 1883, 1886.
Transactions of the Institute of Jamaica, 1885. Kingston: Mortimer C.D. Souza printer, 1885.

Newspapers

Colonial Standard and Jamaican Dispatch, 1883–1890.
Daily Gleaner, March 21, 1889.
Diary and Kingston Daily Advertiser (January–August), 1796.
Falmouth Post (8 March), 1836 (January–December), 1860.
Jamaica Mercury (November–December), 1799.
Outlook (April), 1997.
Royal Gazette (July), 1813–1816, 1830–1831.
The Sunday Gleaner (5 January), 1963, 1981, 1997.
The Weekend Observer (8 August), 1997.
The Jamaica Gazette, 1884, 1885.
The Gleaner, 1902, 1907, 1920, 1960, 2007, 2013.
The New York Times, 2007, 2008.

Primary sources

Anderson, Helen. "Lace." *The Decorator and Furnisher* 15, 6 (March 1890), 199–200.
Bacon, Edgar M., and Eugene M. Aaron. *The New Jamaica*. Kingston: Aston W. Gardner,
    1890.
Barclay, Alexander. *A Practical View of the Present State of Slavery in the West Indies*.
    London: Smith and Elder, 1826.
Beckford, William. *A Descriptive Account of the Island of Jamaica*. 2 vols. London: T.J.
    Egerton, 1790.
Bigelow, John. *Jamaica in 1850*. New York: George P. Putman, 1851.
Bickell, R. *The West Indies As They Are: or A Real Picture of Slavery: Cut More Particularly
    as It Exists in the Island of Jamaica*. London: J. Hatchard and Son, 1825.
Brigham, William T. *Ka Hana Kapa: The Making of Bark-Cloth in Hawaii. Memoirs of the
    Bernice Pauahi Bishop Museum of Polynesian Ethnology and Natural History*, vol. III.
    Honolulu: Bishop Museum Press, 1911.
Browne, Patrick. *The Civil and Natural History of Jamaica*, London: B. White & Son,
    1756.
Carmichael, A.C. *Domestic Manners and Social Conditions of the White, Colored and Negro
    Population of the West Indies*. 2 vols. London: Whittaker, Treacher, 1833.
De la Beche, Sir Henry. *Notes on the Present Condition of the Negroes in Jamaica*. London:
    T. Cadell, 1825.
De la Puerta, Don Gabriel. *Botanica Descriptiva y Determinacion de las Plantas Indigenas y
    Cultivadas en España*. Madrid: Administración de la Revista de Medicina y Cirugia
    Particulars, 1891.
De Lisser, H.G. *In Jamaica and Cuba*. Kingston: Gleaner, 1910.
De Lisser, H.G. "White Man in the Tropics." *Century Review*, February 1900.

Dodge, Mary Mapes. *St Nicholas, an Illustrated Magazine for Young Folks* 13, part 3 (May–October 1886). London: F. Warne, 1886.

Edwards, Bryan. *The History, Civil and Commercial, of the British Colonies in the West Indies.* 3 vols. 2nd ed. London: J. Stockdale, 1796–1801.

Fawcett, William. *A Provisional List of the Indigenous and Naturalized Flowering Plants of Jamaica.* Kingston: Aston W. Gardner, 1893.

Foulks, Theodore. *Eighteen Months in Jamaica with Recollections of the Late Rebellion.* London: Whittaker, Treacher, and Arnott, 1833.

Gardener, W.J. *A History of Jamaica from Its Discovery by Christopher Columbus to the Year 1872.* London: E. Stock, 1872.

Gomez de la Moza, Manuel. *Diccinario Botanico de los Nombres Vulgares.* Havana: La Antilla, 1888.

Gosse, Phillip Henry. *A Naturalist's Sojourn in Jamaica.* London: Longman, 1851.

Grisebach, A.H.R. *Flora of the British West Indian Islands.* London: Lovell Reeve, 1864.

Hakewill, James. *Picturesque Tour of the Island of Jamaica from Drawings Made in the Year 1820 and 1821.* London: Hurst and Robinson, 1825.

Humboldt, Alexander. *The Island of Cuba.* Trans. from the Spanish with notes and preliminary essay by T.S. Thrasher. New York: Derby and Jackson, 1856.

Hutchins, Mary Ann. *The Youthful Female Missionary: A Memoir of Mary Ann Hutchins.* London: Wightman and H. Adams, 1840.

Jay, E.A. Hastings. *A Glimpse of the Tropic: or Four Months Cruising in the West Indies.* London: Sampson Low, Marston, 1900.

Johnston, Jas., MD. *Jamaica: The New Riviera: A Pictorial Description of the Island and Its Attractions.* London: Cassell, 1903.

"Lace-Bark—Lagetta Lintearia." *The Friend: A Religious and Literary Journal* (Philadelphia, William H. Pile, 1872): 261–62.

Lewis, Matthew Gregory. *Journal of a Residence Among the Negroes of the West Indies.* London: John Murray, 1834.

Livingstone, W.P. *Black Jamaica, A Study in Evolution.* London: William Clowes, 1899.

Long, Edward. *The History of Jamaica or General Survey of the Ancient and Modern State of the Island: with Reflections on Its Situation Settlements, Inhabitants, Climate, Products, Commerce, Laws and* Government. vol. 3. London: T. Lownudes, 1774.

Lunan, John. *Hortus Jamaicensis Or a Botanical Description.* Jamaica; Spanish Town: St. Jago De La Vega Gazette, 1814.

MacFadyen, James, MD. *The Flora of Jamaica: A Description of the Plants of that Island Arranged According to the Natural Orders.* London: Longman, Orme, Brown, Green and Longman, 1837.

Madden, Richard Robert. *Twelve Month's Residence in the West Indies during the Transition from Slavery to Apprenticeship.* 2 vols. 1835; reprint, Westport: Negro Universities Press, 1970.

Marly, Or a Planter's Life in Jamaica. Glasgow: Richard Griffin, 1828.

Moreton, J.B. *Manners and Customs in the West India Islands.* 2nd ed. London: J. Parson, 1793.

Morris, Rob. "Negro Life in Jamaica." *Harper's New Monthly Magazine* 44, 261 (March 1872), 553–60.

Nugent, Maria. *Lady Nugent's Journal. Jamaica One Hundred and Thirty-Eight Years Ago.* 3rd ed. Ed. Frank Cundall. London: West India Committee, 1939.

Phillippo, James M. *Jamaica: Its Past and Present State.* London: J. Snow, 1843.

Pullen-Bury, B. *Jamaica As It Is in 1903.* London: T. Fisher, 1903.

Prince, Mrs. Nancy. *A Black Woman's Odyssey through Russia and Jamaica: The Narrative of Nancy Prince*. Boston: N. Prince, 1850.

Pringle, Hall. *The Fall of the Sugar Planters of Jamaica*. London: Trunner, 1869.

"Scenes in Hispanida." *Excelsior: Helps to Progress in Religion, Science, and Literature* (London, James Nesbet, Berners St.), January 1856: 31–38.

Scotus, Philo. *Reminiscences of a Scottish Gentleman, Commencing in 1787*. London: 1861.

Sells, Williams. *Remarks on the Condition of the Slaves in the Island of Jamaica*. London: J. M. Richardson, 1823.

Senior, Bernard Martin. *Jamaica, As It Was, As It Is, and As It May Be*. New York: Negro Universities Press, [1835]1969.

Sloane, Sir Hans. *A Voyage to the Island of Madera, Barbados, Nieves, St. Christopher and Jamaica, with the Natural History of the Herbs and Trees, Four-Footed Beast, Fishes, Birds, Insects, Reptiles, Etc. of the Last of Those Islands*. 2 vols. London: B. M., 1707–25.

Souvenir of Jamaica. London: C.W. Faulkner and Company, 1903.

Stewart, J. *A View of the Past and Present State of the Island of Jamaica: with Remarks on the Moral and Physical Condition of the Slaves and the Abolition of Slavery in the Colonies*. Edinburgh: Oliver and Boyd, 1823.

Sturge, Joseph, and Thomas Harvey. *The West Indies in 1837*. London: Hamilton and Adams, 1838.

Underhill, Edward Bean. *The West Indies: Their Social and Religious Condition*. London: Jackson, Walford and Hodder, 1862.

Williams, Cynric R. *A Tour through the Island of Jamaica from the Western to the Eastern End in the Year 1823*. London: Hunt and Clark, 1826.

Wright, William. "An Account of the Medicinal Plants Growing in Jamaica." *London Medical Journal* 8 (1787): 217–95.

Wright, William. *Memoir of the Late William Wright, MD with Extracts from His Correspondence and Selection of His Papers on Medical and Botanical Subjects*. Edinburgh: William Blackwood, 1787.

Secondary sources

Abiodun, Rowland, Henry John Drewal, and John Pemberton. *The Yoruba Artist: New Theoretical Perspectives on African Arts*. Washington, D.C.: Smithsonian Press, 1994.

Adams, Charles Dennis. *Flowering Plants of Jamaica*. Kingston: University of the West Indies Press, 1972.

Allman, Jean, ed. *Fashioning Africa: Power and the Politics of Dress*. Bloomington: Indiana University Press, 2004.

Altschul, S.V.R. *Drugs and Foods from Little-Known Plants. Notes in Harvard University Herbaria*. Cambridge, MA: Harvard University Press, 1973.

Anderson, Richard L. *Art in Small-Scale Societies*. London: Prentice-Hall, 1989.

Anna, M. "Bark-Cloth Making among the Baganda of East Africa." *Primitive Man* 9, 1 (January 1936), 12–14.

Arnoldi, Mary Jo, Christraud M. Geary, and Kris L. Hardin, eds. *African Material Culture*. Bloomington: Indiana University Press, 1996.

Asprey, G.F., and R.G. Robbins. "The Vegetation of Jamaica." *Ecological Monographs* 23, 4 (October 1953), 359–412.

Atkinson, Lesley-Gail, ed. *The Earliest Inhabitants: The Dynamics of the Jamaican Taíno*. Kingston: University of the West Indies Press, 2006.

Ayre, Michael. *The Caribbean in Sepia: A History in Photographs, 1840–1900*. Kingston: Ian Randle, 2012.

Babcock, Barbara A., ed. *The Reversible World: Symbolic Inversion in Art and Society*. Ithaca: Cornell University Press, 1978.

Bacquart, Jean-Baptiste. *The Tribal Arts of Africa*. New York: Thames and Hudson, 1998.

Bailey, L.H. "The Royal Palm of Hispaniola." *Gentes Herb* 4: 266–70.

Baker, Henry D., and William. S. Dardeau. *Flore d'Haiti – Familles et Genres des Spermatophytes d'Haiti avec la liste de la plupart des espèces*. Service Technique de Department de l'Agriculture et de l'Enseignement Professional, Port-au-Prince, Haiti. 1930.

Barker, David, Carol Newby, and Mike Morrissey. *A Reader in Caribbean Geography*. Kingston: Ian Randle, 1998.

Barrett, Leonard E. *The Rastafarians*. Boston: Beacon, 1977.

Barrett, Leonard E. *Soul-Force: African Heritage in Afro-American Religion*. New York: Anchor Press/Doubleday, 1974.

Barringer, T.J., Gillian Forrester, and Barbaro Martinez-Ruiz. *Art and Emancipation in Jamaica: Isaac Mendes Belisario and His Worlds*. New Haven: Yale Center for British Art in Association with Yale University Press, 2007.

Barriteau, Eudine, ed. *Confronting Power: Theorizing Gender Interdisciplinary Perspectives in the Caribbean*. Kingston: University of the West Indies Press, 2003.

Barthes, Roland. *The Language of Fashion*. Trans. by Andy Stafford. New York: Berg, 2004.

Bartra, Eli, ed. *Crafting Gender: Women and Folk Art in Latin America and the Caribbean*. Durham, NC: Duke University Press, 2003.

Bastide, Roger. *African Civilizations in the New World*. Trans. By Peter Green. New York: Harper and Row, 1971.

Batchelor, Jennie, and Cora Kaplan, eds. *Women and Material Culture, 1660–1830*. New York: Palgrave Macmillan, 2007.

Beckles, Hilary McD. *Centering Woman: Gender Discourses in Caribbean Slave Society*. Kingston: Ian Randle, 1999.

Beckles, Hilary McD. *Natural Rebels: A Social History of Enslaved Black Women in Barbados*. New Brunswick: Rutgers University Press, 1989.

Beckles, Hilary McD. "Sex and Gender in the Historiography of Caribbean Slavery." In *Engendering History: Caribbean Women in Historical Perspective*, eds., Verene Shepherd, Bridget Brereton, and Barbara Bailey, 125–54. Kingston: Ian Randle, 1995.

Benstock, Shari, and Suzanne Ferris, eds. *On Fashion*. New Brunswick: Rutgers University Press, 1994.

Bercht, Fatima, Estrellita Brodsky, John Alan Farmer, and Dicey Taylor, eds. *Taíno: Pre-Columbian Art and Culture from the Caribbean*. New York: Monacelli Press, 1997.

Bergstein, Rachelle. *Women from the Ankle Down: The Story of Shoes and How They Define Us*. New York: Harper Collins, 2012.

Bettelheim, Judith, ed. *Cuban Festivals: A Century of Afro-Cuban Culture*. Kingston: Ian Randle, 2001.

Bettelheim, Judith. "Women in Masquerade and Performance." *African Arts* 31, 2 (Spring 1998), 68–70, 93–94.

Bilby, Kenneth M. *True-Born Maroons*. Gainesville: University Press of Florida, 2005.

Binder, Pearl. *Dressing Up and Dressing Down*. London: Allen and Unwin, 1986.

Bisnauth, Dale. *History of Religions in the Caribbean*. Kingston: Kingston, 1989.

Bisse, J. *Arboles de Cuba*. Havana: Editorial Cientitifisco-Tecnica, 1988.

Black, Clinton. *History of Jamaica*. London: Collins Clear-Type Press, 1965.

Blanco, Rolando García, and Carmen Almodóvar Muñoz. *Cien Figuras de la Ciencia en Cuba*. La Habana: Instituto Cubano del Libro, 2002.

Bland-Sutton, John. *Men and Creatures in Uganda*. London: Hutchinson, 1933.

Blier, Suzanne. *African Vodun: Art, Psychology, and Power*. Chicago: University of Chicago Press, 1995.

Boa, Sheena. "Urban Free Black and Colored Women: Jamaica, 1760–1834." *The Jamaica Historical Review*, 18 (1993), 1–6.

Boone, Sylvia Ardyn. *Radiance from the Waters: Ideals of Feminine Beauty in Mende Art*. New Haven: Yale University Press, 1986.

Borhidi, Attila. *Phytogeography and Vegetation Ecology of Cuba*. Budapest: Akademiai Kiado, 1996.

Boxer, David, and Edward Lucie-Smith. *Jamaica in Black and White: Photography in Jamaica c. 1845–1920: The David Boxer Collection*. Oxford: Macmillan, 2013.

Bradley Foster, Helen. *New Raiments of Self: African American Clothing in the Antebellum South*. Oxford: Berg, 1997.

Bradley-Griebel, Helen. "The African American Woman's Headwrap: Unwinding the Symbols." In Roach-Higgins *et al.*, *Dress and Identity*, 445–60.

Brandon, George. *Santeria from Africa to the New World: The Dead Sell Memories*. Bloomington: Indiana University Press, 1997.

Brathwaite, Edward Kamau. *The Arrivants: A New World Trilogy*. London: Oxford University Press, 1973.

Brathwaite, Edward Kamau. *The Development of Creole Society in Jamaica, 1770–1820*. Oxford: Oxford University Press, 1971.

Brathwaite, Edward Kamau. "Jamaican Slave Society, A Review." *Race & Class* 9, 3 (1968), 331–42.

Brathwaite, Edward Kamau. "The Spirit of African Survival in Jamaica." *Jamaica Journal* 42 (1978): 44–63.

Braudel, Fernand. *The Structures of Everyday Life: Civilization and Capitalism, 15th–18th Century, vol. 1*. Translation from the French revised by Sian Reynolds. New York: Harper and Row, 1979.

Braun, Emily. "Futurist Fashion: Three Manifestoes." *Art Journal* 54, 1. (Spring 1995), 34–41.

Bredemeier, Henry C., and Toby Jackson. "Ideals of Beauty." In Roach and Bubolz, *Dress, Adornment, and the Social Order*, 34–45.

Brennan, Emily, Lori-Ann Harris, and Mark Nesbitt. "Object Lesson Jamaican Lace-Bark: Its History and Uncertain Future." *Textile History* 44, 2 (November 2013), 235–53.

Brody, Jennifer DeVere. *Impossible Purities: Blackness, Feminity and Victorian Culture*. Durham, NC: Duke University Press, 1998.

Bronner, Simon J., ed. *American Material Culture and Folklife: A Prologue and Dialogue*. Ann Arbor: UMI Research Press, 1985.

Bryan, Patrick. *The Jamaican People 1880–1908: Race, Class and Social Control*. London: Macmillan, 1991.

Buckridge, Steeve O. "Artificial Lace or Natural Lace? The Story of Jamaican Lace-Bark." *The Jamaican Historical Society Bulletin* 11 (April 2003): 44–48.

Buckridge, Steeve O. "The Color and Fabric of Jamaican Slave Women's Dress." *Journal of Caribbean History* 33, 1 & 2 (1999), 84–124.

Buckridge, Steeve O. "Dress: From Slavery to Freedom among Jamaican Women, 1790–1890." In *The Faces of Freedom: The Manumission and Emancipation of Slaves in*

Old World and New World Slavery, edited by Mark Kleijwegt. Boston: Brill Academic Publishers, 2006: 233–65.

Buckridge, Steeve O. "Jamaica, Nineteenth Century to Present." In *Encyclopedia of World Dress and Fashion*, series ed. Joanne Eicher, vol. 2, *Latin America and the Caribbean*, edited by Margot Blum Schevill. Oxford: Oxford University Press/Berg publishers, 2010: 264–69.

Buckridge, Steeve O. "Jamaica, Rebellion and Revolt, 1760–1890." In *The International Encyclopedia of Revolution and Protest: 1500 to Present, A–B vol.1*, edited by Immanuel Ness. Oxford: Blackwell, 2009: 1871–74.

Buckridge, Steeve O. *The Language of Dress: Resistance and Accommodation in Jamaica, 1760–1890*. Kingston: The University of the West Indies Press, 2004.

Buckridge, Steeve O. "Overview of Caribbean Dress." In *Encyclopedia of World Dress and Fashion*, series ed. Joanna Eicher, vol. 2, *Latin America and the Caribbean,* edited by Margot Blum Schevill, Oxford: Oxford University Press/Berg, 2010: 247–50.

Buckridge, Steeve O. "The Role of Plant Substances in the Care and Production of Jamaican Slave Women's Dress." *Caribbean Quarterly* 49, 3 (September 2003), 61–73.

Burman, Barbara, ed. *The Culture of Sewing: Gender, Consumption and Home Dressmaking.* London: Berg, 1999.

Burr-Reynaud, Frédéric. *Visages d'Arbres et de Fruits Haïtiens*. Port-au-Prince: Fardin Roman, 1940.

Burt, Eugene C. "Bark Cloth in East Africa." *Textile History* 26, 1, 75–88.

Burton, R. F. *The Lakes Regions of Central Africa*, 2 vols. New York: Horizon Press, 1961.

Burton, Richard D. E. *Afro-Creole: Power, Opposition, and Play in the Caribbean*. Ithaca: Cornell University Press, 1997.

Bush, Barbara. *Slave Women in Caribbean Society, 1650–1838*. Kingston: Heinemann, 1990.

Bushman, Richard L. *The Refinement of America: Persons, Houses, Cities*. New York: Vintage Books, 1993.

Bustamante, Luis J. *Enciclopedia Popular Cubana*. La Habana, Cuba: Cultural, Sociedad Anonima, 1948.

Butler, Judith. *Gender Trouble: Feminism and the Subversion of Identity*. New York: Routledge, 1990.

Butler, Judith, and Joan W. Scott. *Feminists Theorize the Political*. London: Routledge, 1992.

Byfield, Judith A. *The Bluest Hands: A Social and Economic History of Women Dyers in Abeokuta (Nigeria), 1890–1940*. Portsmouth: Heinemann, 2002.

Byfield, Judith A. "Introduction: Rethinking the African Diaspora." *African Studies Review* 43, 1 (April 2000), 1–7.

Byrde, Penelope. *Nineteenth Century Fashion*. London: B.T. Batsford, 1992.

Cabrera, Lydia. *Afro-Cuban Tales*. Trans. by Alberto Hernandez-Chiroldes and Lauren Yoder. Lincoln: University of Nebraska Press, 2004.

Cabrera, Lydia. *La Medicina Popular De Cuba*. Barcelona: Ediciones, 1996.

Cabrera, Lydia. *El Monte*. Havana; Edeboral Letras Cubanas, 1993.

Camirand, Roland, and Owen B. Evelyn. *Jamaica: Trees for Tomorrow Project, Phase II. National Forest Inventory Report*. Vol. 1. Kingston: Jamaica Forestry Department, 2004.

Campbell, Keron C. St. E. *Endemic Trees of Jamaica*. Kingston: University of the West Indies Press, 2010.

Cantizares, Raul. *Cuban Santeria: Walking with the Night*. Rochester, VT: Destiny Books, 1999.

Carney, Judith A., and Richard Nicholas Rosomoff. *In the Shadow of Slavery: Africa's Botanical Legacy in the Atlantic World*. Berkeley: University of California Press, 2011.

Casid, Jill H. *Sowing Empire: Landscape and Colonization*. Minneapolis: University of Minnesota Press, 2005.

Cassidy, Frederic G., and R.B. Le Page, eds. *Dictionary of Jamaican English*, 2nd ed. Kingston: University of West Indies Press, 2002.

Cesaire, Aime. *Discourse on Colonialism*. New York: Monthly Review Press, 2001.

Chadwick, Whitney. *Women, Art and Society*. New York: Thames and Hudson, 2012.

Collier, Ann. *Lace Fans*. London: Batsford, 2003.

A Compendium of Lace Making—Bobbin, Filet, Needle-Point, Netting, Tatting, and Much More—Four Volumes in One. London: Williard Press, 2011.

Chudnoff, M. *Tropical Timbers of the World*. Agric. Handbook, 607. Washington DC: USAID, 1984.

Church, Kathryn. "Try One on for Size: Poetic Notes from Wedding Dress Research" in *Not Just Any Dress: Narratives of Memory, Body and Identity (Counterpoints)* Sandra Weber and Claudia Mitchell, eds. New York: Peter Lang, 2004.

Churches, Christopher, Peter Wampler, Sun Wanxiao, and Andrew J. Smith. "Evaluation of Forest Cover Estimates for Haiti Using Supervised Classification of Landsat Data." *International Journal of Applied Earth Observation and Geoinformation* 30 (2014): 203–16.

Clarke, Duncan. *The Art of African Textiles*. San Diego: Thunder Bay Press, 1997.

Cohen, Erik. "The Commercialization of Ethnic Crafts." *Journal of Design History* 2, 2 & 3, 161–68.

Cooper, Carolyn. *Noises in the Blood: Orality, Gender, and the Vulgar Body of Jamaican Popular Culture*. Durham, NC: Duke University Press, 1995.

Cooper, Carolyn. *Sound Clash: Jamaican Dancehall Culture at Large*. New York: Palgrave Macmillan, 2004.

Cordwell, Justine M. "The Very Human Arts of Transformation" In Cordwell and Schwarz, *The Fabrics of Culture*, 47–75.

Cordwell, Justine M. and Ronald A. Schwarz, eds. *The Fabrics of Culture: The Anthropology of Clothing and Adornment*. New York: Mouton, 1979.

Crahan, Margaret E., and Franklin W. Knight. *Africa and the Caribbean: The Legacies of a Link*. Baltimore: Johns Hopkins University Press, 1979.

Craik, J. *The Face of Fashion: Cultural Studies in Fashion*. New York: Routledge, 1994.

Crane, Diana. *Fashion and Its Social Agenda: Class, Gender, and Identity in Clothing*. Chicago: University of Chicago Press, 2000.

Cumming, Valerie, C. Willett Cunnington, and Phillis Cunnington. *The Dictionary of Fashion History*. New York: Berg, 2010.

Dallas, R. C. *The History of the Maroons*. 1803; reprint, London: Frank Cass, 1968.

Davidson, Basil. *The African Slave Trade*. New York: Back Bay Books, 1980.

Davis, Angela. "Reflections on the Black Woman's Role in the Community of Slaves." *Black Scholar* 3, 4 (December 1971), 3–15.

Davis, Fred. *Fashion, Culture and Identity*. Chicago: University of Chicago Press, 1992; Princeton University Press, 1975.

D'Azevedo, L. Warren, ed. *The Traditional Artist in African Societies*. Bloomington: Indiana University Press, 1973.

De La Torre, Miguel A. *Santeria: The Beliefs and Rituals of a Growing Religion in America*. Grand Rapids, MI: William B. Eerdmans, 2004.

Delle, James A., Mark W. Hauser, and Douglas V. Armstrong, eds. *Out of Many, One People: The Historical Archaeology of Colonial Jamaica (Caribbean Archaeology and Ethnohistory)*. Tuscaloosa: The University of Alabama Press, 2011.

Denzin, Norman K. *Symbolic Interactionism and Cultural Studies: The Politics of Interpretation.* Oxford: Blackwell, 1992.

De Young, Maurice. *Man and the Land in the Haitian Economy.* Gainesville: University of Florida Press, 1958.

Dickson, Kwamina B. *A Historical Geography of Ghana.* London: Cambridge University Press, 1969.

Diouf, Sylviane A. *Servants of Allah: African Muslims Enslaved in the Americas.* New York: New York University Press, 1998.

Drewal, Henry John. "Pageantry and Power in Yoruba Costuming." In *The Fabrics of Culture: The Anthropology of Clothing and Adornment,* edited by Justine M. Cordwell and Ronald A. Schwarz, 189–230. New York: Mouton, 1979.

Drewal, Henry John. *Beads, Body, and Soul: Art and Light in The Yoruba Universe.* Los Angeles: UCLA Fowler Museum of Cultural History, 1998.

Drewal, Henry John and Margaret Thompson Drewal. *Gelede: Art and Female Power among the Yoruba.* Bloomington: Indiana University Press, 1983.

Dubois, W.E.B. *The Gift of Black Folk: The Negroes in the Making of America.* Boston: Stratford, 1924.

Ellert, H. *The Material Culture of Zimbabwe.* Harare: Longman Zimbabwe, 1984.

Evelyn, O.B., and R. Camirand. "Forest Cover and Deforestation in Jamaica: An Analysis of Forest Cover Estimates Over Time." *International Forestry Review* 5, part 4 (2003): 354–63.

Ewins, Rod. *Staying Fijian: Vatulele Island Barkcloth and Social Identity.* Honolulu: University of Hawaii Press, 2009.

Eyre, Lawrence Alan. "Jamaica: Test Case for Tropical Deforestation?" *Ambio* 16, 6 (1987), 338–43.

Fanon, Franz. *Black Skin, White Masks.* Trans. Charles Lam Markham. New York: Grove Weidenfeld, 1967.

Fanon, Franz. *The Wretched of the Earth.* New York: Grove Press, 1963.

Featherstone, Mike. *Consumer Culture and Postmodernism.* Newbury Park, CA: Sage, 1991.

Felshin, Nina. "Clothing as Subject." *Art Journal* 54, 1 (Spring 1995), 20–28.

Fingers, Al. *Clarks in Jamaica.* London: One Love Books, 2012.

Finkelstein, Joanne. *The Fashioned Self.* Cambridge: Polity Press, 1991.

Fisher, Angela. *Africa Adorned.* London: Collins Horvill, 1987.

Fox-Genovese, Elizabeth. "Strategies and Forms of Resistance: Focus on Slave Women in the United States." In *In Resistance: Studies in African Caribbean and Afro-American History,* edited by Gary Y. Okihiro, 143–65. Amherst: University of Massachusetts Press, 1986.

Foucault, Michel. *The History of Sexuality.* 2 vols. London: Penguin, 1978–79; first publication, Paris, 1976.

Foucault, Michel. *The Order of Things: An Archaeology of the Human Science.* New York: Vintage, Reissue edition, 1994.

Frazier, Franklin E. *Black Bourgeoise.* Glencoe: Falcon's Wing, 1959.

French, Joan, and Honor Ford-Smith. *Women, Work and Organization in Jamaica, 1900–1944.* Kingston: Sistren Research, 1986.

Fuentes, Victor R. "Apuntes Para la Flora Economica de Cuba l. Especies Productoras de Fibras." *Revista del Botanico Nacional* XX (1999).

Gaines, Jane M., and Charlotte Herzog, eds. *Fabrications: Costume and the Female Body.* New York: Routledge, 1990.

Gaspar, David Barry, and Darlene Clark Hine. *More Than Chattel: Black Women and Slavery in the Americas*. Bloomington: Indiana University Press, 1996.

Gates, Henry Louis, Jr., ed. *The Classic Slave Narratives*. New York: Mentor, 1987.

Geertz, Clifford. *The Interpretation of Cultures*. New York: Basic Books, 1973.

Genovese, Eugene D. *Roll, Jordan, Roll: The World the Slaves Made*. New York: Vintage, 1976.

Gerard. W.R. "Origin of the Word Lagetto." *American Anthropologist* 14, 2 (April–June 1912), 404.

Gibbons, Jacqueline A. "Ladies' Lace-Making and Imprisonment." *International Visual Sociology* 13, 2 (1998), 91–103.

Gikandi, Simon. *Slavery and the Culture of Taste*. Princeton: Princeton University Press, 2011.

Gillow, John. *African Textiles*. San Francisco: Chronicle Books, 2003.

Gillow, John. *Printed and Dyed Textiles from Africa*. London: British Museum Press, 2001.

Gilroy, Paul. *The Black Atlantic: Modernity and Double Consciousness*. Cambridge, MA: Harvard University Press, 1994.

Glissant, Edouard. "Creolization in the Making of the Americas." In *Race, Discourse, and the Origin of the Americas: A New World View*, edited by Vera Lawrence Hyatt and Rex Nettleford, 268–75. Washington, DC: Smithsonian Institution Press, 1995.

Goodison, Lorna. *Controlling the Silver*. Chicago: University of Illinois Press, 2005.

Goggin, Maureen Daly, and Beth Fowkes Tobin. *Women and the Material Culture of Needlework and Textiles, 1750–1950*. London: MPG Books Group, 2009.

Gordon, Sarah A. "Boundless Possibilities": Home Sewing and the Meanings of Women's Domestic Work in the United States, 1890–1930. *Journal of Women's History*, 16, 2 (2004), 68–91.

Gray White, Deborah. *Ar'n't I a Woman? Female Slaves in Plantation South*. New York: W.W. Norton, 1985.

Gubar, Susan. Race Changes: *White Skin, Black Face in American Culture*. Oxford: Oxford University Press, 1997.

Hafkin, Nancy J., and Edna G. Bay. *Women in Africa: Studies in Social and Economic Change*. Stanford: Stanford University Press, 1976.

Hall, Douglas. *Free Jamaica, 1838–1865: An Economic History*. New Haven: Yale University Press, 1959.

Hall, Douglas. *In Miserable Slavery: Thomas Thistlewood in Jamaica, 1750–80*. London: Macmillan, 1989.

Hall, Stuart, ed. *Representation: Cultural Representations and Signifying Practices*. London: Open University, 1997.

Hallett, Clive, and Amanda Johnston. *Fabric for Fashion: A Comprehensive Guide to Natural Fibres*. London: Lawrence King, 2010.

Harding, Vincent. *There Is a River: The Black Struggle for Freedom in America*. New York: Harcourt Brace Jovanovich, 1981.

Harrington, Michael. "The Best Dressed Poverty." In *Dress, Adornment, and the Social Order*, edited by Mary Ellen Roach-Higgins and Joanne Bubolz Eicher, 163–65. New York: John Wiley and Sons, 1965.

Harris, Jennifer, ed. *5000 Years of Textiles*. Washington, DC: Smithsonian Books, 2010.

Hart, Richard. *Slaves Who Abolished Slavery: Blacks in Rebellion*. Kingston: The University of the West Indies Press, 2002.

Hendrickson, Hildi, ed. *Clothing and Difference: Embodied Identities in Colonial and Post-Colonial Africa*. Durham, NC: Duke University Press, 1996.

Hermkens, Anna-Karina. *Engendering Objects: Dynamics of Barkcloth and Gender among the Maisin of Papua New Guinea*. Leiden: Sidestone Press, 2013.

Herskovits, Melville J. *Life in a Haitian Valley*. New York: Knopf, 1937.

Herskovits, Melville J. *The Myth of the Negro Past*. Boston: Beacon Press, 1959.

Hiery, Hermann, and John Mackenzie, eds. *European Impact and Pacific Influence: British and German Colonial Policy in the Pacific Islands and the Indigenous Response*. New York: I.B. Tauris, 1997.

Higman, Barry. *Jamaican Food: History, Biology, Culture*. Kingston: University of the West Indies Press, 2008.

Higman, Barry. *Plantation Jamaica, 1750–1850: Capital and Control in a Colonial Economy*. Kingston: University of the West Indies Press, 2005.

Higman, Barry. *Slave Population and Economy in Jamaica, 1807–1834*. Cambridge: Cambridge University Press, 1976.

Higman, Barry. *Slave Population of the British Caribbean 1807–1834*. Baltimore: Johns Hopkins University Press, 1984.

Hodder, Ian, ed. *The Meanings of Things: Material Culture and Symbolic Expression*. London: Harper Collins Academic, 1989.

Hollander, Anne. *Seeing Through Clothes*. Berkeley: University of California Press, reprint, 1993.

Honeyman, Katrina. *Women, Gender, and Industrialization in England, 1700–1870*. New York: Palgrave Macmillan, 2000.

hooks, bell. *Black Looks: Race and Representation*. Boston: South End, 1992.

hooks, bell. "My Style Ain't No Fashion." *Z Magazine,* May 1992: 27–29.

hooks, bell. *Yearning: Race, Gender and Cultural Politics*. Boston: South End, 1990.

Hopkins, A. G. *An Economic History of West Africa*. New York: Columbia University Press, 1973.

Howard, Michael, ed. *Bark-cloth in Southeast Asia*. Bangkok: White Lotus, 2006.

Howard, P.L., and G. Nabanoga. "Are There Customary Rights to Plants? An Inquiry among the Baganda (Uganda), with Special Attention to Gender." *World Development* 35, 9 (2007), 1542–63.

Howard, R. A. *Flora of the Lesser Antilles, Leeward and Windward Islands*. Vol. 5. Arnold Arboretum, Harvard University, 1989.

Hurston, Zora Neale. *Mules and Men*. 1935; reprint, Bloomington: Indiana University Press, 1963.

Hurston, Zora Neale. *Their Eyes Were Watching God*. 1937; reprint, Urbana: University of Illinois Press, 1978.

Hurwitz, Samuel J., and Edith F. Hurwitz. *Jamaica: A Historical Portrait*. New York: Praeger, 1971.

Hutchings, Kevin D. *Romantic Ecologies and Colonial Cultures in the British Atlantic World, 1770–1850*. Montreal: McGill-Queen's University Press, 2009.

Hyatt, Vera Lawrence, and Rex Nettleford. *Race, Discourse and the Origin of the Americas: A New World View*. Washington: Smithsonian Institution Press, 1995.

Iannini, Christopher P. *Fatal Revolutions: Natural History, West Indian Slavery, and the Routes of American Literature*. Chapel Hill: The University of North Carolina Press, 2012.

Ingram, Kenneth E. N. *Manuscript Sources for the History of the West Indies*. Kingston: The Press UWI, 1997.

Ipulet, Perpetua. "Uses of Genus Ficus (Moraceae) in Buganda Region, Central Uganda." *African Journal of Ecology* 45, supplement 3 (2007), 44–47.

Jackson, F. Nevill. *A History of Hand-Made Lace*. Detroit: Tower Books, 1971.

Jackson, F. Nevill. *Old Handmade Lace: With a Dictionary*. Reprint, New York: Dover, 1987.

James, C.L.R. *At the Rendezvous of Victory*. London: Alison and Busby, 1984.

James, C.L.R. *The Black Jacobins: Tousssaint L'Ouverture and the San Domingo Revolution*. New York: Vintage, 1989.

Jones, Jacqueline. *Labor of Love, Labor of Sorrow: Black Women, Work and the Family, from Slavery to the Present*. New York: Vintage, 1985.

Jones, Robert W. *Gender and the Formation of Taste in Eighteenth-Century Britain: The Analysis of Beauty*. Cambridge: Cambridge University Press, 1998.

Jousse, Marcel. *The Anthropology of Geste and Rhythm: Studies in the Anthropological Laws of Human Expression and Their Application in the Galilean Oral-Style Tradition*. 2nd revised ed. Translated by Edgard Sienaert and Joan Conolly. Durban, South Africa: Mantis, 2000.

Joyner, Charles. *Down by the Riverside: A South Carolina Slave Community*. Urbana: University of Illinois Press, 1984.

Kaiser, Susan B. *The Social Psychology of Clothing: Symbolic Appearance in Context*. 2nd ed., New York: Macmillan, 1990.

Katzin, Margaret. "The Business of Higglering in Jamaica." *Social and Economic Studies* 9, 3 (1960), 197–331.

Kerr, Paulette. "Jamaican Female Lodging Housekeepers in the Nineteenth Century." *The Jamaican Historical Review* 18 (1993): 7–17.

Kirk, Kris, and Ed Heath. *Men in Frocks*. London: Gay Men's Press, 1985.

Kjaer, Anne. *Traditional Dress in Uganda*. Denmark: Kjaer & Kjaer, 1995.

Knight, Franklin W., and Colin A. Palmer, ed. *The Modern Caribbean*. Chapel Hill: The University of North Carolina Press, 1989.

Kochman, Thomas. *Black and White Styles in Conflict*. Chicago: University of Chicago Press, 1981.

Koohafkan, A.P., and Ch. Lilin. *Arbres et Arbustes de Haiti: Utilisation des Espéces Lingeuses en Conservation des Sols et en Aménagement des Bassins Versants*. Port-au-Prince: Ministère de L'Agriculture de Ressources Naturelle et du Développement Rural, 1989.

Kooijman, Simon. *Ornamented Bark-Cloth in Indonesia*. Leiden: E.J. Brill, 1963.

Kooijman, Simon. *Tapa on Moce Island, Fiji: A Traditional Handcraft in a Changing Society*. Leiden: E.J. Brill, 1977.

Kriger, Colleen E. *Cloth in West African History*. New York: Altamira Press, 2006.

Kriz, Kay Dian. *Slavery, Sugar and the Culture of Refinement: Picturing the British West Indies, 1700–1840*. Hew Haven: Yale University Press, 2008.

Kriz, Kay Dian and Geoff Quilley, eds. *An Economy of Colour: Visual Culture and the Atlantic World, 1660–1830*. Manchester: Manchester University Press, 2003.

Kroll, Carol. *The Whole Craft of Spinning: From the Raw Material to the Finished Yarn*. New York: Dover, 1981.

Lamb, Venice, and Alastair Lamb. *Au Cameroun Weaving-Tissage*. Hertingfordbury, UK: Roxford Books, 1981.

Leiva, Angela. *Trees of Cuba*. New York: Macmillan Caribbean, 2007.

Leon [J.S. Sauget], and Alain [E.E. Liogier]. *Flora De Cuba*. Reprint. Koenigstein: Otto Koeltz Science, 1974.

Leonard, Anne, and John Terrell. *Patterns of Paradise: The Styles and Significance of Bark Cloth around the World*. Washington, DC: Field Museum of Natural History, 1980.

Lovén, Sven. *Origins of the Tainan Culture, West Indies*. Göteborg: Elanders Bokfryckeri Akfiebolag, 1935.

MacGregor, Arthur, ed. *Sir Hans Sloane: Collector, Scientist, Antiquary, Founding Father of the British Museum*. London: British Museum Press, 1994.

Martin, Claude. *The Rainforests of West Africa: Ecology, Threats, Conservation*. Basel; Boston: Birkhäuser Verglag, 1991.

Mathurin-Mair, Lucille. *A Historical Study of Women in Jamaica 1655–1844*, edited by and with an introduction by Hilary McD. Beckles and Verene A. Shepherd. Kingston: The University of the West Indies Press, 2006.

Mathurin-Mair, Lucille. *The Rebel Woman in the British West Indies during Slavery*. Kingston: Institute of Jamaica, 1975.

McAlister, Elizabeth. *Rara! Vodou, Power, and Performance in Haiti and Its Diaspora*. Berkeley: University of California Press, 2002.

McDonald, Roderick A. *The Economy and Material Culture of Slaves: Goods and On the Slave Plantations of Jamaica and Louisiana*. Baton Rouge: Louisiana State University Press, 1993.

McKendrick, Neil, John Brewer, and J.H. Plumb. *The Birth of a Consumer Society*. London: Europa, 1982.

McLeod, M.D. *The Asante*. London: British Museum, 1981.

Memmi, Albert. *The Colonizer and the Colonized*. Boston: Beacon Press, 1965.

Merchant, Carolyn. *The Death of Nature: Women, Ecology and the Scientific Revolution*. New York: HarperOne; Reprint edition, 1990.

Meyers, Amy R., ed. *Knowing Nature: Art and Science in Philadelphia, 1740–1840*. New Haven: Yale University Press, 2011.

Miers, Suzanne, and Igor Kopytoff, eds. *Slavery in Africa*. Madison: The University of Wisconsin Press, 1977.

Miller, Daniel, ed. *Material Cultures: Why Some Things Matter*. Chicago: The University of Chicago Press, 1998.

Miller, Monica L. *Slaves to Fashion: Black Dandyism and the Styling of Black Diasporic Identity*. Durham, NC: Duke University Press, 2009.

Mintz, Sidney W., and Richard Price. *The Birth of African-American Culture: An Anthropological Perspective*. Boston: Beacon Press, 1992.

Mohammed, Patricia, ed. *Gendered Realities: Essays in Caribbean Feminist Thought*. Kingston: University of the West Indies Press, 2002.

Molineux, Catherine. *Faces of Perfect Ebony: Encountering Atlantic Slavery in Imperial Britain*. Cambridge, MA: Harvard University Press, 2012.

Momsen, Janet, ed. *Women and Change in the Caribbean*. Kingston: Ian Randle, 1993.

Monzote, Reinaldo Funes. *From Rain Forest to Cane Field in Cuba: An Environmental History since 1492*. Trans. Alex Martin. Chapel Hill: The University of North Carolina Press, 2008.

Morris, Brian, and Jerome D. Msonthi. *Chewa Medical Botany: A Study of Herbalism in Southern Malawi*. Hamburg: LIT Verlag, 1996.

Morrison, Toni. *Beloved*. New York: Penguin, 1987.

Moore, Brian L., and Michele A. Johnson. *Neither Led nor Driven: Contesting British Cultural Imperialism in Jamaica, 1865–1920*. Kingston: University of the West Indies Press, 2004.

Murray, Stephen O., ed. *Oceanic Homosexualities*. New York: Garland, 1992.

Munro, Martin, ed. *Haiti Rising: Haitian History, Culture and the Earthquake of 2010*. Kingston: University of the West Indies Press, 2010.

Munro, Martin and Elizabeth Walcott-Hackshaw, eds. *Echoes of the Haitian Revolution, 1804–2004*. Kingston: University of the West Indies Press, 2008.

Musisi, Nakanyike B. "Women, 'Elite Polygyny' and Buganda State Formation." *Signs: Journal of Women in Culture and Society* 16, 4 (Summer 1991), 757–86.

Nakazibwe, Venny M. *Bark-Cloth of the Baganda People of Southern Uganda: A Record of Continuity And Change from the Late Eighteenth Century to the Early Twenty-First Century*. Thesis/Dissertation, London: Middlesex University, 2005.

Nash, G.V. "The Lace-Bark Tree." *Journal of the New York Botanic Gardens* 9 (1908): 116–19.

Neich, Roger, and Mick Pendergrast. *Traditional Tapa Textiles of the Pacific*. New York: Thames and Hudson, 1998.

Neptune-Rouzier, Marilise. *Plantes Médicinales d'Haiti: Description, Usages et Propriétés*. Port-au-Prince: les Editione du CIDIHCA, 1997.

Nettleford, Rex M. *Caribbean Cultural Identity: The Case of Jamaica*. Los Angeles: UCLA Latin American Center, 1978.

Nettleford, Rex M. *Identity, Race and Protest in Jamaica*. New York: William Morrow, 1972.

Nettleford, Rex M. *Inward Stretch, Outward Reach: A Voice from the Caribbean*. London: Macmillan Press, 1993.

Newell, Jennifer. *Trading Nature: Tahitians, Europeans, and Ecological Exchange*. Honolulu: University of Hawaii Press, 2010.

Noa, Alfredo. *Taxonomia de la familia Thymlaeaceae Jussiaeu en Cuba*. Havana: University of Havana, 1992.

Nunez, M.E. *Plantaz Medicinales de Puerto Rico*. Rio Piedras: Universidad de Puerto Rico, 1982.

Okihiro, Gary Y. *In Resistance: Studies in African Caribbean and Afro-American History*. Amherst: The University of Massachusetts Press, 1986.

Oliver, Douglas. *Return to Tahiti: Bligh's Second Breadfruit Voyage*. Melbourne: Melbourne University Press, 1988.

Oliver-Bever, B. *Medicinal Plants in Tropical West Africa*. Cambridge: Cambridge University Press, 1986.

Ortiz, Fernando. "Nuevo Catauro de Cubanismos." *La Habana: Editorial de Ciencias Sociales*, 1974.

Pacius, Gerald L., ed. *Living in a Material World*. St. John's: Institute of Social and Economic Research, Memorial, University of Newfoundland, 1991.

Padavic, Irene, and Barbara F. Reskin. *Women and Men at Work*. London; Thousand Oaks, CA: Pine Forge Press, 2002.

Padmanabhan, Martina. "Women and Men as Conservers, Users and Managers of Agrobiodiversity: A Feminist Social-Ecological Approach." *Journal of Socio-Economics* 40, 6 (2011), 968–76.

Parker, Rozsika. *The Subversive Stitch: Embroidery and the Making of the Feminine*. New York: I.B. Tauris, 2010.

Parrish, Susan Scott. *American Curiosity: Cultures of Natural History in the Colonial British Atlantic World*. Chapel Hill: University of North Carolina Press, 2006.

Parry, Linda. *Textiles of the Arts and Crafts Movement*. New Edition. London: Thames and Hudson, 1988.

Paydar, Niloo Imami, and Ivo Grammet, eds. *The Fabric of Moroccan Life*. Indianapolis: Indianapolis Museum of Art, 2002.

Payne-Jackson, Arvilla, and Mervyn C. Alleyne. *Jamaican Folk Medicine: A Source of Healing*. Kingston: University of the West Indies Press, 2004.

Pearman, Georgia, and D.V. Prendergast. "Plant Portraits." *Economic Botany* 54, 1 (2000), 4–6.

Pichardo, Esteban. *Pichardo Novisimo o Diccionario Provincial Casi Razenada de Vozes y Frases Cubanas*. La Habana: SELECTA, 1953.

Pierre-Noël, Arsène V. *Les Plantes et les Légumes d'Haiti qui Guérissent: Mille et Une Recettes Pratiques*. Port-au-Prince: Imprimerie De L'Etat, 1959.

Powell, Dulcie. "The Voyage of the Plant Nursery, HMS Providence 1791–1793." *Bulletin of the Institute of Jamaica, Science Series* 15 (1973).

Pressini, Mauro, and Rachel Beauvoir-Dominique. *Vodou*. Gatineau-Quebec: Canadian Museum of Civilization Corporation, 2012.

Pritchard, Mary J. *Siapo: Bark Cloth Art of Samoa*. American Samoa: Council on Culture, Arts and Humanities, Special Publication 1, 1984.

Proctor, George. "A New Jamaican Species of Ctenitis," *American Fern Journal* 48, 3 (July–September, 1958), 108–110.

Pule, John, and Nicholas Thomas. *Hiapo: Past and Present in Niuen Barkcloth*. Dunedin: University of Otago Press, 2005.

Quilley, Geoff, and Kay Dian Kriz, eds. *An Economy of Colour: Visual Culture and the Atlantic World, 1660–1830*. New York: Manchester University Press/Palgrave, 2003.

Quiros-Moran, Dalia. *Guide to Afro-Cuban Herbalism*. Bloomington: AuthorHouse, 2009.

Rabine, Leslie W. *The Global Circulation of African Fashion*. New York: Berg, 2002.

Radner, Joan, ed. *Feminist Messages: Coding in Women's Folk Culture*. Urbana: University of Illinois Press, 1993.

Record, Samuel, and Robert W. Hess. *Timbers of the New World*. New York: Arno Press, 1972.

Ribeiro, Aileen. *Dress and Morality*. London: B.T. Batsford, 1986.

Roach, Joseph. *Cities of the Dead: Circum-Atlantic Performance*. New York: Columbia University Press, 1996.

Roach, Mary Ellen. "The Social Symbolism of Women's Dress." In *The Fabrics of Culture: The Anthropology of Clothing and Adornment,* edited by Justine M. Cordwell and Ronald A. Schwarz, 415–22. New York: Mouton, 1979.

Roach, Mary Ellen and Joanne Bubolz Eicher, eds. *Dress, Adornment, and the Social Order*. New York: John Wiley and Sons, 1965.

Roach, Mary Ellen. "The Language of Personal Adornment." In *The Fabrics of Culture: The Anthropology of Clothing and Adornment,* edited by Justine M. Cordwell and Ronald A. Schwarz, 7–21. New York: Mouton, 1979.

Roach-Higgins, Mary Ellen, Joanne B. Eicher, and Kim K.P. Johnson, eds. *Dress and Identity*. New York: Fairchild, 1995.

Roberts, Helene E. "Exquisite Slave: The Role of Clothes in the Making of the Victorian Woman." *Signs* 2, 3 (Spring 1977), 554–69.

Robertson, Claire C. "Africa into the Americas? Slavery and Women, the Family, and the Gender Division of Labor." In *More than Chattel: Black Women and Slavery in the Americas,* edited by David Barry Gaspar and Darlene Clark Hine, 3–40. Bloomington: Indiana University Press, 1996.

Robertson, Claire C. *Trouble Showed the Way: Women, Men, and Trade in the Nairobi Area, 1890–1990*. Bloomington: Indiana University Press, 1997.

Robertson, Claire C. and Martin A. Klein, eds. *Women and Slavery in Africa*. Madison: University of Wisconsin Press, 1983.

Robertson, Claire C. "Women's Importance in African Slave Systems." In *Women and Slavery in Africa,* edited by Claire C. Robertson and Martin A. Klein, 3–25. Madison: University of Wisconsin Press, 1983.

Robertson, Glory. "Pictorial Sources for Nineteenth Century Women's History." In *Engendering History: Caribbean Women in Historical Perspective,* edited by Verene Shepherd, Bridget Brereton, and Barbara Bailey, 111–22. Kingston: Ian Randle, 1995.

Robertson, James. "Knowledgeable Readers: Jamaican Critiques of Sloane's Botany." In *From Books to Bezoars: Sir Hans Sloane and His Collection,* edited by Alison Walker, Arthur MacGregor and Michael Hunter, 80–90. London: British Library, 2012.

Root, Regina A., ed. *The Latin American Fashion Reader.* New York: Berg, 2005.

Roscoe, Will. *Changing Ones: Third and Fourth Genders in Native North America.* New York: St. Martin's Griffin, 2000.

Rouse, Irving. *The Taínos: Rise and Decline of the People Who Greeted Columbus.* New Haven: Yale University Press, 1992.

Rovine, Victoria L. *Bogolan: Shaping Culture through Cloth in Contemporary Mali.* Bloomington: Indiana University Press, 2008.

Safa, Helen Icken. *The Myth of the Male Breadwinner: Women and Industrialization in the Caribbean.* Boulder, CO: Westview Press, 1995.

Salmond, Anne. *Aphrodite's Island: The European Discovery of Tahiti.* Berkley: University of California Press, 2009.

Sanchez, Angela T. *Trees of Cuba.* Trans. Juliet Barclay. Oxford: Macmillan Caribbean, 2007.

Sanders, C. R. *Customizing the Body: The Art and Culture of Tattooing.* Philadelphia: Temple University Press, 1989.

Satchell, Veront M. *Hope Transformed: Historical Sketch of the Hope Landscape, St. Andrew, Jamaica, 1660–1960.* Kingston: University of the West Indies Press, 2012.

Scott, James C. *Weapons of The Weak: Everyday Forms of Peasant Resistance.* New Haven: Yale University Press, 1985.

Schiebinger, Londa. "Agnotology and Exotic Abortifacients: The Cultural Production of Ignorance in the Eighteenth Century." *Proceedings of the American Philosophical Society* 149, 3 (September 2005), 316–43.

Schiebinger, Londa. *Plants and Empire: Colonial Bioprospecting in the Atlantic World.* Cambridge, MA: Harvard University Press, 2004.

Séverin, François. *Plant AK Pyebwaté d'Ayiti.* Port-au-Prince: Imprimerie Henri Deschamps, 2002.

Seward, Ingrid, ed. "In Fine Style: The Art of Tudor and Stuart Fashion." From the exhibition at the Queen's Gallery, Buckingham Palace. *Majesty* 34, no5. (May 2013): 21–25.

Shepherd, Verene A., Ahmed Reid, Cavell Francis, and Kameika Murphy. *Jamaica and the Debate over Reparations for Slavery: A Discussion Paper Prepared by the Jamaica National Bicentenary Committee.* Kingston: Pelican, 2012.

Shepherd, Verene A., Bridget Brereton, and Barbara Bailey, eds. *Engendering History: Caribbean Women in Historical Perspective.* Kingston: Ian Randle, 1995.

Shepherd, Verene A. and Glen L. Richards, eds. *Questioning Creole: Creolisation Discourses in Caribbean Culture* (Kingston: Ian Randle, 2002).

Smith, Edward Lucie, and David Boer. *Jamaica in Black and White: Photography in Jamaica c. 1845–c.1920: The David Boxer Collection.* London: Macmillan Caribbean, 2013.

Spradley, James P., and David W. McCurdy, ed. *Conformity and Conflict: Readings in Cultural Anthropology.* Boston: Little, Brown, 1980.

Spring, Chris. *African Textiles Today.* London: British Museum Press, 2012.

Steele, Valerie. *Fashion and Eroticism: Ideals of Feminine Beauty from the Victorian Era to the Jazz Age*. New York: Oxford University Press, 1985.

Stoller, Debbie. *Stitch 'N Bitch Nation*. New York: Workman, 2004.

Swabey, C. "The Principal Timbers of Jamaica." Department of Science and Agriculture, *Jamaica Bulletin*, 29. Government printer, Kingston, 1941.

Tandberg, Gerilyn G. "Field Hand Clothing in Louisiana and Mississippi during the Ante-bellum Period." In *Dress: The Journal of the Costume Society of America* 6, 1 (January, 1980), 89–103.

Tandberg, Gerilyn and Sally Graham Durand, "Dress Up Clothes for Field Slaves of Ante Bellum Louisiana and Mississippi." *Costume* 15 (1981), 40–48.

Tcherkézoff, Serge. *"First Contacts" in Polynesia: The Samoan Case (1722–1848) Western Misunderstandings about Sexuality and Divinity*. Canberra: Australian National University, 2008.

Thompson, Robert Farris. *African Art in Motion*. Los Angeles: University of California Press, 1974.

Thompson, Robert Farris. *Flash of the Spirit: African and Afro-American Art and Philosophy*. New York: Random House, 1983.

Thompson, Robert Farris. *Painting from a Single Heart: Preliminary Remarks on Bark-Cloth Designs of the Mbute Women of Haut-Zaire*. Munchen: F. und J. Jahn, 1983.

Thompson, Robert Farris. *African Art in Motion*. Los Angeles: University of California Press, 1974.

Thornton, John. *Africa and Africans in the Making of the Atlantic World, 1400–1680*. New York: Cambridge University Press, 1992.

Timyan, Joel. *Bwa yo: Important Trees of Haiti*. Washington, DC: SECID, 1996.

Tobin, Beth Fowkes. *Picturing Imperial Power: Colonial Subjects in Eighteenth-Century British Painting*. Durham, NC: Duke University Press, 1999.

Tomlinson, A., ed. *Consumption, Identity and Style: Marketing, Meanings and the Packaging of Pleasure*. New York: Routledge, 1990.

Tselos, Susan Elizabeth. "Threads of Reflection: Costumes of Haitian Rara." *African Arts* 29, 2 (Spring 1996), 58–65.

Tulloch, Carol, ed. *Black Style*. London: Victoria and Albert Museum, 2004.

Tulloch, Carol, ed. "Fashioned in Black and White: Women's Dress in Jamaica, 1880–1907." *Things* 7 (Winter 1997–98), 29–53.

Turner, Mary. *Slaves and Missionaries: The Disintegration of Jamaican Slave Society, 1787–1834*. Urbana: University of Illinois Press, 1982.

Turner, Victor. *Dramas, Fields, and Metaphors: Symbolic Action in Human Society*. Ithaca: Cornell University Press, 1974.

Tyler, S. Lyman. *Two Worlds: The Indian Encounter with the Europeans, 1492–1509*. Salt Lake City: University of Utah Press, 1988.

Vincent, Margaret. *The Ladies' Work Table: Domestic Needlework in Nineteenth-Century America*. Allentown, PA: University Press of New England, 1988.

Walker, Alison, Arthur MacGregor, and Michael Hunter. *From Books to Bezoars: Sir Hans Sloane and His Collections*. London: British Library, 2012.

Warner-Lewis, Maureen. *Central Africa in the Caribbean: Transcending Time, Transforming Cultures*. Kingston: The University of the West Indies Press, 2003.

Wardle, Patricia. *Victorian Lace*. New York: Frederick A. Praeger, 1969.

Wass, Betty M. "Yoruba Dress in Five Generations of a Lagos Family." In Cordwell and Schwarz, 331–48.

Weibel, Kathryn. *Mirror, Mirror: Images of Women Reflected in Popular Culture*. New York: Anchor, 1977.

Weiner, Annette B., and Jane Schneider. *Cloth and Human Experience*. Washington, DC: Smithsonian Institution Press, 1989.

Welters, Linda, and Abby Lillethun. *The Fashion Reader*. New York: Berg, 2009.

West, Cornel. "The New Cultural Politics of Difference." In *Out There: Marginalization and Contemporary Culture*, edited by Russell Ferguson, Martha Gwen, Trinh T Minh-ha, and Cornel West, 19–38. Cambridge, MA: MIT Press, 1990.

West, Shearer. *The Victorians and Race*. Hants: Scholar Press, 1996.

Williams, Raymond. *Culture and Society, 1780–1950*. 2nd ed. New York: Columbia University Press, 1983.

Williamson, Karina, ed. *Contrary Voices: Representations of West Indian Slavery, 1657–1834*. Kingston: University of the West Indies Press, 2008.

Wilson, Samuel M., ed. *The Indigenous People of the Caribbean*. Gainesville: University Press of Florida, 1997.

Wolf, Diane Lauren. *Factory Daughters: Gender, Household Dynamics, and Rural Industrialization in Java*. Berkeley: University of California Press, 1992.

Wood, Marcus. *Blind Memory: Visual Representations of Slavery in England and America, 1780–1865*. New York: Routledge, 2000.

Wood, Marcus. *Slavery, Empathy and Pornography*. Oxford: Oxford University Press, 2002.

Woolf, Virginia. *Orlando*. London: Wordsworth Editions, 2003.

Wright, Margot. *Barkcloth: Aspects of Preparation, Use, Deterioration, Conservation and Display*. London; New York: Archetype, 2001.

Wulf, Andrea. *Brother Gardeners: Botany, Empire and the Birth of an Obsession*. New York: Alfred A. Knopf, 2009.

Yancy, George. *Black Bodies, White Gazes: The Continuing Significance of Race*. London: Rowman & Littlefield, 2008.

Young, Robb. "Africa's Fabric Is Dutch." *The New York Times*, November 14, 2012.

INDEX

Lightning Source UK Ltd.
Milton Keynes UK
UKHW01f0235080818
326928UK00001B/2/P

9 781350 058507